Old Salem

~ in ballad and song ~

Old Salem

~ in ballad and song ~

Old Salem ~ in ballad and song ~
Second Edition

Researched and Compiled by

ROBERT E. STROM

Foreword by Jim McAllister
Photography by Mary Barker

SELF-PUBLISHED IN SALEM, MASSACHUSETTS

To my family:
Jennifer, Eric, Emily,
Eleanor, Lena James,
Dana, Felicia,
and Rosie

~ *Foreword* ~

Salem, Massachusetts, is one of America's oldest and most historic small cities. Permanently settled in 1626, the coastal community later became famous for its architecture, maritime history, and connections to author Nathaniel Hawthorne and infamous for its 1692 witch trials. Not surprisingly, "Historic Salem" today is a popular destination for tourists from all over the world.

Historians are especially fond of the city. Some are content to walk the streets and visit the sites where Salem's history was made. Others research and write books about that history, most of them related to one of the aforementioned important Salem themes.

But many other deserving aspects of the city's past have been largely ignored by historians. Rare is the volume, for example, that pays tribute to Salem's lengthy and diverse musical heritage. A survey of my own shelves, crammed with nearly 200 full-length books and shorter publications, turns up a single pamphlet devoted to the topic. But that is finally about to change, thanks to the publication of Bob Strom's *Old Salem in Ballad and Song*.

When I met Bob twenty years ago, he was already a fixture on the Salem folk scene. When he wasn't working at his day job or gardening, Bob could usually be found playing guitar or stand-up bass at a local concert, contra dance, First Night celebration, Celtic or maritime festival, or some other public event. He was usually joined on stage by his wife and fellow musician, Jennifer Strom, and other traditional "folkies" from the Greater Salem area. In addition to performing, the Stroms hosted or co-hosted folk "jam sessions" for fellow musicians. The couple also found time to produce a pair of albums, *'round the Bend* and *Heading Home*, of traditional songs from the British Isles and America.

Bob's longstanding immersion in, and passion for, the world of traditional folk songs and ballads paved the way for his new role as historian and author. Eight years ago, Strom began searching out "lost" or little-known works that had either been written or performed by Salemites or were based on people, places, or events from Salem's past. His internet research "travels" led him to the collections of the Library of Congress, Brown University, Middle Tennessee State University, Salem's Peabody Essex Museum, and a host of other institutions. The author also drew on historical research previously undertaken by other musicians, most of them personal friends. T. William Smith, and Sarah Smith, Daisy Nell and Captain Stan, Bob Franke, Larry Young, John Roberts, Jim Dalton, and Maggie Smith-Dalton all shared gems they had uncovered in their own folk music treasure hunts. In some cases, their contributions were their own original Salem songs, like Bill Smith's *High Street* or Bob Franke's *Under the Willows*, or personal adaptations of older tunes or ballads.

The rich material Strom unearthed in his search laid the foundation for *Old Salem in Ballad and Song*. In his Introduction, the author briefly examines the role ballads and songs played in chronicling current events and saving them for posterity. The pages that follow are crammed with lyrics, verses, musical scores, illustrations, and historical tidbits relating to works with Salem connections. Some names will be familiar to many readers. Strom notes that the famed 19th century bandleader Patrick Sarsfield Gilmore, who wrote the best-known version of *When Johnny Comes Marching Home*, led the Salem Brass Band from 1855 until 1858. The equally famous Hutchinson Family Singers performed at a New England Anti-Slavery Society convention held in Salem in 1844, and the group's temperance song *King Alcohol*, says the author, was inspired by the town's controversial Deacon Giles Distillery. And while Manuel Fenollosa is hardly a household name, the Salem composer's *Emancipation Hymn* (1863) was one of the most popular tunes of the Civil War era – at least in the northern states.

Also included in Strom's book are ballads related to the murder of Capt. Joseph White in 1831 (sung, ironically, to the tune of *Auld Lang Syne*), the pressing to death of Giles Corey during the 1692 witch trials, and other tragic Salem events. The "Commerce" chapter features historical pieces like *The First Trip*, which was written for the opening celebration of the Salem-Lowell Railroad in 1850. The song was first sung at the event by the *Salem Glee Club*, one of the many 19th century musical societies and military bands highlighted by the author. Other songs reprinted in the book are downright fun and frivolous. The *Salem Willows for Mine* (1919) captures the excitement and color of a popular park and amusement area on the Salem waterfront. *Chestnut Street*, written by Salem composer and four-term Salem mayor Henry Kemble Oliver, does the same for what has been called "the most beautiful street in America."

The above tidbits are offered as a sampling of the treasures to be found in the 300 pages of *Old Salem in Ballad and Song*. I enjoyed the book immensely: the combination of fascinating content, the author's style, and a plethora of illustrations make for easy and enjoyable reading. The book can be read piecemeal, and it doesn't require the reader to have to have a background in music or even local history. The fact that few of the songs and ballads included in the ten themed chapters have much to do with Salem's witch trials, maritime history, architecture, or Nathaniel Hawthorne means that the reader is introduced to many new and different pieces of Salem history "pie."

Old Salem in Ballad and Song will be a welcome addition to my Salem book collection and a new and reliable (i.e. well footnoted) local history resource for which I am very grateful to Bob Strom. There will be many times in the years to come that information gleaned from this book and his companion book *Old Salem at Sea in Ballad and Song*, will filter, with credit given of course, into my tours and lectures.

~ Jim McAllister

[Since 1983, Jim McAllister has been bringing Salem's history to life through tours, lectures, courses, and newspaper columns. He is the author of *Salem From Naumkeag to Witch City* and co-author of *Salem Cornerstones of a Historic City*. In 2015 he was designated Salem's Official Historian. – RS]

Contents

Foreword   VII

Introduction   XVIII

In Salem Town
by Oliver Jenkins   XXIII

II. ON DYING, TRAGEDY

V. CONFLICT

VII. DANCING, COURTSHIP

VIII. CHILDREN SONGS

IX. TEMPERANCE

Introduction

In the first edition of *Old Salem in Ballad and Song,* I published 79 ballads, songs, and tunes. The music reflected 18th and 19th century ballads from Salem as an integral part of the community. Ballads of every theme were sung throughout the town, printed and sold on the streets, and eventually spread around the country. The songs and ballads in this collection are rooted in Salem's history through oral and written tradition. Songs and stories passed orally from generation to generation, written ballads saved by libraries, museums, and collectors on a broadside, in newspapers, posters, and manuscripts. In selecting the material for the second edition, I have limited the scope to ballads, broadsides, and events in Salem related to its maritime history. Part II of this two-book series, *Old Salem at Sea In Ballad and Song,* will focus on Salem's maritime history in song.

In the second edition of *Old Salem in Ballad and Song,* I have decided to publish a larger format for ease of reading, add the *Roud Folk Song Index Numbers,* if available, and include 50 recently uncovered songs. As my research continued and the folk music enthusiasts and Salem history buffs became aware of my project, more ballads and songs appeared. I recently met Salem ephemera collectors Nelson Dionne and Bonnie Hurd Smith. They have welcomed me to review their collection, and I have included their advertising ditty, *The Pickering Oil Company.* The *Dionne Collection* contains several examples of sheet music published by Salem writers, band leaders, and local printers. Documenting this material in the future will further the knowledge and understanding of Salem's musical history. After a Zoom presentation one evening, Salem bandleader Cynthia Napierkowski informed me that the Patrick S. Gilmore Award is given yearly to an outstanding Salem High School musician. I have added more historical context to Gilmore's time in Salem during the 1850s, reflecting on the music he wrote while leading the Salem Brass Band and Gilmore's collaboration piece with Salem writer Henry K. Oliver called *Hail Gentle Peace* and performed at the *World's Peace Jubilee.*

Thanks to Craig Burnham for sharing his great-grandmother's scrapbooks. I have culled several songs and ballads, including the *Skating Song,* a song about Salem folks skating on the now nonexistent Mill Pond, and *We Are Ped(d)lars,* a ballad typed into the scrapbook. As I continued culling through old newspapers on microfilm, I discovered that Salem had a yearly *May Day Festival* on Castle Hill and how one of the girls from the Higginson School is Queen and named the Effie of Dempster. I have included the song, the *Colored Millionaires,* dedicated to the *Salem Amateur Minstrels,* a local minstrel group that performed in the Salem area during the 1880s. I have touched on some minstrel song material, including *Ordway's Aeolians,* but have not gone into great depth.

I have also touched on Salem's long history of military and marching bands, starting with Patrick S. Gilmore, and limited the entries because this music is already well-documented. Bandleader Jean Missud of Salem was known for writing the *March of the Salem Witches* and the *New Faneuil Hall March*. Later, George Rigby kept the marching band tradition alive from his predecessor, Missud, and continues today with bandleader Cynthia Napierkowski.

The songs, ballads, and broadsides presented here describe specific events and hint at Salem's past and its influence in helping to shape America both politically and socially. *Old Salem in Ballad and Song* begins with Bob Franke's *Under the Willows*, a contemporary song describing the Salem Willows' seaside park. The book continues with a description of *The Pageant of Salem*, which portrays Salem as a City of Peace and then touches on events in Salem that affected social change, commerce, and war. Some lyrics have tunes associated with them while others do not, thus giving the singer freedom to create melodies to the words. Some singers sing ballads to familiar airs or tunes. On occasion, I have altered one or two words in a ballad for clarity and understanding.

The *Charlestown Land Shark* is an example of a broadside ballad about a man imprisoned because of his debts. *Dreaming of Mother and Home* and the *Emancipation Hymn* were popular songs about the Civil War. The collection concludes with ballads that reflect the temperance movement in Salem. Each ballad holds a place in history that led to the development and growth of Salem, which today is a city notable for its rich culture as well as for the tourism it attracts

Harriet E. Peet taught at the State Normal School (now Salem State University) in 1907 and published an article titled *English Composition in the Elementary School: Studies in Ballad Literature*. She stated, "The ballad tells its story in such a simple dramatic way that we have within it its charm of rhythm and rhyme and its echoes of far-off times." * The ballad, *Young Man of Salem: Execution of Stephen M. Clark*, tells the story of a young sixteen-year-old boy who was hanged on Winter Island for the crime of arson in 1821. Harriet Peet goes on to say:

> Long before printing had been invented, and books and newspapers were common, strolling musicians went from hamlet to hamlet in England and Scotland, chanting old tales while accompanying themselves on harps or zithers. People gathered around these musicians on the village greens in the summer or around the chimney nook of a tavern or farmhouse on a wintery night. The listeners often join in on the song's refrain or add a new verse. *

[* Harriet E. Peet, (Salem Normal School Professor) "English Composition in the Elementary School: Studies in Ballad Literature." *The School Journal*, vol. 75 (New York: A. S. Barnes & Company, 1115 Last Twenty-Fourth Street, vol. LXXV, 1907 and 1908), 574. – RS]

Imagine hearing William Warner or his agent selling Union Oil Polish to preserve boots inside local public houses or on the streets of Salem and Lynn while singing *The New England Blacking Man* to the tune of *Yankee Doodle*.

> When Warner's agent went to Lynn,
>   The polish'd men did hail him,
> They cheer'd him for the song he sang,
>   And so they did in Salem.
>
> He sold a box and sung a verse,
>   And then the dimes seemed handy,
> For people always like to hear
>   Of Yankee Doodle Dandy.

Redfern Mason describes in his book, *The Song Lore of Ireland*, "The rallying tune of the American Revolution *Yankee Doodle*, is an Irish air," called *All the Way to Galway*. Because copyright laws did not exist, people wrote ballads and songs to familiar tunes, a common practice not only in Salem's bustling seaport town but in most towns and cities throughout the New World and Europe. When teaching her students about ballads, Harriet Peet wrote, "A ballad is a literary form almost perfectly adapted to children. But even a ballad, for all its simplicity, must have its method of presentation carefully thought out if it is to be used as a basis for study in a school room." *

We all remember the ditty *The Ants Go Marching One By One* for its humor and simplicity. Both the unforgettable tune and words meet Peet's criteria:

> The ants go marching one by one,
>   Hurrah, Hurrah
> The ants go marching one by one,
>   Hurrah, Hurrah
>
> The ants go marching one by one
>   The little one stops to suck his thumb
> And they all go marching down to the ground
>   To get out of the rain.

Patrick S. Gilmore, bandleader of the *Salem Cadet Band* from 1855 – 1858 was inspired by the Battle of Gettysburg in 1863, soon after he left Salem, and wrote the song *When Johnny Comes Marching Home*. There is an ongoing debate about whether Gilmore originally heard the tune sung by hearing children sing it

(*The Ants Go Marching One by One*) or by various minstrel groups, or whether it was a variant of one of Gilmore's Irish songs from his youth.[5] Either way, the song's popularity grew because of the sentiment of wanting to celebrate Johnny coming home from the Civil War no matter which side he fought on.

> The old church bell will peal with joy
>   Hurrah! Hurrah!
> To welcome home our darling boy,
>   Hurrah! Hurrah!
>
> The village lads and lassies say
>   With roses, they will strew the way,
> And we'll all feel gay
>   When Johnny comes marching home.

As Salem moved into the mid-1800s, so did copyright laws. The U.S. Supreme Court tried its first case relative to copyright law in 1834, some 44 years after the first copyright law. This act formalized the way music was written, presented, and sold. Sheet music and songbooks were now copyrighted and published, with royalties going directly to writers and publishers.

Manuel Fenollosa, a Spanish immigrant who immigrated to Salem, wrote the music for the *Emancipation Hymn* in 1863. Oliver Ditson & Co. published the sheet music, and Fenollosa received the royalties for his work. He continued performing concerts throughout New England.

Reflecting on the times, Fenollosa wrote::

> Asking for a Land, for a Land united,
>   We forgot the slave.
> Pray'd we for our Country, for our Country blighted –
>   For our falling brave.

The ballads and songs in this book help tell the rich and fascinating story of Salem's past. Collecting material for this book has brought to light the ballad singers and the songs they sang. Each ballad tells a story about Salem in a way that can be remembered and retold. Some songs were sung to familiar tunes, while others were published, received copyrights, and sold throughout the land. The song tradition continues to live on today with contemporary songs written in the tradition of the past about Salem. I hope you get to know these ballads and sing these songs. Feel the rhythm of the tunes and share them with friends and family, but most of all, enjoy the music.

~ Bob Strom

In Salem Town

Quaint gabled house squat and frown
    Along the streets in Salem Town,
And meeting elm-trees sway and nod
    In memory of those who trod
The winding street in days gone by
    When gay romance lured men to die.

What must they think the modern day
    When things rush madly on their way
Along the streets in Salem Town
    Where gabled houses squat and frown? *

OLIVER JENKINS – 1922

[* Oliver Jenkins, *Open Shutters, a Volume of Poems*
    (Chicago: W. Ransom, 1922), 39 – RS]

~ 1 ~

Salem

Under The Willows

Under the Willows [1] was composed by Bob Franke and included on his *Brief Histories* CD. Franke refers to Salem Willows, a historic seaside amusement park, and the "old carousel," the "sweet Salem breeze," and the "Lemon Gibraltar" an old-fashioned rock candy favorite. Eleanor Putman writes in her book *Old Salem*, "The Gibraltar is a white and delicate candy, flavored with lemon or peppermint, soft as cream at one stage of its existence, but capable of hardening into a consistency so stony and so unutterably flinty hearted that it is almost a libel upon the rock whose name it bears. The Gibraltar is the aristocrat of Salem confectionery." [2]

Franke lives in Peabody, Massachusetts, and has been a well-known folk singer in the States for over forty years.

Under the Willows

There's a spun-sugar smell in the penny arcade,
    The old carousel is an endless parade;
Of horses and bunnies and camels and chicks,
    Whose riders hang on to their peppermint sticks.

Chorus: And it's under the willows come walk with me, love,
    The sea at our feet and the sky up above.
    The children at play know there's nothing to fear,
    In the sweet Salem breezes, come walk with me, dear.

See the bathers, so bold as their noses turn blue,
    The young and the old build a castle or two;
Though the tide may bring tears when those castles depart,
    There's a hope and a memory in each summer heart.

Chorus: And it's under the willows come walk with me, love,
    The sea at our feet and the sky up above.
    The children at play know there's nothing to fear,
    In the sweet Salem breezes, come walk with me, dear

Now, the rich merchant families look haughty and high,
    But the big clipper packets have all passed us by;
And the captains of legend have all sailed away,
    But they left us the sea and this fine summer day.

Chorus: And it's under the willows come walk with me, love,
    The sea at our feet and the sky up above.
    The children at play know there's nothing to fear,
    In the sweet Salem breezes, come walk with me, dear.

Now, the storm clouds may roll on the wind far away,
    But what's that to us on a day like today?
For the corn, it grows high; and the mill wheels still roll,
    And the Lemon Gibraltar is good for the soul.

Chorus: And it's under the willows come walk with me, love,
    The sea at our feet and the sky up above.
    The children at play know there's nothing to fear,
    In the sweet Salem breezes, come walk with me, dear.

BOB FRANKE – 1992

Salem Willows Postcard, courtesy of Sal Pangallo

Ode to Salem
City of Peace
tune: *Federal Street*

Pageant of Salem Postcard,
courtesy of Sal Pangallo

Alice Osborne Atwood, Salem resident and graduate of Smith College,[3] class of 1879, wrote the song *Ode To Salem (City of Peace)* for the House of Seven The Gables Settlement Association's production of *The Pageant of Salem* in 1913. The Pageant was a weekend-long event highlighting the history of Salem, beginning with the Naumkeag Indians, Roger Williams' banishment by the government, the persecution of the Quakers, maritime commerce, and the Witchcraft conflict.[4]

The Pageant of Salem was one of the Settlement Association's biggest fundraisers. During the Pageant, the *Salem Brass Band*, under the direction of bandleader Jean Missud, performed the song *Ode To Salem (City of Peace)* to the melody of *Federal Street* written by composer and Salem resident Henry K. Oliver.[4]

Gospel Hymn and Tune Book, courtesy of the Boston Public Library

Ode to Salem
City of Peace

Can sculptured stone or painted wood
    Build up a city great and good?
How well the clear-eyed Greek replies;
    "Where there are Men, the cities rise."

True men of faith, whose hearts are sure
    That only things unseen endure;
So they toil on, by day and night,
    Obedient to the Vision bright.

True men of love, who see the chain
    Their brother wears, and feels his pain;
Who cannot rest, but run to share,
    All that they have with Want and Care.

What though a city's numbers grow
    When half are sunk in sin and woe?
What though her towers touch the sky,
    Unless the thoughts of man be high?

O Salem! Let your children live
    In peace the world can never give;
The peace of those who do God's will,
    And see His kingdom coming still.

ALICE OSBORNE ATWOOD – 1913

Pageant of Salem
Kernwood Salem
Massachusetts

Friday, June 13, at 8 P. M.
Saturday, June 14, at 3 P. M.
Monday, June 16, at 8 P. M.
Tuesday, June 17, at 3 P. M.

Pageant accompanied by the SALEM
CADET BAND and a large chorus of
mixed voices. 1500 people in the cast.
Arrangements will be made for trans-
portation to Kernwood.

Admission............ .... .50
With reserved seat:.......$1.00
Automobile space.........$5.00

Boston Herald, May 25, 1913

In 1908, Caroline Emmerton purchased the Turner-Ingersoll mansion (now the House of the Seven Gables), restored the structure, and opened the stately home to the public in 1910.[5] Emmerton used the proceeds from *The House of the Seven Gables* to fund the Settlement Association. The Settlement Association was considered a progressive organization that helped newly arriving immigrant families adapt to their new lives in the city.[5]

5

Henry K. Oliver

Henry K. Oliver was born in Beverly, Massachusetts, on November 24, 1800, and died in Salem on August 12, 1885. Oliver served as the 21st Mayor of Salem from 1876 to 1880, the 5th mayor of Lawrence, Massachusetts, a member of the Massachusetts House of Representatives, an Adjutant General of Massachusetts, and the 26th Treasurer of Massachusetts. Oliver lived at 142 Federal Street, was a master of the theory and history of music, and was the author of several familiar compositions. The tune *Federal Street* has become permanent in musical literature and sacred harp singing. [6]

Henry K. Oliver, 1859,
courtesy of the Lawrence Public Library

Federal Street
by Henry K. Oliver

Transcribed from the *Plain Dealer*, August 6, 1885
   How Oliver wrote *Federal Street*:
   "He was 31 years old when he sat in his library one afternoon reading Theodore Hook's novel, *Passion and Principle*." A passage suggested to him Mrs. Steele's lines, "So fades the lovely, blooming flower." As he ran through the last verse, "Thus gentle patience smiles on pain," an unbidden melody floated into his mind. He was not attempting composition, but without effort, words somehow melted into music. He sat quickly down at the piano and played the tune by improvising the harmonies. Then he transcribed it upon paper and threw it into a drawer. There, it lay for two years,until Dr. Lowell Mason came to Salem to teach a class in music. Happening one day to ask if anyone present had ever written music, General Oliver thought of his composition and brought it forth. Dr. Mason asked for the privilege of publishing it in the academy collection. It was granted, but they were at a loss for a name. General Oliver promptly suggested, "Sally" that of his wife. But that would not do for a sacred tune, so *Federal Street* the street on which the Olivers lived, was chosen, and the world has ever since been grateful to Henry K. Oliver for this grand old tune.[7]

Merton C.M.

by Henry K. Oliver

142 Federal Street, Salem, home of
Henry K. Oliver, courtesy of Mary Barker

Transcribed from the *Plain Dealer*, August 6, 1885

Merton was composed in much the same way as *Federal Street*. General Oliver was the organist at the Old North Church in 1843. During the service one Sunday he searched in vain for the music to (Philip) Doddridge's hymn, *Ye Golden Lamps of Heaven Farewell*. The Rev. Dr. Brazer was halfway through the sermon when the melody came to General Oliver. He hastily jotted down the notes, and the choir, all of them fine musicians, sang the tune at sight. The next day, the venerable pastor remarked to his organist that he had never heard that tune before. General Oliver replied that he himself hadn't and then confessed. The old doctor responded reprovingly, that he ought to chide him for making notes while during his sermon.[7]

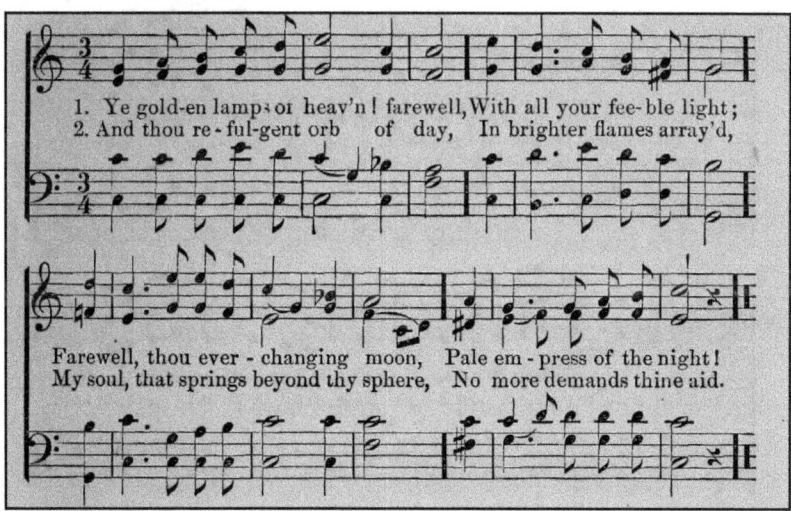

1. Ye gold-en lamps of heav'n! farewell, With all your fee-ble light;
2. And thou re-ful-gent orb   of day,   In brighter flames array'd,

Farewell, thou ever - changing moon,   Pale em - press of the night!
My soul, that springs beyond thy sphere,   No more demands thine aid.

Merton C.M., Evangelical Lutheran Hymnal, courtesy of the Boston Public Library

Oliver taught school in Salem for twenty years (the Oliver School was named after him). Oliver was a member of the *Salem Glee Club,* [8] played organ at St. Peter's Church, and led the choir at the North Church in Salem. Oliver's *Collection of Church Music* and Dr. Tuckerman's *The National Lyre* are examples of his work.

To Cold Spring In North Salem

G.L. Streeter wrote an article in the *Historical Collection of the Essex Institute* entitled *Historical Notices of Salem Scenery*, in which he included the ballad *To Cold Spring in North Salem*. Streeter wrote:

> As we stand upon Liberty Hill above the spring and look out towards the North, the eye takes in some spots of historic as well as scenic interest. Liberty Hill itself has its history as the common property of the original proprietors of North Fields. On the right to the North is Orne's Woods, and on the opposite side is Leavitt's Woods, a patch of fine oaks surrounded by a smooth-shaven lawn. Beyond Orne's Woods is Kernwood, the sightly and beautiful estate of Col. F. Peabody. [9]

According to Duffalo's account in *The Lineage of the Goodell Family of Westminster, England*, the Goodell's made their home at Salem, "in the field northeasterly of Cold Spring in North Salem," [10] where they were granted a house lot and an acre of land in 1636. This spring was known for the first half-century of the 18th century as Goodell's spring. [10]

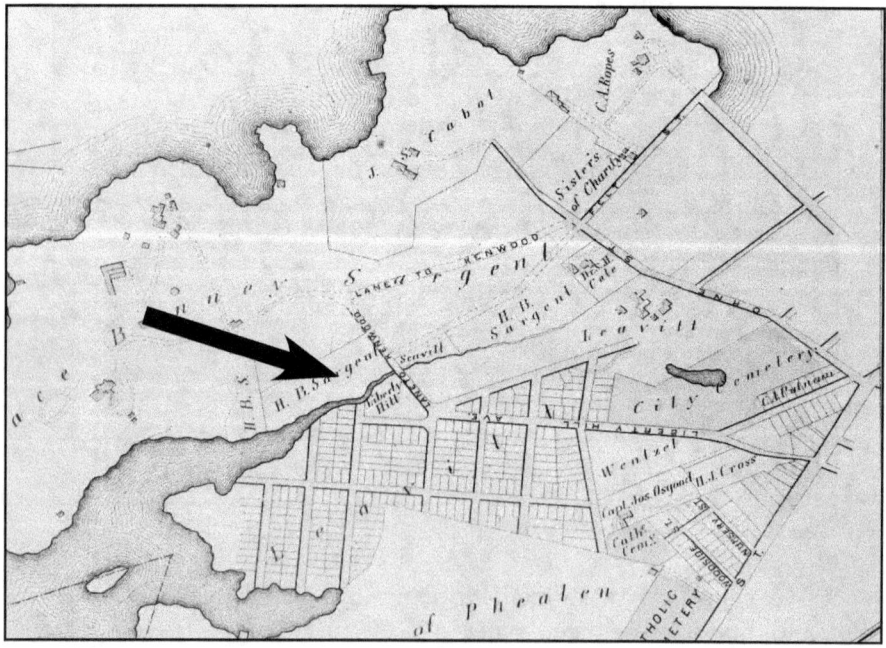

North Salem Map, Author's Personal Collection

To Cold Spring In North Salem

Perchance this aged oak o'er head,
    Now bending as a sheltering friend,
Once lay an acorn in its bed,
    And sought the strength thy waters lend.

These pleasant groves on either side;
    This time-worn inlet of the sea;
Yon swelling bills that stay the tide;
    All share their life and years with thee.

Here once the Indian loved to quaff
    Thy cooling bowl, in summer's day;
To see thy wavelets dance and laugh;
    And watch thy sands in mimic play.

Yet now, as then.—so long ago—
    Thy tiny fountains flood the brim;
Thy singing waters seaward go,—
    A rill of praise, a constant hymn.

Thou art a joy, a gift divine.
    Thy cup o'er flows for every lip;
The timid bird, the thirsty kind,
    The weary traveler, stoop to sip.

Gush ever forth, thou ancient Spring!
    Refresh, delight, inspire the heart.
Thou art, indeed, a lovely thing,
    But faithful to thy humble part.

TRADITIONAL – 1800s

A Skating Song

tune: *A Hunting I Will Go*

Sung to the melody, *A Hunting I Will Go*, *A Skating Song* is from the scrapbook of the Smith Family of Salem. Published in the *Salem Gazette*, cut out, and put into their family scrapbook, the article was undated but assumed to be circa 1880. The *Gazette* reported that:

That portion of the public who tried on their skates last Wednesday to have "just one more" trial of their skills before the Mill Pond ice was buried in snow was delighted on waking yesterday morning to find a drenching rain falling. If cold succeeds, as is probable, an icy surface of renewed smoothness may be expected when, once more, the state of things prevails, such as induces clever performances like the following, which very likely touches off the extreme to which some people carry things, quite deservedly.[11]

The Sky with clouds is over east,
    It has begun to snow,
Yet swiftly they will go,
    For a skating they will go.

Chorus: A skating they will go
        A skating they will go,
        A skating they will go-o-o,
        A skating they will go.

The clothes are soaking in the tub,
    The lines hung out in vain,
For skating now is all the rub,
    And housework's on the wane.

Chorus: A skating they will go
        A skating they will go,
        A skating they will go-o-o,
        A skating they will go.

The baby's voice rings shrill and loud,
    While mother skates away,
And little sis with figure bowed,
    Must tend it all the day.

Chorus: A skating they will go
         A skating they will go,
      A skating they will go-o-o,
         A skating they will go.

Just as it left the wharf,
    The wood is lying in the shed,
While father grinds bark on the ice,
    Or falls and splits his head.

Chorus: A skating they will go
         A skating they will go,
      A skating they will go-o-o,
         A skating they will go.

Old Winter laughs to see how brave,
    The ladies have become;
The never heed his pinched now,
    He cannot drive them home.

Chorus: A skating they will go
         A skating they will go,
      A skating they will go-o-o,
         A skating they will go.

And stern Dark laughs to see the feet,
    With thin cloth gaiters shod,
And says, before the year is out,
    I'll lay them 'neath the sod.

Chorus: A skating they will go
         A skating they will go,
      A skating they will go-o-o,
         A skating they will go.

UNKNOWN – LATE 1800s

Smoking – on 76 Chestnut Street

Smoking – on 76 Chestnut Street [12] was found in the log journal of the Ship *Ringleader* based in Boston. Its writer, Edwin Humphreys from Salem, wrote this song and ends the song with, is "76 Chestnut Street, Salem, Mass."

According to The Registry of Deeds, [13] 76 Chestnut Street in Salem does not exist because numbered houses only go up to 48. There is a house in Boston with the address of 76 Chestnut Street, and it could very well be the house Humphrey is referring to. We'll let the mystery be.

Smoking, many people say,
    Is good to drive the blues away.
It makes men social, drowns their cares,
    To puff their troubles in the air
But to be brief and stop all joking,
    There's nothing (taste) like Goodwin's smoking.

Just so with chewing – all, of every rank,
    Use Goodwin's celebrates Yellow Bank.
Tis lively, bright and full of juice,
    The best tobacco now in use.

Others with habits firmly fixed,
    Prefer the Sarsaparilla mixed.
He say 'tis of the finest grade,
    And knocks all others in the shade.

To all the various brands you'll find,
    Of every shade and every kind.
But none superior on the list,
    To convert's celebrated twist.

You know all men of every creed,
    Who use this most delicious weed?
The place to find it all complete,
    Is 76 on Chestnut Street.
          Salem, Mass.

EDWIN HUMPHREYS – 1858

The homes on Chestnut Street were built by wealthy sea captains during the 1800s. To this day, Chestnut Street is considered "The most beautiful street in America." It is the address of Hamilton Hall, which has been an assembly hall for cultural and social events for over 200 years, and it is also the address of the historic Phillips House located at 34 Chestnut Street.

Chestnut Street Postcard, courtesy of Sal Pangallo

Chestnut Street C.M.
by Henry K. Oliver

Chestnut Street, written by Henry K. Oliver of Salem, is still sung today at Sacred Harp gatherings, traditional sacred choral music that originated in New England.[14]

Hamilton Hall, located on Chestnut Street in Salem, has hosted elaborate celebrations honoring various local historians and visiting dignitaries. [15] Famous architect and master woodcarver Samuel McIntire of Salem designed Hamilton Hall in 1805. The Hall is considered an impressive Federal-style building in America and is designated a National Historic Landmark. It has been a vibrant part of the community for over two hundred years.

Chestnut Street, Carmina Sacra: or, Boston Collection of Church Music, courtesy of the Boston Public Library

The Pickering School

tune: *Auld Lang Syne*

Smith Family of Salem cut out the theme song *The Pickering School* [16] from an undated *Salem Gazette* and pasted the cutout into their family Scrapbook. The graduates typically sing the song at school reunions and graduations. The *Pickering School* served as an elementary school since its inception in 1893. Located at 181 North Street, the building exists today and is home to *Pickering North Condominiums.*

We meet again tonight my dear friends,
From many a distant home,
Old pupils and Teachers, too,
No longer care to roam.

Chorus: For Pickering and our past dear friends,
For present pleasures too,
We join in living greeting here
And loyal hopes renew.

As Pigeons fly afar dear friends,
And find their home place dear,
So we are gathered here once more,
To join in words of cheer.

Beneath the sod some now my sleep,
Free from earthly care,
We bless them all, the loved and lost,
Let History speak them fair.

Chorus: For Pickering and our past dear friends,
For present pleasures too,
We join in living greeting here
And loyal hopes renew.

North, South, and West our mates have flown,
And borne their honors well,
And every heart will throb with joy,
As we the story tell.

Brave men and women have gone forth,
   To give the world their best,
Yet all who live to see all right,
   Must honor our old nest.

Chorus: For Pickering and our past dear friends,
      For present pleasures too,
      We join in living greeting here
      And loyal hopes renew.

So here's a cheer for every lad,
   Who started here in life,
We can't be Moody if we would,
   But glory in his strife.

And here's to every lassie too,
   So many and so fair,
May each one find her own true mate,
   In some congenial air.

Chorus: For Pickering and our past dear friends,
      For present pleasures too,
      We join in living greeting here
      And loyal hopes renew.

And here's to our old Teachers too,
   Our Hayward, and the rest,
We love and honor every one,
   They gave to us the best.

And here's a "three times three" dear friends,
   For Pickering old and new,
God grant he pupils all may prove,
   Both wise and noble too.

Chorus: For Pickering and our past dear friends,
      For present pleasures too,
      We join in living greeting here
      And loyal hopes renew.

UNKNOWN – circa 1880

Only Waiting

The *Salem Register* [17] published *Only Waiting* in their December 11, 1854 issue. The writer asked an older man outside the Almshouse, "What he was doing now?" He answered *Only Waiting*, hence the ballad.

According to The Salem Public Library historical reference site, *Salem Links and Lore*, the *Almshouse*, or *Poor Farm*, is located in the Collins Cove area of Salem. The structure was constructed in 1816 based on the designs of the renowned architect Charles Bulfinch and housed up to one hundred residents. In 1884, a contractor built a second building, which served as a hospital for contagious diseases. A local developer dismantled the *Almshouse* in 1954, and in the 1980s, a contractor purchased the property and built condominiums overlooking Collins Cove. [18]

ONLY WAITING.

A very aged man in an almshouse was asked what he was doing now. He replied, "Only waiting."

Only waiting till the shadows
  Are a little longer grown;
Only waiting till the glimmer
  Of the day's last beam is flown;
Till the night of earth is faded
  From the heart, once full of day;
Till the stars of heaven are breaking
  Through the twilight soft and gray.

Only waiting till the reapers
  Have the last sheaf gathered home,
For the summer time is faded,
  And the autumn winds have come.
Quickly, reapers! gather quickly
  The last ripe hours of my heart,
For the bloom of life is withered,
  And I hasten to depart.

Only waiting till the angels
  Open wide the mystic gate,
At whose feet I long have lingered.

Only Waiting,
Salem Register,
December 11, 1854

The Poor Farm, Salem, Mass.

The *Poor Farm* or *Almshouse*, courtesy of the Nelson Dionne Collection and the Salem Public Library

Only Waiting

Only waiting till the shadows
    Are a little longer grown;
Only Waiting till the glimmer
    Of the day's last beam is flown;
Till the night of the earth is faded
    From the heart, once full of day;
Till the stars of heaven are breaking
    Through the twilight soft and gray.

Only Waiting till the reapers
    Have the last sheaf gathered home,
For the summer time is faded,
    And the autumn winds have come.
Quickly, reapers! Gather quickly
    The last ripe hour of my heart,
For the bloom of life is withered,
    And I hasten to depart.

Only waiting till the angles
    Open wide the mystic gate,
At whose feet I long have lingered,
    Weary, poor, and desolate.
Even now I hear their footsteps,
    And their voices far away;
If they call me I am waiting,
    Only waiting to obey.

Only waiting till the shadows
    Are a little longer grown,
Only waiting till the glimmer
    Of the day's last beam is flown.
Then from out the gathering darkness,
    Holy, deathless stars shall rise,
By whose light my soul shall gladly
    Tread its pathway to the skies.

BY AN AGED MAN IN THE ALMSHOUSE – 1854

Gentle Queen, Ascend Thy Throne, (May Day)

On May 1, 1849, a group of school-aged girls met at Castle Hill in Salem to "commemorate the time-honored pageant, First of May." The *Salem Register* stated:

> A large number of young girls connected with the Higginson School had ventured, despite the chilling admonitions of former years, to believe that the day might pass unvisited by the wind, the hail, the snow, or the rain, those most unwelcome guests at a rural fete. The group met at the summit of Castle Hill. It was a beautiful day. One of the girls from the Higginson School was chosen Queen and named the "Effie" of Dempster. The Maypole, with its tiny flag, its "wavering streamers, and its flowery decorations," was a most conspicuous and attractive object.[19]

The "Queen" then read the words of an Alfred Tennyson poem, called *The May Queen*, as she descended into the valley: [20]

YOU must wake and call me early, call me early, mother dear;
    To-morrow 'ill be the happiest time of all the glad New-year;
Of all the glad New-year, mother, the maddest merriest day,
    For I'm to be Queen o' the May, mother, I'm to be Queen o' the May.

As the "Queen" ascended to the summit of Castle Hill, the girls sang Liverpool poet Felicia Dorothea Browne's (Mrs. Hemans) song, *I Come, I Come! Ye Have Called Me Long*: [21]

I COME, I come! ye have called me long,
    I come o'er the mountains with light and song!
Ye may trace my step o'er the wakening earth,
    By the winds which tell of the violet's birth,
By the primrose-stars in the shadowy grass,
    By the green leaves, opening as I pass.

The ceremony of coronation was performed and accompanied by the song *Gentle Queen, Ascend Thy Throne*.

Gentle Queen, Ascend Thy Throne

"Gentle Queen, ascend thy throne,
  Wear thy fragrant, flowery crown;
Let its beauty deck thy brow,
  While before thy will we bow.

A rosy crown we twine for thee,
  Of Flora's richest treasure;
We lead thee forth to dance and glee,
  To mirth and youthful pleasure.

We bade the fairest flowers that grow
  Their varied tribute render,
To shine above that brow of snow,
  In all their sunny splendor.

Then deign to wear the wreath we twine,
  Thy beauteous ringlets shading;
And be its charm type of thine,
  In all except in fading."

UNKNOWN – 1849

The diadem was of natural flowers of rare beauty, woven together in the most tasteful manner. After dancing around the Maypole and partaking in some simple refreshments, a procession was again formed, and the happy company returned to their homes.[19]

Salem "Great Pasture"

Chris Burke, Salem local and self-taught naturalist, gives monthly walking tours of the *Great Pasture* [22] and takes a romantic look at the pasture and the ballad.

The poem is set in the *Great Pasture* in Salem, a series of walled pastures that began, in the writer's time, with a gate at the present *Broad Street Playground*. The land above that park remains open and undeveloped. There is a cliff with a view of the city with the ocean and Marblehead in the distance. There are indeed crevices between the rocky outcrops. The soil is thin here and can only support a grassy meadow of blue stems and plants such as columbine, blue toadflax, and green briar. Lying on these rocks, the young romantic of today, as did our author, could easily imagine himself in the misty Scottish Highlands where Roderick Dhu of Clan Alpine laid in ambush for the Lowlander Fitz-James, as told by Sir Walter Scott in the *Lady of the Lake*.

Oh! How I languish for the green!
    And budding forest; where is seen,
Among the rocks, the columbine:
    That flower, a favorite of mine!
Because, in youth's most happy days,
    That, the first wildflower of my gaze.

When old Salem's "pasture great,"
    Upon the hoary rocks, I sat,
And saw that blushing flower all around,
    Strewing the rocks, as well as the ground,
So brilliant, 'mist the sterile scene,
    Where only the thin grass was green.

There, on some rocky height it grew,
    All glistening with morning dew;
Bowing its crimson to the gale,
    (As sheltering the violet, pale:)
Like warrior's plumes; when "Roderick Dhu,"
    In ambush, hid his clans-men true.

There too, the briar, odors sweet
    Sent forth, when trampled under feet.
And, the pond lily, watery star,
    Its modest perfume shed afar.
And, there the robin built his nest,
    To live a hermit-life, of rest,

In the lone bush; fearless of ill,
    Where all was desolate, and still;
Where wandering feet but seldom trod,
    Amidst that dreary solitude.

I loved to lie down on the rocks;
    And see, far off, the peaceful flocks;
The farm-house neat; the garden's bloom;
    The blue sea, with its veil of gloom;
Ships, turning white wings to the sun;
    The gold-tipped waves, when day was done;
The music of the pebbly beach;
    The seagull's plunge, and thrilling screech;
The tolling bell; as seaman dead,
    Was carried to his sandy bed;
And, the faint echoes of the drum,
    As troops, returning, hailed their home.

Ah! Those were the days of youth; – no more
    I wander, on my native shore;
They, who once knew me, now, all rest,
    Where slate-stones rise above their breast;
Another race, who know not me,
    Launch their bold prows upon the sea,
The eyes, that once bosom fired,
    Are dim in death! All I desired,
In life's glad morn, are gone, e'ermore!
    I only see a desert shore!
And walk among a race new-grown;
    Alike; unknowing; and, unknown!

Yes! I could pace the longest street,
    And, not a single face should meet,
I saw before! My school-mates, too.
    Are scattered far; All, all is new;
The glory of my race is gone!
    Even their name almost unknown;
The eldest holds this trembling pen!
    A pauper poet! Among men,
Who knows his wealthy family,
    Some of the fleeting years, gone by;
And say, whene'er this last they see,
    How rich, were they; how poor, is he!

J.B.D. – 1857

The Latest Song

This editorial cartoon, *The Latest Song*, was published in *The Salem Daily Gazette* [23] on January 25, 1896, and comments on the city parks. The writer of the cartoon highlights the *Willows, Lynn, and Boston Railroad Park, Cold Springs in North Salem, Liberty Hill, Mack's Hardscrabble Hill, Gallows Hill* – habitat for beasts and reptiles, *Rosewell Field* – for hoodlums and the *Great Pasture* – rendezvous for Robin Hood. The discussion and issues related to the Salem parks are unfamiliar, while the singer in the editorial is standing on *Liberty Hill*. Maybe the only underutilized park in Salem to visit may be *Liberty Hill*.

> Only one, "Park" in the world for me,
>   Only one park has my sympathy,
> It's not very pretty,
>   Nor yet of high degree–
> Only one, "Park" in the world for me."

UNKNOWN – 1896

The Latest Song, Salem Daily Gazette, January 26, 1896

Be Salem Home

```
BE SALEM HOME.
Be Salem home.  'Tis sweet to live in Peace
Where commerce flourishes, and trades in-
     crease ;
Where manufacture germs in fertile fields,
Which, rightly cultur'd, rich abundance
     yields—
Where intellect exuberantly springs,
Amidst examples of life's useful things ;
Where Pageantry is not the Idol serv'd ;
But Industry to worth intrinsic nerv'd.
Where few amusements, lavish, or of chance
Impede the Arts and Sciences advance ;
Where blest Religion reigns, with conscience
     free
For all to differ, who cannot agree.
To fit the soul for duty and release,
'Tis wise, and good, to live and die in peace
  Boston, March 17, 1826.      ALFRED.
```

Essex Register, March 17, 1826, courtesy of Christine Elizabeth Mistretta's private collection

The *Essex Register* published *Be Salem Home* [24] on March 17, 1826. By 1826, the wars with England were over, and the trade embargos lifted. Salem economically began to flourish with shipping, trade, manufacturing, and the arts. The last line in the song, 'Tis wise, and good, to live and die in Peace, reflects the sentiment of Salem and the country's prosperity.

Be Salem home. 'Tis sweet to live in Peace
 Where commerce flourishes, and trade increase;

Where manufacture germs in fertile fields,
 Which, rightly cultured, rich abundance yields.

Where intellect exuberantly springs,
 Amidst examples of life's useful things;

Where Pageantry is not the Idol serv'd;
 But Industry to worth intrinsic nerv'd.

Where few amusements, lavish, or of chance
 Impede the Arts and Sciences advance;

Where blest Religion reigns, with conscience free
 For all to differ, who cannot agree,

To fit the soul for duty and release,
 'Tis wise, and good, to live and die in Peace.

ALFRED – 1826

Who's to Foot the Bills?

This editorial cartoon, *Who's to Foot the Bills?* [25] published in the *Salem Daily Gazettes,* references the town of Danvers complaining to the cities of Salem and Beverly about the build-up of silt in the Danvers River and who will dredge the river. Salem and Beverly's response is Who's to foot the bills?

Danvers:	Lord, I can't get through that slit, It'll have to spread some ways,
Salem & Beverly in chorus:	Yes, It's all very well to talk about spreading, but who's to foot the bills?

UNKNOWN – 1896

Who's to Foot the Bills? Salem Daily Gazette, February 1, 1896

The Origin of the "Salem Shag"

The origins of the *Salem Shag* are unclear. Still, according to Huntress & Dennis Aylward, in an article in the *Essex Institute Collection*, a New York philologist summering in Salem said, "he was unwilling to go home until he had discovered the origin of the *Salem Shag*." The Essex Institute could not find a better explanation to offer him than these verses. [26]

In martial panoply arrayed,
    Welcomed of sire, beloved of maid,
See our brave youngsters file in view,
    What time the century was new,–

The gilded youth of Salem town,
    In leggins white, with muskets brown,
Coats blue, picked out in dainty red.
    Casques fit to cap a Spartan's head,

High topped with nodding ostrich plume
    White as the angry ocean's foam.
While each proud crest must flaunt in air
    Its shaggy tuft of blood-red hair.

As though in gore some battle-steed
    His streaming mane had drenched indeed.
Thus bravely dight for war or love,
    To muster marched,– in ball-room strove,–

The youth of Salem's halcyon time.
    Proud striplings of our golden prime,
So shaggy, all who saw them swore,
    "These should be shags"– and shags they were!

TRADITIONAL – 1894

True Facts About Salem, Mass.

TRUE FACTS ABOUT SALEM, MASS.

The ancient old city of Salem,
  It never was builded by men,
But just as you see it at present
  It always and always has been.

The houses the people now live in
  Were made when the world was first made
And when the great darkness was lifted
  They stood, as they stand, in the shade.

The streets, they were laid out and graded
  The very first day of the six,
And long before nine in the morning
  The mortar was made, and the bricks.

And when he was only an infant—
  An hour or two old, as I think—
Young Adam walked down to the market
  And purchased his first morning drink.

And Eve, after eating the apple,
  She went into Peabody's store,
And bought the first pattern of fig leaf
  Which ever the good woman wore.

And Cain, after taking off Abel,
  He walked right away on his feet,
And married his first wife in Salem,
  And lived upon Washington street.

Methuselah read the old Gazette,
  And wrote for it once in a while,
And the faintest hint of wit would cause
  That ancient old fellow to smile.

And though he lived to a green old age,
  And never was counted a dunce,
In all of the weary years he lived
  The poor man he smiled only once.

The Salem folk were a quiet folk,
  Their ways were peculiar and odd,
And, being a sort of drowsy place,
  It was known as the Land of Nod.

'Tis pleasant—it must be—to live in
  A place that is finished and still;
No sound of the axe or the hammer,
  Or vulgar dull hum of the mill.

The beautiful city of Salem,
  It grows, as the trees grow, you see!
And that it has always existed
  Is proof that it always will be.
      (Salem Gazette)

Facts About Salem,
Salem Gazette,
November 13, 1898

The *Salem Gazette* published Hiram Ozias Wiley's ballad, *True Facts about Salem, Mass.*,[27] on November 13, 1898. H.O. Wiley was born in Middlebury, Vermont, on May 20, 1831, and was a Unitarian layman who practiced law in Peabody from 1855 until he died in 1873. On occasion, he contributed his verse to local newspapers.[28] This ballad does not appear in his published book of poems.

The ancient old city of Salem,
  It never was built by men,
But just you see it at present,
  It always and always has been.

The houses the people now live in,
  Were made when the world was first made,
And when the great darkness was lifted,
  The stood, as the stand, in the shade.

The streets, they were laid out and graded,
  The very first day of the six,
And long before nine in the morning,
  The mortar was made and the bricks.

And when he was only an infant,
  An hour or two old, as I think,
Young Adam walked down to the market,
  And purchased his first morning drink.

And Eve, after eating the apple,
  She went into Peabody's store,
And bought the first pattern of fig leaf,
  Whichever the good women wore.

And Cain, after taking off Abel,
    He walked right away on his feet,
And married his first wife in Salem,
    And lived upon Washington Street.

Methuselah read the old Gazette,
    And wrote for it once in a while,
And the faintest hint of wit would cause,
    That ancient old fellow to smile.

And though he lived to a green old age,
    And never was counted a dunce,
In all of the weary years he lived,
    The poor man he smiled only once.

The Salem folk were a quiet folk,
    Their ways were peculiar and odd,
And being a sort of a drowsy place,
    It was know as the land of the nod.

'Tis pleasant, it must be, to live in,
    A place that is finished and still,
No sound of the axe or the hammer,
    Or vulgar dull hum of the mill.

The beautiful city of Salem,
    It grows as the trees grows you see,
And that it has always excited,
    Is proof that it always will be.

HIRAM OZIAS WILEY – 1898

Lines
Occasioned by the Author's leaving Salem, Mass. to reside in New York

The *Portsmouth Oracle* printed the ballad *Lines on the Occasioned by the Author's Leaving Salem, Mass. To Reside in New York* [29] in its July 24, 1819 issue.

Adieu! My native town, Salem farewell!
    Soon from thy dear and hollowed spot I go;
Soon will my aching heart will sorrow swell,
    And soon the tears of bitter anguish flow.

How dark the ways of Providence to man,
    How deep this truth is written on the heart,
That, though a long connection we may plan,
    Fate had decreed, "The best of friends must part!"

Within thy walls, I've spent my youthful days,
    Here have I felt a mother's anxious care,
Here has she brought me up in virtue's ways,
    And taught me too, to shun the tempter's snare.

Here from a brother's lips has council flowed,
    To warn the young and inexperienced mind,
Here has a sister's tongue with rapture glow'd,
    To reach me where true happiness to find.

"Adieu! My youthful friends, a long adieu,
    With you I've spent the morning of my life,
The sweet Friendship were enjoyed with you,
    Unmixed with envy, passions, or with strife.

Soon we must part, but ah! repress the pain,
    Soon these sad scenes of parting will be over,
For when death parts,– we soon shall meet again,
    On Canaan's land and ever blissful shore.

The tears no more shall wet the sunken eye,
　No more shall sorrow fill the heaving breast;
The breast composed, the tear forever dry,
　And every painful feeling be represt.

Adieu! My native town, Salem farewell!
　Soon from thy dear and hollowed spot I go;
Soon will my aching heart with sorrow swell,
　And soon the tears of bitter anguish flow.

UNKNOWN – 1819

*Lines on the occasioned by the Author's leaving
Salem, Mass. To reside in New York, Portsmouth
Oracle, July 24, 1819*

The Salem Singers

tune: *Camptown Races,* Stephen Foster

Edwin Jocelyn, an occasional contributor to the *Salem Register*, wrote this piece, *The Salem Singers*, [30] and used the well-known Stephen Foster melody *Camptown Races*. Jocelyn published the ballad in the *Register* on July 8, 1852. The city of Salem presented the song during a celebration.

The Salem Singers will sing you a song,
    It sha'n't be dull, and it sha'n't be long,
It shall be all about the times of old,
    When women were witches, and men were bold.

Chorus: We've kept it up all night,
        And we'll keep it up all day;
    If you would celebrate aright,
        We'll show you all the way.

Old Salem Towne was a bluff'd old man,
    He took his pipe, and he took his can,
He lived all along on the rough sea-shore,
    And a grey old fear-naught he sometimes wore.

Chorus: We've kept it up all night,
        And we'll keep it up all day;
    If you would celebrate aright,
        We'll show you all the way.

To foreign ports he sent his ships,
    And his fishing smacks to make short trips,
A plenty of land, all around he had,
    And some was good and some was bad.

Chorus: We've kept it up all night,
        And we'll keep it up all day;
    If you would celebrate aright,
        We'll show you all the way.

A lot of lusty sons he had,
    And some staid at home, and some went to sea,
He taught them all to handle a gun,
    But never to turn their backs and run.

Chorus: We've kept it up all night,
        And we'll keep it up all day;
    If you would celebrate aright,
        We'll show you all the way.

He call'd his sons, like the man of old,
    Around him one day, and their lots he told,
He measured to each a farm apiece,
    Of which he gave a good life lease.

Chorus: We've kept it up all night,
        And we'll keep it up all day;
    If you would celebrate aright,
        We'll show you all the way.

To Danvers, he gave a farm on the west,
    And told him to work, and do his best;
Let his aim be high, and his gain would be much,
    Tan leather, makes shoes, raise onions and such.

Chorus: We've kept it up all night,
        And we'll keep it up all day;
    If you would celebrate aright,
        We'll show you all the way.

To Marblehead, who was tough and stout,
    He gave some land that wouldn't wear out,
And bid him do ought that his genius would suit,
    Catch haddock and cod, and raise stone fruit.

Chorus: We've kept it up all night,
        And we'll keep it up all day;
    If you would celebrate aright,
        We'll show you all the way.

To Lynn he gave some marshes and wood,
   And bid him be frugal, industrious and good,
If he would save well, "in time take his stiches,"
   In the end he would wax in honor and riches.

Chorus: We've kept it up all night,
       And we'll keep it up all day;
     If you would celebrate aright,
       We'll show you all the way.

To Bev'ly he gave a farm on the north,
   And told him of trading, of fishing, & etc.,
For the "main chance" take heed, get rich by all means,
   Till his soil at the best, and raise plenty of beans.

Chorus: We've kept it up all night,
       And we'll keep it up all day;
     If you would celebrate aright,
       We'll show you all the way.

To Manch'ster, Wenham, gave land that were nice,
   And bid them raise hay, good poultry, and ice,
To Topsfield, the meadow, the hilltop and vale,
   Bid them turn up the soil, and thrift wouldn't fail.

Chorus: We've kept it up all night,
       And we'll keep it up all day;
     If you would celebrate aright,
       We'll show you all the way.

Now, mother Britain, who lived on the Isle,
   Set out to tax our folks, awhile,
When Old Salem Towne flar'd up outright,
   And swore he'd sooner stand and fight.

Chorus: We've kept it up all night,
       And we'll keep it up all day;
     If you would celebrate aright,
       We'll show you all the way.

Then he sent his privateers to sea,
 And many a good, rich prize took he;
To fight the "keg 'lars" his sons must go,
 And the way they whipp'd them "wasn't slow."

Chorus: We've kept it up all night,
   And we'll keep it up all day;
  If you would celebrate aright,
   We'll show you all the way.

They stopp'd the "Red Coats" at North River,
 And quickly backward made them "shiver;"
At Lexington and Bunker Hill
 They dealt out many a leaden pill.

Chorus: We've kept it up all night,
   And we'll keep it up all day;
  If you would celebrate aright,
   We'll show you all the way.

Throughout the War, at every scratch,
 The Britons found they had more than their match;
And concluded at last, they got such a whacks,
 They'd better stop, and give up the tax.

Chorus: We've kept it up all night,
   And we'll keep it up all day;
  If you would celebrate aright,
   We'll show you all the way.

The peace return's with its blessings sweet,
 And Old Salem Towne increased his fleet;
He traded "right sharp" like a Yankee true,
 And into his coffers the money flew.

Chorus: We've kept it up all night,
   And we'll keep it up all day;
  If you would celebrate aright,
   We'll show you all the way.

He saw his children around him thrive,
　　Like busy bees in the humming hive,
And he shook his wig, and slapped his knee,
　　In very joy, for right glad was he,

Chorus: We've kept it up all night,
　　　　　And we'll keep it up all day;
　　　　If you would celebrate aright,
　　　　　We'll show you all the way.

Then he thought one day, "I'll make a feast,"
　　And gather my sons from the west and east,
From the north and south, my board around,
　　And joy, and glee, and song shall abound."

Chorus: We've kept it up all night,
　　　　　And we'll keep it up all day;
　　　　If you would celebrate aright,
　　　　　We'll show you all the way.

So here we meet in a happy way,
　　On this our "Independent Day!"
A Day we will always keep in mind,–
　　That bound is once, and shall ever bind.

Chorus: We've kept it up all night,
　　　　　And we'll keep it up all day;
　　　　If you would celebrate aright,
　　　　　We'll show you all the way.

But we must stop, and cut short our song,
　　For we find we're getting rather long;
An excuse we have,– we're apt, you know,
　　When joy gets high, in excess to flow.

Chorus: We've kept it up all night,
　　　　　And we'll keep it up all day;
　　　　If you would celebrate aright,
　　　　　We'll show you all the way.

SONG.

BY EDWIN JOCELYN.

TUNE.—*"Camptown Races."*

The Salem Singers will sing you a song,
It sha'n't be dull, and it sha'n't be long,
It shall be all about the times of old,
When women were witches, and men ↑

Chorus—We've kept it up all night,
    And we'll keep it up all day
    If you would celebrate arigl
    We'll show you all the way

Old *Salem Towne* was a bluff old man,
He took his pipe, and he took his can,
He lived all along on the rough sea-shor
And a grey old fear-naught he sometime

We've kept, &c.

To foreign ports he sent his ships,
And his fishing smacks to make short tri
A plenty of land, all around he had,
And some was good and some was bad.

We've kept, &c.

A lot of lusty sons had he,
And some staid at home, and some wen
He taught them all to handle the gun,
But never to turn their backs and run.

We've kept, &c.

He call'd his sons, like the man of old,
Around him one day, and their lots he told.
He measured to each a farm apiece,
Of which he gave a good life's lease.

We've kept, &c.

To Danvers, he gave a farm on the west,
And told him to work, and do his best;
Let his aim be high, and his gain would be much,
Tan leather, make shoes, raise onions and such.

We've kept, &c.

To Marblehead, who was tough and stout,
He gave some land that would'nt wear out,
And bid him do aught that his genius would suit,
Catch haddock and cod, and raise *stone-fruit.*

We've kept, &c.

To Lynn he gave some marshes and wood,
And bid him be frugal, industrious and good,
If he would save well, "in time take his stitches,"
In the *end* he would *wax* in honor and riches.

We've kept, &c.

To Bev'ly he gave a farm on the north,
And told him of trading, of fishing, &c.
For the "*main chance*" take heed, get rich by a
    means,
Till his soil at the best, and raise plenty of beans.

We've kept, &c.

To Manch'ster, Wenham, gave lands that wer
    nice,
And bid them raise hay, good poultry, and ice.
To Topsfield, the meadow, the hill-top and vale,
Bid them turn up the soil, and thrift would'nt fail,

We've kept, &c.

Now, Mother Britain, who lived on the Isle,
Set out to tax our folks, awhile—
When Old *Salem Towne* flar'd up outright,
And swore he'd sooner stand and fight.

We've kept, &c.

Now, no feud have we with foreign lands,
    But a fray among ourselves, on hand;
So, we'll Pierce our foes with thrusts and shots,
    And fight the field like very Scotts.

Chorus: We've kept it up all night,
    And we'll keep it up all day;
    If you would celebrate aright,
    We'll show you all the way.

EDWIN JOCELYN – 1852

The Salem Singers,
Salem Register, July 8, 1852

Our Ride to Lynn

tune: *Willie's on the Dark Blue Sea*

Found in the Broadside collection at the Phillips Library, *Our Ride to Lynn* [31] refers to the adventures of several young men on their ride to Lynn and their trip back to Salem. As they enter Salem, they pass the tollhouse, pay their toll, and head home. *Our Ride to Lynn* is sung to the tune of *Willie's on the Dark Blue Sea*, written by Boston composer H. S. Thompson. [32]

> This day we've got a horse and chaise,
>   To ride far over to Lynn
> And many a pleasant hour will pass,
>   Ere we come home again.
>
> Chorus: We're bound to have a first rate time,
>   Of pleasure drink our fill;
>   And as the day is very fine,
>   Enjoy ourselves we will.
>
> The sun is shining bright and clear,
>   The breeze is blowing free,
> The trees in autumn's hues are drest,
>   The birds sing merrily.
>
> Here, on the crest of this high hill,
>   We view the ocean blue;
> Now through the valley swift we speed,
>   With our merry, happy crew!
>
> Ah! Here we are, in sight of Lynn!
>   Now, through its streets we ride:
> And as we swiftly go, we see
>   New scenes on every side.
>
> In every street, in every lane,
>   Some pretty lass we meet;
> But when compared with Salem bells,
>   They are not half so sweet.

The sun is sleeping in the west,
  The night comes on apace:
We'll leave Lynn city far behind,
  Home, through the woods we'll race.

The moon is sailing through the sky,
  The twinkling stars appear;
And over the road, the tall trees cast
  Their shadows far and near.

Chorus: We're bound to have a first rate time
      Of pleasure drink our fill;
      And as the night is very fine,
      Enjoy ourselves we will.

We pass the toll-house swiftly by,
  Scarce stop to pay our scot;
And now we enter Essex Street
  Upon a handsome trot.

Chorus: Yes, we a pleasant time have had,
      Seen many a thing that's new,
      Seen many a joyous, sprightly, lad,
      And many a lassie too.

J.C. DUCHOW – 1850

Willie's on the Dark Blue Sea

The Legend of the Club House

The ballad writer, Patricia (last name unknown), published *The Legend of the Club House* in a California paper called the *Hemet News* on March 18, 1921, along with a letter to Salem Willows resident Miss Sarah Saltonstall.

Dear Sallie, You remember that snippy Collins girl who used to be in our bridge club? I never liked her, but I thought I would send her my column just to show her she wasn't the only literary one in our set. She wrote back: "I shall lose no time in reading it!" What do you suppose she meant by that? She needn't think her time is so valuable just because she writes poetry. She isn't the only one. I have written a poem myself just to spite her. I wish you would show it to her, though I know it is like "casting pearls before swine." [33]

Should you ask me, "Whence these stories?
   Whence these ravings of Patricia,
With the odor of the doughnut,
   With the caring of the children,
With the blanket of the savage,
   And the cleaning of the silver?"

I should answer, I should tell thee
   "From the Woman's Club of Hemet,
From the club of many women,
   Working for the mighty dollar."

If still further you should ask me,
   "Why the struggle of these women,
Why their striving and their grasping,
   For piles of filthy lucre?"
I should answer, I should tell thee
   Straightway in such words as follow:

"In the lovely town of Hemet,
   In the green and fruitful valley,
Where the snows of San Jacinto,
   From above the orange blossoms,

There is still one thing that lacking,
    For the pleasure of the women,
For the joy and their contentment.
    And they fain would build a clubhouse.

On their lot, besides the Lib'ry,
    Where they all could come together,
For their feasts and merry-makings,
    Gatherings of all the people."

And if further you should question,
    Saying, "Can I aid this project
For the good of all the valley?"
    I should say in accents forceful,
In the language of the doughboy,
    "Then it was, you said a mouthful!"

"You who love the tender pie-crust,
    Love the frosting and the doughnut,
Love the cake, food of the devil,
    Love the sherbet and the wafer,
And the marmalade so golden.
    Buy these recipes, to aid you
In the feastings of your households,
    Buy and help those noble women
Working bravely for their clubhouse.

"Buy lemon pie, so toothsome,
    Heritage of far New England.
But the clothing for your children,
    Buy the comforts for your old folks,
Comforts to keep off the east wind
    When it blows from San Jacinto –"

Ye, whose clothes are growing shabby,
    Who takes pride in festive raiment?
Hie ye to the home of Myers,
    There to buy the gorgeous sweater,

Haste ye to the house of Ankrum,
 There to get the rich embroidery,
And be sure to buy the dress form,
 Replica of your own figure.

Thus it is that your Patricia,
 In this language, quaint and olden,
Could rave on to you forever
 Of the doings of the clubmates.

In the lovely town of Hemet.
 'Neath the peak of the mighty Tahquitz.
Homely phrases, yet each letter,
 Filled with hope and filled with longing.

BY PATRICIA – 1921

Hemet Woman's Club Exchange

(With Comments by Patricia)

Miss Sarah Saltinstall,
 Salem Willows, Mass.

Dear Sallie:—You remember that snippy Collins girl who used to be in our bridge club? I never liked her but I thought I would send her my column just to show her she wasn't the only literary one in our set. She wrote back: "I shall lose no time in reading it!" What do you suppose she meant by that? She needn't think her time is so valuable just because she writes poetry. She isn't the only one.

I have written a poem myself just to spite her. I wish you would show it to her, though I know it is like "casting pearls before swine."

Anyone else would see that it is beautiful because it is just like Longfellow's Hiawatha. I have called it:

The Legend of the Club House

Should you ask me, "Whence these stories?
Whence these ravings of Patricia,
With the odor of the doughnut,
With the caring of the children,
With the blanket of the savage,
And the cleaning of the silver?"

I should answer, I should tell thee
"From the Woman's club of Hemet,
From the club of many women
Working for the mighty dollar."

If still further you should ask me,
"Why the struggle of these women,
Why their striving and their grasping
For the piles of filthy lucre?"
I should answer, I should tell thee
Straightway in such words as follow:

"In the lovely town of Hemet,
In the green and fruitful valley,
Where the snows of San Jacinto
From above the orange blossoms,
There is still one thing that lacking
For the pleasure of the women,
For their joy and their contentment.
And they fain would build a club house
On their lot, beside the 'Lib'ry,'
Where they all could come together
For their feasts and merry-makings,
Gatherings of all the people."

And if further you should question,
Saying, "Can I aid this project
For the good of all the valley?"
I should say in accents forceful,
In the language of the doughboy,
"Then it was, you said a mouthful!"

The Legend of the Club House,
Hemet News,
March 18, 1921

The Moon So Round and Mellow

This postcard of the Salem Willows at night is from the Nelson Dionne Collection. The verse on the postcard, *The Moon So Round and Mellow,*[34] is a variant of the Scottish children's poem *The Moon So Round and Yellow* [35] written by Matthias Barr.

> The Moon so round and mellow
> Looks down from up on high;
> It's sure a pretty picture
> Of whispering waves and sky.

UNKNOWN – circa 1920

> Moon, so round and yellow,
> Looking from on high,
> How I love to see you
> Shining in the sky.

MATTHIAS BARR – 1922

The Moon So Round and Mellow, courtesy of the Nelson Dionne Collection

Observations of Their Travel

Roger Williams was born in London circa 1603 and died in March 1683. Williams was a minister who founded the first Baptist Church (Meeting House) in America in 1638. He worked closely with Native Americans in New England and wrote the first dictionary of Native American languages. Williams, banished from Salem because of his separatist teachings voiced in the *Christian Pioneer Intended To Uphold The Great Doctrines of the Reformation*, a book of unknown authorship, "God can comfort, feed and safely guide even through a desolate howling wilderness." [36] After his exile from Salem in mid-winter, ill and on his way to form the colony of Rhode Island and Providence Plantations, pilgrim poet Roger Williams [36] wrote these verses in 1643:

God makes a path, provides a guide,
　　And feeds in wilderness;
His glorious name, while breath remains,
　　Oh that I may confess.

Lost many a time, I've had no guide,
　　No house but hollow tree;
In stormy winter night, no fire,
　　No food, no company.

In him I have found a house, a bed,
　　A table company;
No cup so bitter but made sweet,
　　When God shall sweetening be. [37]

ROGER WILLIAMS – 1643

What Cheer or Roger Williams in Banishment
The Fire-Side of Salem

In 1829, Job Dufree (1790 – 1847) of Tiverton, Rhode Island, wrote *Roger Williams in Banishment: The Fire-Side of Salem*. Durfee, a Rhode Island politician, decided not to run for re-election, retired to private life, and "mingled with agricultural labors and the more delightful pursuits of literature." [38] During his retirement, he wrote the epic poem *Roger Williams in Banishment*. The poem accounts for Williams' journey through the wilderness, his subsequent settlement in Seekonk, Massachusetts, and before he founded Providence. [39] Verses 1, 2, & 3 are included here.

> I sing of trials stern and sufferings great,
>> Which Father Williams in his exile bore,
> That he the conscience bound might liberate,
>> And her religious rights the soul restore;
> How after flying persecution's hate,
>> And roving long by Narragansett's shore,
> In lone Moshassuck's vale at last he sate,
>> And gave soul liberty her Guardian State.
>
> He was a man of spirit true and bold;
>> Feared not to speak his thoughts what e'er they were;
> His frame, though light, was of an iron mould,
>> And fitted well fatigue and change to bear;
> For God ordained that he should breast the cold
>> Of northern Wilderness in winter drear;
> And of red savages protection pray,
>> From Christians, but– more savage far than they.
>
> Midwinter reigned and Salem's town,
>> Where late were cleft the skirts away,
> Showed its low roofs and from thatching brown,
>> The sheeted ice sent back the last ray;
> The schoolboys left the slippery crown,
>> So keen the blast came o'er the bay.
> And the fun in vapors thick down,
>> And the glassed forest cast a somber frown.

JOB DURFEE – 1829

Patrick S. Gilmore
Time in Salem 1855 – 1858

Essex Institute Historical Collection,
courtesy of the Salem Public Library

Born in Ballygar, County Galway, in 1829, Gilmore emigrated from Ireland to Boston in 1849. Coming to America with a strong background in music, his musical talents and ambitions became apparent, and he soon became the leader of the *Boston Brigade Band*. Gilmore's reputation grew as a bandleader, and his endeavors widened.[40]

While leader of the Boston and Charlestown bands, Gilmore wrote and published several compositions. *The Everlasting Polka,* played by the *Suffolk Brass Band* and penned by Gilmore in 1852 and dedicated to Miss S.E. Daily. During this period, Gilmore also wrote the larger piece, *On The Road To Salem Quick Step*, which includes the *Salem Hornpipe*, a tune still played today, possibly anticipating his move to Salem.

In early 1854, Gilmore wrote the piece *Sad News From Home* [41] and dedicated the song to Miss Maria Hall. Another piece, *Good News from Home*, is a ballad written in 1854 by Gilmore and dedicated to his mother.

In the fall of 1854, Mr. Jerome H. Smith, leader of the *Salem Brass Band*, took sick and soon passed away. On January 15, 1855, the *Salem Register* reported that Gilmore, leader of the *Boston Brigade Band*, "has accepted the leadership of the *Salem Brass Band*." [42] The newspaper article continued saying that Gilmore was a gentleman and highly qualified for the position.

Sad News From Home, courtesy of Lester S. Levy Collection of Sheet Music, Sheridan Libraries, Johns Hopkins University

The Early Days of
The Salem Brass Band

One year after Gilmore left Salem and headed back to Boston, the *Salem Register* published an article called *The Early Days of The Salem Brass Band* [43] outlining the history of the *Salem Brass Band* from its inception in 1837 to 1859.

Transcribed from the *Salem Register*:

The *Salem Brass Band* was organized in 1837, with Mr. George W. Felton as Leader, who, with twelve others, constituted the band at the time. The next season, Mr. F. W. Morse received and accepted a call as Leader and Director, who, although a young man not quite twenty years of age, possessed fine musical talent and taste and united at once, energetically and full of interest, with his associates, to raise the band to quite a degree of excellence. That he succeeded in this is evident from the fact that the band received, at home and abroad, a very good share of patronage, being employed by the military, fire, and other associations. The band, too, during his connection with them, performed for Commencement services at Colleges and at Academies(Universities). In 1848 and '49, the band was obliged to procure a substitute for Mr. Morse as Leader, being seized with sickness, which finally proved fatal. He was a good musician, as all must know who ever heard his unsurpassed Bugle and Cornet tones.

Sometime in 1849, the band procured the services of Mr. Jerome H. Smith as Leader, who came highly recommended, and all who remember his unrivaled execution and had become acquainted with his genial and gentlemanly manners, together with his great business tact were not surprised that he, too, fully sustained the growing reputation of the band.

It is proper for him, perhaps, to state, as evidence of the popularity of Messers. Morse and Smith, that the citizens of Salem presented to each, at different times, a splendid silver Bugle.

In the fall of 1854, Mr. Smith was suddenly taken sick and, after a short illness, died, lamented, and mourned by all who knew him.

Mr. P.S. Gilmore succeeded Mr. Smith. Heretofore, the principal melody instruments were Bugles, but Mr. Gilmore's joining the band, he being a fine Cornet player and musician, as is well known, Bugles were laid aside and Cornets substituted. This was done at some sacrifice, as Messrs. Parsons and Faxon possessed fine silver Bugles. The change was also an improvement doubtless, the Cornet being in every way superior to the Bugle. As the band had increased in experience, ability, and numbers and enjoyed the undivided support and exertion of all the members, it was a comparatively easy task for Mr. Gilmore, with his fine taste and tact, to further develop the talent and extend the patronage of the band, which has certainly attained a reputation second to no other in New England, to say the least. At the close of the present season (1858), Mr. Gilmore decided to move to Boston, and Mr. Kehrbahn was chosen as his successor. [43]

Salem Hornpipe
On The Road To Salem Quick Step

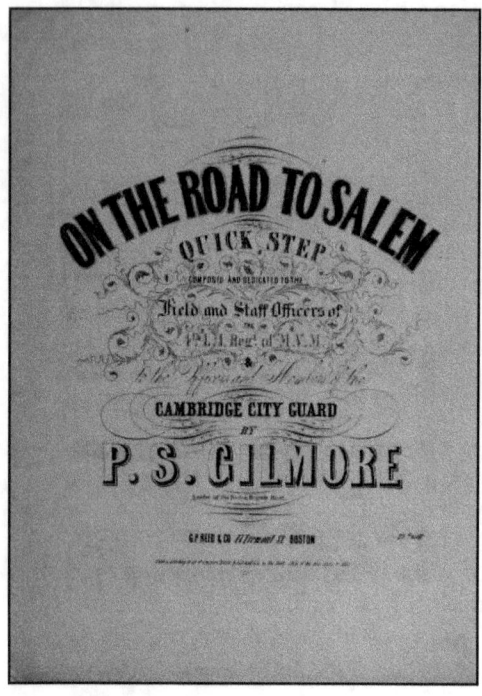

On the Road to Salem,
courtesy of the Boston Public Library

Patrick S. Gilmore wrote the *Salem Hornpipe* [44] in 1853. Jim Dalton, Salem resident and Professor of Core Studies at Boston Conservatory at Berklee, unearthed an early written version of the tune at the Phillips Library in Rowley, Massachusetts. He discovered that the *Salem Hornpipe* was part of a longer piece called *On The Road To Salem Quick Step*. Dalton stated in an article published in the *Salem Gazette*, "The names of the officers were listed in order of rank, right on the music as if Gilmore was dedicating a few beats of the music to each." [45] Dalton continued looking for the connection and noticed, "On the fourth page of the music, it was labeled *Road to Salem*, the same tune as the *Salem Hornpipe*." [45] Elias Howe published the *Salem Hornpipe* in Boston in 1883 and included the tune in *Ryan's Mammoth Collection: 1050 Reels and Jigs* by William Bradbury.

Jim and Maggi Smith-Dalton, perform 19th and 20th century American music.

Salem Hornpipe, courtesy of Jim and Maggi Dalton's private collection

I Never Can Be Thine

The *Salem Register* included this little-known ballad by Gilmore in 1856 called *I Never Can Be Thine*.[46] There is minimal evidence on whether Gilmore officially published this song along with a corresponding tune.

Oh. no I never can be thine;
　　Then bid the hopes depart,
And let thy thoughts to one incline,
　　More worthy of thine heart.
I would not have thee shed a tear,
　　Nor breathe a sign in vain;
Then go, and charm some other ear,
　　Ne'er think of me again.

Go seek for one of higher birth
　　Than fortune have to me;
Go choose a better home on earth
　　Then I could hive to thee,
I will not tell thee, what I would
　　If kingdoms were mine own;
But, blessed angel, if I could,
　　I'd place thee on a throne.

The rich so seldom love the poor,
　　How strange the act would be,
If one like thee could e'er endure
　　To give thine hand to me.
Oh, no, 'twere better ne'er to wed
　　Then choose the lot that's mine,
'Till I am numbered with the dead,
　　I never can be thine.

Look up, there is a place above,
　　Away from earthly woe;
A home of everlasting love,
　　Where all the good shall go.
Then, let thy thoughts that would be mine,
　　To Him on high he given,
On earth, I never can be thine,
　　But, oh, I may in heaven.

PATRICK S. GILMORE – 1856

Gilmore Concerts with
The Salem Brass Band

GRAND CONCERT!
—o—
THE
SALEM BRASS BAND,
P. S. GILMORE, LEADER,
—— Will give a ——
GRAND CONCERT,
—AT—
MECHANIC HALL,
—ON—
TUESDAY EVENING,
on which occasion they will be ass...
its American Arti...
Mr. Edward Ke...
the greatest Bugle player in t...
Mr. M. P. Ho...
the celebrated Baritone
The Programme will consist of
formed by Mr Kendall; Songs, by
Obligatos, by Mr Gilmore; Trum
Kehrhahn—who will also appear for
Solo on his favorite instrument, th
Selections from the most favorite
the Anvil Chorus, from Il Trovato
companiment, Remembrance of Mi
lop, and many other favorite gems,
clude with the popular Quickstep,
Mr Kendall (who was the first to

Grand Concert,
Salem Register,
July 28, 1856

Gilmore continued writing ballads and putting them to music. In 1855, he published several compositions while leading the *Salem Brass Band*, including *Come Buy the Bridal Ring*, *Oh Let Me Dream of Former Years*, and *The Prize Baby Polka*.

Over the next couple of years, Gilmore and the *Salem Brass Band* toured all over New England, building a nationwide reputation as one of the best bands in the country. In 1855, Gilmore put on a Grand Concert at *Mechanics Hall* in Salem featuring Bugle solos by Edward "Ned" Kendall and baritone singer H.P. Horne.[47]

The Salem Brass Band, Concert poster, from the Smith Family Scrapbook

Gilmore's productivity continued in 1856, publishing several compositions, including the songs *Music is the Only Charm* and *Bonnie Woman's Smile*. In July of 1856, the *Salem Register* reported that Gilmore's Band put on a public concert on Gallows Hill in Salem with views of downtown and the harbor, adding, "From the eminence, and the elevation is such, and the atmosphere was so clear on Friday, the music could be heard favorably in almost every part of the city."[48]

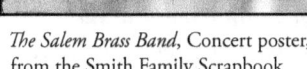

The following is the programme for to-morrow evening:

PROGRAMME.

PART I.
1—March—On the road to Salem. Gilmore.
2—Pot Pourri—Remembrance of the Military. Weiprecht.
3—Belgian Gallery Polka. Dodworth.
4—Grand Fantaisie for E flat Cornet, variations on Old Folks at Home. Belsheim.
5—Jessamine Waltzes. Labitzky.
6—Divertissement from Robert le Diable. Meyerbeer.

PART II.
7—Grand Selection from Il Trovatore. Verdi.
8—When the Swallows homeward fly. Abt.
9—Wedding March. Mendelssohn.
10—Serenade—Departed Days. Louis.
11—Prize B by Polka. Gilmore.
12—Grand Finale—National Airs. Jonathan.

Program at Gallows, Hill
Salem Register, July 28, 1856

On March 2, 1857, Gilmore's Band headed to Washington D.C. and performed at U.S. President James Buchanan's inauguration. Salem historian Jim McAllister wrote on the SalemWeb blog:

> The band's reputation earned it a highly sought-after invitation from the *New England Militia Company* to play at the inauguration of U.S. President James Buchanan. *The Salem Brass Band's* performance in the nation's capitol was praised by the Washington press, further enhancing its reputation as one of the nation's leading outfits. But the publicity also enraged the Boston area bands who had not been chosen to make the trip. Their egos were bruised, and a group of Bostonians decided to ambush Gilmore's group at the Boston train depot when they returned from Washington. The Bostonians planned to destroy the instruments of the Salem musicians and render their lips unserviceable for playing. Fortunately for the unsuspecting Salem band members, they caught an earlier train home and missed their surprise rendezvous with their jealous counterparts.[49]

Gilmore's popularity grew while he led the *Salem Brass Band*. One reason was his ability to know what the people wanted to hear. In the program booklet of his *Grand Concert by Gilmore's Salem Brass Band*, Gilmore performed a sampling of classical pieces, popular songs of the day, and brass band pieces such as marches and quicksteps.[50]

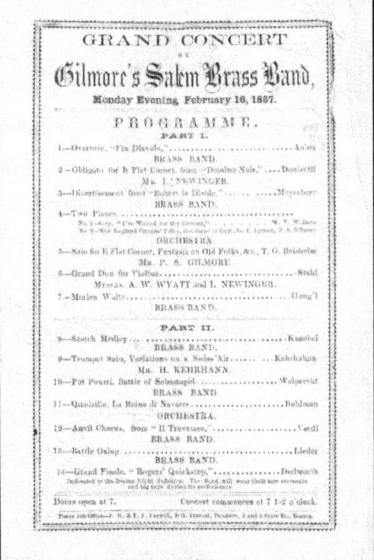

Grand Concert – Gilmore's *Salem Brass Band*, courtesy of Jarlath MacNamara

Gilmore's stay in Salem would end in 1858, but not without continued touring and publishing three additional song sheets, including *Sons of Temperance Quickstep*,[51] *Dinner Bell Polka*, and the *Breakfast Bell Polka*. Gilmore moved back to Boston to lead the *Boston Brigade Band*.

Gilmore's World's Peace Jubilee

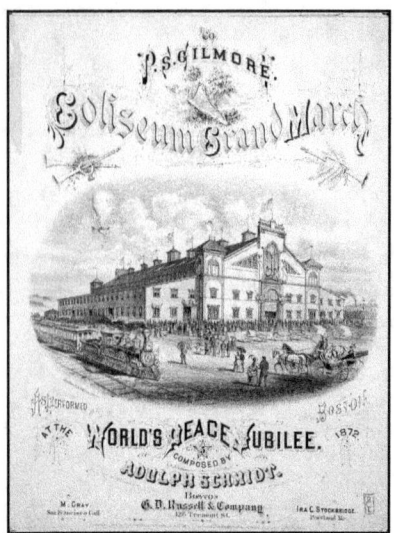

Coliseum Grand March, courtesy of the Boston Public Library

The *World's Peace Jubilee* took place in Boston, with the opening ceremonies on June 17, 1872, *Bunker Hill Day*, and ending on the 4th of July. [52] It was the second of a series of performances commemorating the end of the Civil War and an effort to unite the country. Gilmore directed both festivals. The *National Peace Jubilee* took place on the weekend of June 15 – 19, 1869. The *World's Peace Jubilee* lasted over two weeks and consisted of a 2000-piece orchestra and a 20,000-voice chorus.

Gilmore held the events in the *Boston Coliseum*. Constructed in the Back Bay of Boston and designed by William Preston, the *Boston Coliseum* was 550 in length and 350 feet wide and reached a height of 120 feet. Built as a temporary structure, the Coliseum was large enough to hold 100,00 people. The newly formed Jordan March Company partially funded the building. [53]

Two groups that performed at the *World's Peace Jubilee* and received national and local attention were *The Fisk Jubilee Singers*, a group of black college students from *Fisk University* in Nashville, and according to the *Boston Daily Journal,* 100 Boston firemen were part of *Gilmore's Anvil Choir.* Under the direction of Gilmore, they performed *Verdi's Il Trovatore* and became local celebrities. [54]

Austrian-born Johann Strauss also performed at the Jubilee and conducted his composition *Beautiful Blue Danube.* The newspaper reported that the "selection was most beautifully rendered and was repeated at the enthusiastic demands of the Audience." [54]

Gilmore did not forget his days in Salem. At some point, he met music teacher and church organist Henry K. Oliver of Salem. Oliver is well known throughout Massachusetts. On a Tuesday evening, at the *World's Peace Jubilee*, with President Grant in attendance, Gilmore invited Oliver to "wield the baton" and lead the large orchestra and the chorus of 20,000, singing Oliver's newly composed hymn, *Hail, Gentle Peace,* written to the tune he called *Federal Street.* [55]

Hail, Gentle Peace

tune: *Federal Street*

Hail, gentle Peace! Good Will to Man!
    God's blessing o'er the world's wide span!
War's fearful storms are passed away,
    The Prince of Peace o'er earth bears sway.

No sounds of battle rend the air,–
    No shrieks of passion or despair;
But, from the woods, the vales, the hills,
    Sweet Peace the air with music fills.

So the full choir of angels bright,
    Heralds of Christ, ere early light,
To shepherds sang melodious strains,
    On the still air of Bethlehem's plains.

Take up, ye voices, all the song,
    With high acclaim the strain prolong;
Earth, join to angel choir your voice,
    And in full harmony rejoice.

HENRY K. OLIVER – 1872

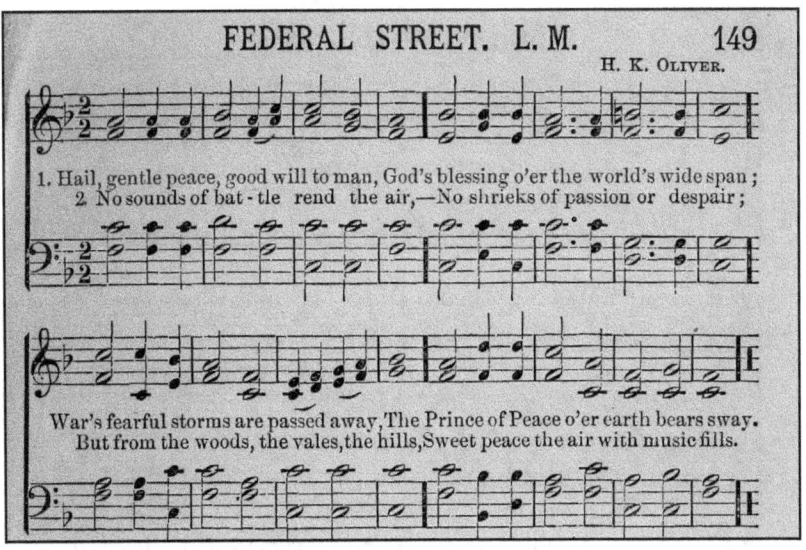

Hail Gentle Peace, The Devotional Chimes: A Collection of New & Standard Hymns, courtesy of the Boston Public Library

The Colored Millionaires
Marching Song

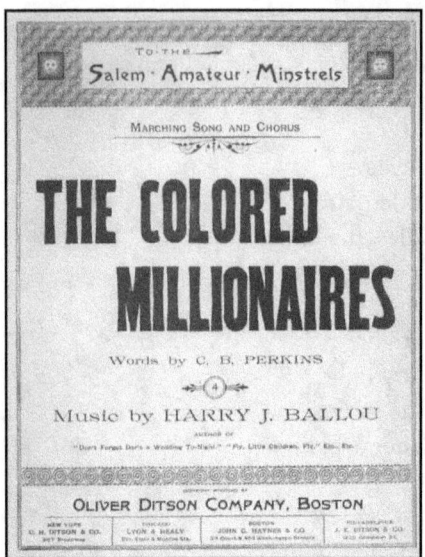

The Colored Millionaires,
author's personal collection

Local songwriter C.B. Perkins wrote the words to *The Colored Millionaires* while Harry J. Ballou wrote the music. Boston publisher Oliver Ditson published the song in 1891. The song was dedicated to The *Salem Amateur Minstrels*, a local Salem/Beverly minstrel group.[56] They performed minstrel variety shows on the North Shore of Massachusetts. The group included several local singers, including locals J.P. Brown and C.H. Weston. William John Mahar, described in his book *Behind the Burnt Cork Mask: Early Blackface Minstrelsy and Antebellum American Popular Culture,* "By the middle of the 19th century, blackface minstrel shows had become a distinctive American artform, translating formal works such as opera into popular terms for a general audience".[57] By today's standards, Minstrel shows as a form of entertainment are considered unacceptable.

The Colored Millionaires – Marching Song

Just throw your eyes upon our shape, We think we're out of sight,
    Ar-rayed in clothes of latest cut, and deck'd with jewels bright!
Our hands are soft, just like a girl's, We always wear kid's gloves;
    And all the ladies that we met, They call us turtle doves.

We ride in hacks and four in hands, and tally hos so gay.
    And set the pace for any kind of sport that comes our way.
And ev'ry body knows our name, And greets us with their states,
    For we're the pet of ev'ry set, the Colored Millionaires!

Oh, did you ever see such style?
　It is really worth your while
To watch us as we go by
　With our eyeglass in our eye.
Our pocket books are fat,
　We wear diamonds and all that,
And with us no one compares,
　For we're the colored Millionaires.

We never put on any airs, We are too richer che!
　And all the dudes they copy us, Or just try to, anyway.
In all the best society, we never are out classed,
　But take the lead in ev'ry thing and hold it to the last;

At ev'ry dance we have the choice of all the ladies there;
　In etiquette we lead them all, And teach both dark and fair.
And all the swell ones tip their hats, to slight us no one dares,
　For far and wide they know us well, the Colored Millionaires,

Oh, did you ever see such style?
　It is really worth your while
To watch us as we go by
　With our eyeglass in our eye.
Our pocket books are fat,
　We wear diamonds and all that,
And with us no one compares,
　For we're the colored Millionaires.

You ought to see the steam yachts fine, we own them, to a man!
　To take a trip to foreign climes just now it is our plan;
At all the racetracks we are known, the bookies fight us shy.
　We always pick the winners for we are so very fly,

We never mind expense or care a pin of any cost,
　For want of cash you just can bet there is no pleasure lost.
The very richest of them all we really have no cares.
　The jolliest crowd in all the world, the Colored Millionaires.

WORDS: C.B. PERKINS, MUSIC: HARRY J. BALLOU – 1891

~ 2 ~
On Dying
and Tragedy

Written on Reading an Account of the Execution of
Stephen M. Clark

The Harris Broadside Collection at the John Hay Library at Brown University houses the Broadside ballad called *Written on Reading, an Account of the Execution of Stephen M. Clark.*[1] A jury found Clark guilty of arson and recommended commutation of his sentence, but the state followed through on his execution. Clark was put to death on Winter Island in Salem on Thursday, May 10, 1821, at the early age of sixteen years and nine months.[2]

Clark's case fueled the movement in Massachusetts to reduce the number of capital crimes, if not abolish the death penalty altogether. By 1852, only murder remained on the books as a capital offense, and in 1984, the Supreme Judicial Court ruled the death penalty unconstitutional.[3]

SALEM,

TUESDAY MORNING, APRIL 24, 1821.

EXECUTION OF STEPHEN M. CLARK.

The Execution of Clark, now confined in our gaol, heretofore ordered to take place next Thursday, is respited by the Governor and Council till the 10th of May next. The Sheriff has made known to the unhappy young man that the dreadful sentence of the law will then be carried into effect.

It has been usual in this State to grant short reprieves to those who have been executed.

Salem Gazette,
April 24, 1821

Written on Reading an Account of the Execution of Stephen M. Clark
courtesy of the Harris Broadside Collection at Brown University

Written on Reading an Account of the Execution of Stephen M. Clark

OH! Massachusetts! Name to me most dear,
    And Salem too, thou art my native spot,
For thee I have to drop pitying tear,
    For on thy name there's a disgraceful blot.

Oh! Could'st thou not thy legal arm outstretch,
    Show mercy to the Youth who now is gone,
Snatch from the grave the poor deluded wretch,
    And mitigate the grief of those who mourn?

Could not this Youth – could not the hoary hairs
    Of his afflicted broken-hearted sire,
Could not a People's cries, a People's prayers,
    A human breast with pity's glow inspire?

Me thinks I see the afflicted Father stand,
    His quivering lips, his stammering tongue employ,
To implore the ruler of a pious land,
    To spare this guilty but repenting boy.

But all his supplications were in vain,
    Mercy was due, but mercy was denied,
Nothing an Earthly pardon could obtain,
    Die, says the law – the young offender dies.

Here ends the scene – his spirit now is flown,
    Unto that God by whom, all crimes are tried,
And there I trust that mercy will be shown,
    Which unrelenting man on earth denied.

WRITTEN BY A YOUNG MAN OF SALEM – 1831

A Funeral Elegy

A Funeral Elegy is a ballad about seven women and three men who tragically drowned in Salem in June of 1773 while out on a "party of pleasure" to Baker's Island. [4] According to Raymond H. Bates Jr. in his book *Shipwrecks North of Boston, Volume I, Salem Bay*, the group sailed aboard the Salem Custom House Boat called "*The King's Boat*," a large, two-mastered vessel. During the afternoon, the weather began to turn dark—foreboding clouds and strong gusts of wind developed. [5] "As *The King's Boat* cruised by Eagle Island, an intense gust of wind hit the sail hard." [5] *A Funeral Elegy* is available at the Harris Broadside Collection at Brown University.

A Funeral Elegy, courtesy of the Harris
Broadside Collection at Brown University

A Funeral Elegy

Awake, my Muse, and tune the Song
    To harp a doleful sound,
Enough to melt the mournful Throng,
    Which echoes oe'r the Ground.

What Heart but feels the heavy Stroke
    Sent by GOD's awful Hand,
When ten poor Souls were lately cast
    Ashore upon the Sand.

Think, O poor Salem, think upon,
    And hear this dreadful Thing,
Ne'r let it pass without regret;
    But fear your heav'nly King.

Yes, ten poor Souls, I've heard them say
    Went lately to the Bottom: Salem,
O let it not be said
    Their Names were e'er forgotten.

May we not say fifteen poor Souls
    Were plunged in the Sea,
As Five th' unhappy Women were
    Advanc'd in Pregnancy.

A shocking Sight must it not seem,
    And dismal for to see
The loving Husband and the Wife
    Who once did well agree?

Now they embrace each other's Arms,
    And take a watery Grave;
All Nature sure it must alarm
    To see that men can't save.

O who could bear to hear the Shrieks
    And Cries none could prevent
Among these wretched dismal Souls,
    It makes my heart relent.

The tender Hand of Help was near,
    No Help it could afford,
Though Friends were nigh, behold and cry
    They could not get aboard.

May grateful Thanks be ever paid
    To Marblehead's kind Town;
Whose Hearts relent, their Strength they
    And sav'd two Souls not drown'd.

When Gentle, Simple, all agree
    To lend an aiding Hand,
With Heart and Voice they now rejoice
    To form a helping Band.

Their pitying Hand was kindly shewn,
    May it remember'd be.
When Friends, Relatives, Neighbours were
    So late drown'd in the Sea.

The dismal Boat and Relicts they
    With much adieu did save,
To Salem Wharf they landed them,
    For which kind Thanks they have.

Alas, who then but grieves and mourns,
    With Many a sigh and Tear,
Beholding of their dismal Urns,
    Their Corpse is drawing near.

Hark, Hark! We hear the passing Bell,
    Along as they do go;
Traveler, stop and shed a Tear;
    This is a Scene of Woe.

TRADITIONAL – 1773

The Salem Tragedy

This varient, of the broadside ballad, *A Funeral Elegy* called *The Salem Tragedy* [6] describes the same tragic event and the death of ten people that occurred in Salem Harbor in 1773. The Library of Congress houses a copy of the broadside.

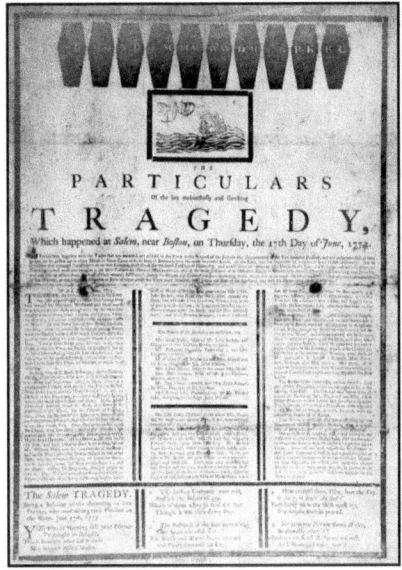

The Salem Tragedy, courtesy
of the Library of Congress

You who at Morning call your friends
    To mingle in Delight,
Think furiously what sad events
    May happen before Night.

This smiling Company were met,
    And left the Wharf all gay,
Which of them when he trod the Boat
    Thought it was their dying Day.

The pastimes of the day were o'er
    They sat at cheerful Tea;
The Winds and Waves began to roar,
    And Death demands his prey.

How couldst thou, Pilot, hear the Cry,
    O low'r, O'low'r the Sail!
Fool-hardy thou thy Skill must try,
    Nor female Shriek's prevail.

See how the Picture shews all this,
    So dismally adorn'd!
Frolicks are finish'd, Sports are past,
    And Boats to Coffins turn'd.

TRADITIONAL – 1773

Baker's Island Postcard,
courtesy of Sal Pangallo

Murder of Joseph White

tune: *Auld Lang Syne*

The *Harris Broadside Collection* at Brown University archives a copy of the Broadside ballad, *The Murder of Joseph White*. [7] Sung to the popular tune, *Auld Lang Syne*. The brutal murder of Joseph White was the subject of the book titled Death of an Empire, *The Rise and Murderous Fall of Salem, America's Richest City*, by Robert Booth. [7]

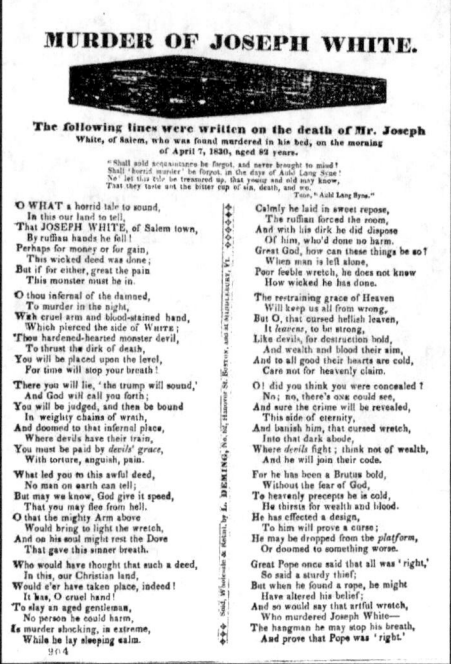

Murder of Joseph White, courtesy of Harris Broadside Collection at the John Hay Library, Brown University

Murder of Joseph White

O WHAT a horrid tale of so-und,
In this our land to tell,
That Joseph White, of Salem town,
By ruffian hands he fell!
Perhaps for money or for gain,
This wicked deed was done;
But it for either, great the pain,
This monster must be in.

O thou infernal of the damned,
  To murder in the night,
With cruel arm and bloostained hand,
  Which pierced the side of White;
Thou hardened-hearted monster devil,
  To thrust the dirk of death,
You will be placed upon the level,
  For time will stop your breath!

There you will lie, 'the trump will sound,'
  And God will call you forth;
You will be judged, and then be bound,
  In weighty chains of wrath,
And doomed to that infernal place,
  Where devils have their train,
You must be paid by devil's grace,
  With torture, anguish, pain.

What led you to this awful deed,
  No man on earth can tell;
But may we know, God give it speed,
  That you may flee from hell.
O that the mighty Arm above,
  Would bring to light the wretch,
And on his soul might rest the Dove
  That gave this sinner breath.

Who would have thought that such a deed,
  In this, our Christian land,
Would e'er have taken place, indeed!
  It has, O cruel hand!
To slay an aged gentleman,
  No person he could harm,
In murder shocking, in extreme,
  While he lay sleeping calm.

Calmly he laid in sweet repose,
  That ruffian forced the room,
And with his dirk he did dispose,
  Of him, who'd done no harm.

Great God, how can these things be so!
    When man is left alone,
Poor feeble wretch, he does not know,
    How wicked he has done.

The restraining grace of Heaven,
    Will keep us all from wrong,
But O, that cursed hellish leaves,
    It leavens, to be strong,
Like devils, for destruction bold,
    And wealth and blood their aim,
And to all good their hearts are cold,
    Care not for heavenly claims.

O! Did you think you were concealed?
    No; no, there's one could see,
And sure the crime will be revealed,
    This side of eternity,
And banish him, that cursed wretch,
    Into that dark abode,
Where devils fight; think not of wealth,
    And he will join their code.

For he has been a Brutus bold,
    Without the fear of God,
To heavenly precepts he is cold,
    He thirsts for wealth and blood.
He has affected a design,
    To him will prove a curse;
He may be dropped from the platform,
    Or doomed to something worse.

Great Pope once said that all was 'right,'
    So said a sturdy thief;
But when he found a rope, he might
    Have altered his belief;
And so would say that artful wretch,
    Who murdered Joseph White–
The hangman he may stop his breath,
    And prove that Pope was 'right.'

TRADITIONAL – 1830

George A. Brown

tune: *Pleyel's Hymn*

The ballad of *George A. Brown* was composed and sung to the tune of *Pleyel's Hymn* at his grave. George Brown drowned in Salem on February 18, 1857. [8] The text was found in the Broadside Collection at the Center for Popular Music at Middle Tennessee State University.

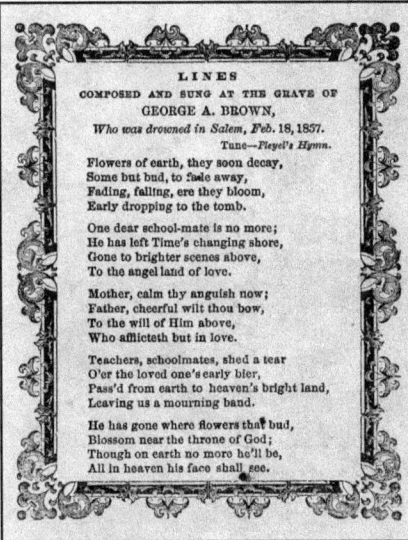

George A. Brown, courtesy of the Kenneth S. Goldstein Collection of American Song Broadsides Center for Popular Music, Middle Tennessee State University

Flowers of earth, they soon decay,
    Some but bud, to fade away.
Fading, falling, ere they bloom,
    Early dropping to the tomb.

One dear school-mate is no more;
    He has left Time's changing shore,
Gone to brighter scenes above,
    To the angel land of love.

Mother, calm thy anguish now;
    Father, cheerful wilt thou bow,
To the will of Him above,
    Who affecteth but in love.

Teacher, schoolmates, shed a tear,
    O'er the loved one's early bier,
Pass'd from earth to heaven's bright land,
    Leaving us a mourning band.

He has gone where flowers that bud,
    Blossom near the throne of God,
Though on earth no more he'll be,
    All in heaven his face shall see.

TRADITIONAL – 1857

Ballad of Giles Corey

The *Ballad of Giles Corey* [9] is a shortened version of *Giles Corey & Goodwyfe Corey, A Ballad of 1692.* [10] In 1962, folk singer John Allison recorded the shortened version called the *Ballad of Giles Corey* on his LP *Witches and War-Whoops: Early New England Ballads.* According to an article in the *Essex Institute Bulletin* called *The Witchcraft Delusion in New England*, Fitch Poole, Esquire of Peabody, Massachusetts, wrote the ballad and first published it in the April 13, 1850 issue of the *Salem Observer.* [11]

Giles Corey was a Wizard strong,
    A stubborn wretch was he;
And fit was he to hang on high,
    Upon the Locust-Tree.

So when before the magistrates,
    For trial he did come;
He would no confession make,
    But was completely dumb.

"Giles Corey," said the Magistrate,
    What hast thou here to plead;
To those who now accuse thy soul,
    Of crime and horrid deed?"

Giles Corey he said not a word,
    No single word spoke he.
Giles Corey," said the Magistrate,
    "We'll press it out of thee."

They got them then a heavy beam.
    They laid it on his breast;
They loaded it with heavy stones,
    And hard upon him pressed.

"More weight!" Now said this wretched man;
    "More weight!" Again he cried;
And he did no confession make,
    But wickedly he dyed.

FITCH POOLE – 1850

Few Are Our Days

Roud # V65467

The Phillips Library in Rowley, Massachusetts, houses this broadside ballad called *Few Are Our Days*. The ballad was presented and sung at Samuel McIntire's funeral at his home on Summer Street in Salem on Saturday, February 9, 1811.[12] Salem native and renowned architect and woodcarver Samuel McIntire developed his skills after being influenced by Charles Bullfinch of Boston. Several buildings designed by McIntire still stand in Salem today, including the Pierce-Nichols House, the Gardner-Pingree House, the Peabody-Silsbee House, Assembly Hall, and Hamilton Hall.[13]

> Few are our days, those few we dream away,
>> Sure is our fate, to moulder in the clay;
> Rise, immortal soul! Above thine earthly fate,
>> Time yet is thine, but soon it is too late.
>
> Lo! Midnight's gloom invites the pensive mind,
>> Pale is the scene, but shadows there you'll find;
> Rise! Immortal soul! Shun gloom, pursue thy flight,
>> Lest hence thy fate be like the gloomy night.
>
> Hark! From the grave oblivion's doleful tones,
>> There shall our names be moulder'd like our bones;
> Rise, immortal soul! that hence thy fame may shine;
>> Time flies, and ends; eternity is thine.

UNKNOWN – 1811

 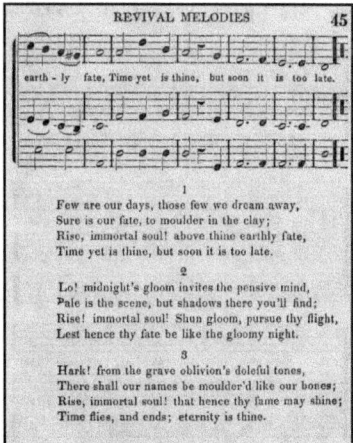

Few Are Our Days, Revival Melodies, or Songs of Zion, courtesy of Hymnary

Ring The Bell Softly,
There's Crape on the Door

Dexter Smith, Nancy Lutts'
Personal Collection

Salem-born Dexter Smith wrote the ballad *Ring The Bell Softly, There's Crape on the Door*, in 1867. Smith graduated from college and became a postman in Boston. While delivering mail, he noticed black crape paper draped around the doorknob, a sign of mourning. He approached the home, and the sign on the door entrance read, "not to disturb the sorrowing occupants," and delivered the mail as quietly as possible.[14] Smith, inspired by the saying, wrote the song *Ring The Bell Softly, There's Crape on the Door*. The song became very popular, and nearly every newspaper and magazine in America and England published the song. "Had Dexter Smith never written any other poem, *Ring The Bell Softly* would have established his reputation as a true poet and secured to him a high niche in *Temple of Fame*" [14]

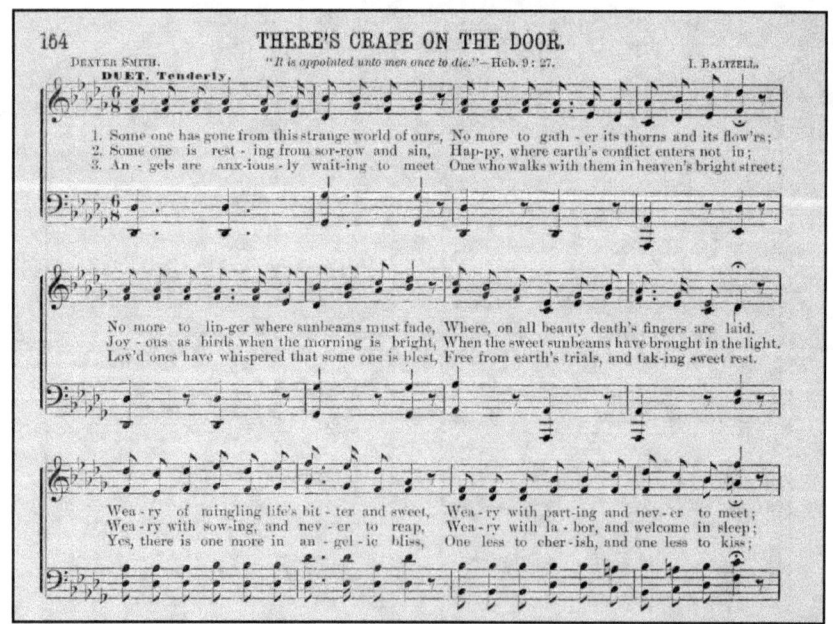

Ring The Bell Softly, There's Crape on the Door, courtesy of Hymnary

Ring The Bell Softly,
There's Crape on the Door*

Someone has gone from this strange world of ours,
    No more to gather its thorns with its flowers,
No more to linger where sunbeams must fade,
    Where, on all beauty, Death's fingers are laid.

    Chorus: Weary with mingling Life's bitter and sweet,
        Weary with parting and never to meet,
        Someone has gone to the bright golden shore.
        Ring the bell softly, there's crepe on the door.
        Ring the bell softly, there's crepe on the door.

Someone is resting from sorrow and sin,
    Happy where earth's conflicts enter not in,
Joyous as birds, when the morning is bright,
    When the sweet sunbeams have brought us their light.

    Chorus: Weary with sowing and never to reap,
        Weary with labour and welcoming sleep,
        Someone's departed to Heaven's glad shore.
        Ring the bell softly, there's crepe on the door.
        Ring the bell softly, there's crepe on the door.

Angels are anxiously longing to meet,
    One who walks with them in Heaven's bright street,
Loved ones have whispered that someone is blest,
    Free from earth's trials, and taking sweet rest.

    Chorus: Yes, There's one more in angelic bliss,
        One less to cherish, and one less to kiss,
        One more departed to Heaven's bright shore.
        Ring the bell softly, there's crepe on the door.
        Ring the bell softly, there's crepe on the door.

DEXTER SMITH – 1867

[* The spelling of Crape or Crepe have appeared both ways – RS]

~ 3 ~

Imprisoned

The Escape of Old John Webb
or Billy Broke Locks
Roud #83

John Roberts, a folk singer from England now living in New York, sang *The Escape Of Old John Webb* at Larry Young's session at O'Neil's Irish Pub in Salem in 2003. Since John was playing in Salem, he wanted to sing a Salem song. Roberts said he learned his version from the *Kingston Trio* and added lyrics from *British Ballads from Maine*.[1]

As John Roberts indicated, Phillips Barry, Fannie Hardy Eckstrom, and Mary Winslow Smyth published the song *John Webber* in his book *British Ballads from Maine* in 1929. The song was given to him by Mrs. Seth S. Thornton of Southwest Harbor, Maine. Barry quotes Mrs. Thornton, "The one about Billy and Johnny. I have gathered line by line from my cousins who remember their parents and grandparents singing it." [2] Also published in *British Ballads from Maine* are four variants culled from Boston newspapers and James M. Watson's version published by Harvard Professor Francis Child's in his ballad book *English and Scottish Ballads Volume III*. On April 10, 1889, Watson, boat builder and singer from Clark Island in Plymouth, Massachusetts, communicated with Child and sent his version of the song, which Child published in his ballad book as *Archie O Cawfield* (an old Scottish ballad) Varient F. Watson's version could be the earliest published American version of the ballad.[3] The ballad has a similar storyline of a prisoner who breaks out of jail with the help of his friends. [4] The storyline in both ballads is similar, indicating that the writer of *The Escape Of Old John Webb* was aware of the ballad, *Archie O Cawfield*.

John Allison recorded a version called *The Escape of Old John Web*b in 1943 on 78 rpm and released the song on *Keynote Records,* [5] probably using the version from *British Ballads from Maine*. In 1960, *The Kingston Trio* recorded the song with credit given to Tom Drake. [6]

Burl Ives and Alan Lomax' published versions of the song, *The Escape Of Old John Webb*, in their books, *The Burl Ives' Songbook* [7] and *The Folk Songs of North America*.[8] They referred to a 1730s [*Boston Evening Post*, October 16, 1738] article about the event and how the authorities imprisoned John Webb in Salem for purchasing a saddle on the docks of Salem with counterfeit money printed in Rhode Island. His imprisonment was unpopular, and a mob set him free. The *Boston Evening Post* article is on the following page, referencing the infamous John Webb.

THE
Boston Evening-Post.

Numb. 166.

Monday, October 16. 1738.

Of making War with Spain to the best Advantage.

WHEN one Nation goes to War with another, I take it for granted, (if their Conduct be directed by *wise Counsels*) that They extend their Views much farther than merely to fitting out a *Fleet* or two, bombarding *a few Towns*, and taking some *rich Ships* of the Enemy, and then supposing that it will fright Them into Submission; in which Expectation They may possibly be very much disappointed, tho' They may have acted with Vigour, and their Undertakings be attended with Success.

I can therefore make no Doubt that, at the very Entrance into a War, or when the Intent is to begin only with making *Reprisals*, which, in some Situations, is the worst Way of going to Work, as it will put a Stop to a beneficial Trade, and give an Handle for *fresh Seizures*, without humbling the *Enemy*, or gaining the Advantages, which might easily have been got; I doubt not, I say, that at the very Entrance into a *War*, or the Commencement of *Hostilities*, which I look upon as the same Thing, the whole Strength and Weakness of the *Enemy* is consider'd throughout, and that a long Train of wise and shrewd Designs are form'd; many of them, perhaps, at some Distance, as to the Execution, yet each depending on, and contributing to the Success of the Whole; in the same Manner as a skilful Player at *Chess* forms his Stratagems, and conducts his Game, not merely by sudden Starts and short Views, but by a settled Plan; and yet it is not amiss for *private Persons*, as long as any *Liberty of the Press* remains amongst us, to offer their Speculations; for tho' they have not all the Advantages of Information, which Those in *publick Stations* have, yet their crude Thoughts may serve to suggest better and more ripen'd Designs to the Others. I will therefore take the Liberty to offer mine, and to set down in this Paper where I think *Great Britain* may best attack *Spain*, in Case of a War, and what Advantages She may reap from such a Contest.

the greatest Probability of Success. None but a *free Government* can well make Use of *this Method*, and They only against an *arbitrary One*; but it is most likely to succeed, when it is exerted against *such Governments*, where the *People* were formerly *free*, and still retain some Sense of that Happiness. What I mean is the drawing up clear and well-digested Plans and Representations of the *Liberties* and *Privileges* such People once enjoy'd, and have lost; then declaring and undertaking to recover and restore *those Liberties* to Them, instead of endeavouring to ravage and destroy, or at best to make a Conquest, and retain Them in the same Servitude as before, only with *another Master*. Of all Nations in the World *Britain* is the best fitted to make Use of *this Method of War*, which I have mention'd, it being well known that We seek no farther Possessions for Ourselves on the Continent in *Europe*; and We had a small Specimen shewn Us, in the late War, how ready People are to revolt in *such a Case*, when They have a Prospect of being supported. The Instance I mean is That of the *Catalans*, who revolted from King *Philip*, not from any Affection to the House of *Austria*, but from the Desire and Hope of recovering their *antient Liberties*; and who knows what might have been the Consequences amongst the spirited *French Nation*, if the *Allies* had declared that They would restore the *Rights*, add *Assemblies of the States of France*? For there are no People on the Earth more sensible than the *French* of their having lost *their Liberties*, and who will in their Freedoms, where They think They may speak with safety, express with a greater Zeal their Readiness to reassume them.

FOREIGN AFFAIRS.
BRISTOL, June 27.

THEY write from *Ilminster*, a Market Town 9 Miles from *Taunton*, that last Saturday se'night a Fire broke out there in the Day Time, at a Dyer's House; and that upwards of twenty Houses were laid in Ashes.

Last Monday, towards Evening, a Man, whose Name is since found to be *John Webb*, of *Salem*, came to the Shop of Mr. *Isaac Casno*, Sadler, upon the Town Dock, and cheapned a Saddle, which being agreed for, he offer'd a *Five Pound* Bill on the Colony of *Rhode-Island* for pay, but the Bill being scrupled by Mr. *Casno*, and censured as a Counterfeit by several Persons who happened to be present, the Man left the Bill, mounted his Horse, and rode away with such Expedition, that he had

Boston Evening Post, October 16, 1738, courtesy of the Boston Public Library

As the story goes, John Webb surfaces in his hometown of Salem and begins circulating counterfeit Rhode Island Bills dated 1728 and 1731. As stated in the *Boston Post* article, last Monday, October 13, 1738, John Webb purchased a saddle on the docks in Salem using counterfeit money from tavern/shopkeeper Isaac (Sadler) Martin. When discovered, Webb fled to Rhode Island on horseback. The local sheriff pursued Webb, and on Tuesday, October 14, 1738, he was arrested and held overnight in the sheriff's home. Webb escaped from the sheriff's house that evening and soon returned to Salem. The next day, the authorities apprehended Webb, hiding in his mother's garret in Salem. At his arrest, Webb pretended to stand in his defense. He was soon taken and committed to jail in Salem. [9]

After his arrest, the authorities searched Webb and found several letters in his possession that identified his accomplices. According to the *Boston Post* article, one or two of his associates were already in Gaol, and there was a good possibility the sheriff could arrest the whole gang. The sheriff began integrating Webb's wife. She indicated that a clockmaker from Marblehead manufactured plates found in Webb's possession, and unfortunately, the clockmaker has since died. [10] The bills and the plates were of high quality, and the sheriff believed each gang member took their share of the money and signed the Bills individually, misspelling the signatures. One example is the name George incorrectly spelled with the e missing (Gorge). [11]

According to a later article in the *Boston Evening Post*, on October 23, 1738, John Bennet, suspected to have been the "Accomplice with John Webb and others in Counterfeiting the Rhode Island Five Pound Bills, was taken up and committed to Prison here, " [12] in Salem.

> Laſt Week *John Bennet*, ſuſpected to have been an Accomplice with *John Webb* and others, in Counterfeiting the *Rhode Iſland* Five Pound Bills, was taken up and committed to Priſon here. 'Tis ſaid the principal Perſon concern'd in this Scene of Iniquity, and who has the Plate in his Cuſtody, is marched off.

Boston Evening Post, October 23, 1738

On November 20, 1738, the *Boston Post* reported the authorities had insufficient evidence to hold John Webb and John Bennet (Webb's partner-in-crime) in jail. They were both released from prison on bail and given a court date of May 1739 to appear at the Court of Assize in Ipswich.[13]

> We hear from *Salem*, that the Perſons lately in Goal there on Suſpicion of counterfeiting the *Five Pound* Bills on the Colony of *Rhode Iſland*, which were to have been tried at the Aſſizes held at *Salem* aforeſaid the laſt Week, are diſcharged from their Confine-ment, having Recognized to appear at the Court of Aſſize and General Goal Delivery to be held at *Ipſwich* in *May* next. The Cauſe of this Delay, we are told, was want of Evidence.

Boston Evening Post, November 20, 1738

Kenneth Scott wrote and published a book called *Counterfeiting in Colonial Rhode Island*, and he stated, "Despite the setback encountered by Webb and Bennet, others were busily putting off the bogus £5 Rhode Island notes. About the end of January 1739, two men were committed to jail in Springfield, Massachusetts, for passing counterfeit Connecticut currency and £5 Rhode Island bills, while about them were found some £400 of the £5 denomination." [14]

There is little evidence through the local newspapers that John Webb attended his trial in Ipswich in May of 1739.* Court officers Sam Sewall, Samuel Adams, and Dan Henchman questioned Isaac (Sadler) Martin of Chebacco (now Essex, Massachusetts) in court on September 21, 1739. He testified that "He lives at Chebacco, has formerly followed the trade of a Shoemaker, but of late has kept a Tavern in Said Town -Sais that about a year & half past he received of John Webb Junior of Salem a Five pound Bill of the Colony of Rhoad (SIC) Island and gave him back in change three pounds, & the remaining Forty Shillings he paid sd Martin for one Garteron Gennings a Poppet Showe." [15]

This testimony confirms that in the *Boston Post* article, John Webb purchased a saddle from Martin, and Webb paid him with counterfeit Rhode Island currency. Martin went on testifying that "soon after he had received the Bill from Webb, he heard that Webb was apprehended and put in Goal on suspicion of being concerned in the counterfeit Bills, but he was soon after out of Goal on Bail, and it was after this that he sent to said Webb to Change the Five Pound Bill." [16] Also confirming another article in the *Boston Evening Post* published on November 20, 1738.

Martin continues his testimony stating Webb kept stalling on paying for his purchase with legal tender, offering Martin opportunities to join him in the counterfeiting activities with the promise of high-quality printing plates. Martin's testimony continues, "he then asked him (Webb) where he got his Plates made he answered at Rhoad (SIC) Island by the Engraver who made the Government Plates, and therefore they were very good and exact but that they cost him deer viz. Fifty pounds a Plate, Said Webb further said that the Six & Eight penny plate would be ready in a front this he told Martyn the Latter End of March last, and that he had recd Such advice from ye Engraver at Rhd (SIC) Island by Letters," [17] Martin concludes his testimony declaring "that John Webb of Salem told him if anyone yt knew of those Secrets and did discover ym he would kill him," [18]

[*Martin's testimony is taken word for word from the court documents, misspellings and all. Chamberlain Manuscripts Cham F 1.43, *Historical Manuscripts in the Public Library of the City of Boston, Volumes 1–5*, Boston Public Library, (Boston: Published by the Trustees A.D.) 1900 – RS]

At some point between the years 1739 and 1746, Webb ended up imprisoned in Salem. The *Boston Evening Post* published an article on March 29, 1746, stating that John Webb had escaped from a Salem Goal. [19]

> BRoke out of *Salem* Goal laft Night an abfconded, *John Webb*, junr of faid *Salem*. He is a middle-ftatur'd, well-fet Man, of about Thirty-five Years of Age, and wears a Wigg or Cap: Whofoever fhall take up faid *Webb*, and bring him back to faid Goal, or otherwife fecure him; or fha'l difcover fuch as affifted his Efcape, fo that they be convicted thereof, in either Cafe, fhall be paid *Twenty Pounds* old Tenour, and all neceffary Charges by me
> *Beverly, March* 29, 1746. *Robert Hale*.

Boston Evening Post March 31, 1746

On September 9, 1754, sixteen years after Webb's initial arrest in Salem for passing counterfeit money and eight years after escaping from a Salem goal, the a court in Sussex County (Boston) tried him and found him guilty of being a common cheat. The *Boston Evening Post* reported that Webb would stand in the Pillory for one hour, with a paper on his breast, having the words COMMON CHEAT in capitols, whipped twenty-five times, to serve one-year imprisonment, and he should have good behavior for five years. [20]

> BOSTON.
> Wednefday laft, at the Superiour Court of Judicature, Court of Affize, &c. held here for the County of *Suffolk*, came on the Trial of *John Webb*, late of *Salem*, but now of *Danvers*, indicted as a Common Cheat, when the Proof turn'd out fo full and clear againft him by a great Number of credible Witneffes, that the Jury declared him *Guilty*, without ftirring off their Seats, and then the Court paffed the following Sentence upon him, *viz.* To ftand in the Pillory one Hour, with a Paper on his Breaft, having the Words COMMON CHEAT wrote thereon in Capitals, to be publickly whipped twenty five Stripes, to fuffer one Year's Imprifonment, and after that to be bound to his good Behaviour for five Years. The former Part of the Sentence was faithfully executed on Thurfday, in the Prefence of a great Concourfe of People, who all expreffed their Satisfaction both at his Exaltation and Flagellation, and earneftly wifhed that an Amputation had alfo been added.——The Day of his Trial, *Jofeph Perry* of faid *Danvers*, one of his great Cronies, and an Accomplice, commonly called by the Gang, *'Squire Perry*, was committed to Goal for the fame Crime; and we hear that feveral more of his Brethren in Iniquity are complained of, and will foon be profecuted.

Bostom Evening Post, September 9, 1754

We will leave you with these questions about Salem's John Webb. Was his imprisonment unpopular, and did a mob set him free, or did he escape from the unsecured Sheriff's home as the 1738 *Boston Evening Post* article reported, or was he a "Common Cheat" documented in several news articles over the last sixteen years? Was printing his occupation, which made counterfeiting a reality, or did he take advantage of the complications of the currency situation in New England, rebelling against the use of the British pound sterling notes as currency?

The Escape Of Old John Webb

There were nine to guard the British ranks
 And five to watch the town about,
And two to stand at either hand,
 And one to let old Tenor out.

There was eighty weight of Spanish iron
 Between his neck bone and his knee,
But Billy took Johnny up on his back,
 And he carried him away right manfully.

 Chorus: And Billy broke locks, and Billy broke bolts,
    And Billy broke all that he came nigh,
   Until he came to the dungeon door,
    And that he broke right manfully.

So he stole them a horse and away did ride,
 And who but they rode gallantly,
Until they came to the river wide,
 The river running wide and free.

The British were coming close on their heals,
 And who but they stood fearfully,
And Billy took Johnny upon his back,
 And he carried him away quite manfully.

 Chorus: And Billy broke locks, and Billy broke bolts,
    And Billy broke all that he came nigh,
   Until he came to the dungeon door,
    And that he broke right manfully.

Oh Billy, oh Billy the sheriff says he,
 Your the damnedest rascal I ever did see,
Oh give me back the iron you stole,
 And I will set your prisoner free.

Oh no, oh no, no Billy says he,
 Oh no, oh no that never can be,
But the iron will do my horses this year,
 The blacksmith rides in our company.

Chorus: And Billy broke locks, and Billy broke bolts,
          And Billy broke all that he came nigh,
      Until he came to the dungeon door,
          And that he broke right manfully.

So they swan 'til they came to the other side,
      And who did but they stood shivering thee,
But soon they came on to an inn,
      When they call for ale most cheerfully.

And then they called for a room to dance,
      And who but they danced merrily,
And the very best dancer among them all,
      Was old John Webb, who was just set free.

Chorus: And Billy broke locks, and Billy broke bolts,
          And Billy broke all that he came nigh,
      Until he came to the dungeon door,
          And that he broke right manfully.

TRADITIONAL – UNKNOWN

The Old Salem Gaol

Located at 4 Federal Street in Salem, the Old Salem Gaol was built in 1684. Known today as the Old Salem Witch Gaol, there is a high probability that this is the Gaol for which imprisoned John Webb later escaped with the help of his friends. In 1692, some 40 years prior, the Gaol held the local residents accused of witchcraft.

The original Salem jail was closed in 1813, and on an adjacent lot on what is now called St. Peter Street, the county constructed a new, larger jail. This area of Salem has been referred to as "Prison Lane" because of the location of the various Gaols built in the area.[21]

The old jail was purchased in 1863 by Abner Cheney Goodall, who built a home around the structure of the old prison. The Goodalls and their descendants lived in the house until 1956. Beginning in 1935, Goodall's grandson, Alfred, and his wife offered tours of the home for a small fee. The tourists could view artifacts and visit the basement of their home, which they believed was the location of the Old Salem Witch jail. The New England Telephone Company purchased the property in 1956, razed the house, and built their local headquarters.[21]

The Second Salem Jail,
Sal Pangallo's personal collection

Abner Cheney Goodall,
4 Federal Street, Salem, MA
Nancy Lutts' personal collection

The Charlestown Land Shark

The Charlestown Land Shark is a lament about a man imprisoned in Salem for being a debtor. John Greenway included the ballad in his book *American Songs of Protest*. Greenway states, "In 1830, five out of six prisoners in New England and middle states jails were debtors, most of whom owed $20 or less." [22] Martin Van Buren introduced the first bill to the New York legislature in 1817 to completely repeal the law on debtor imprisonment. Colonel Richard M. Johnson, soon to be Vice President under Martin Van Buren and himself a former debtor, introduced another bill in 1823 in the United States Senate to repeal the debtor's law. The federal government abolished the law in 1832, and every state followed suit. Greenway adds, "The 1815 freedom from class law was still beyond the vision of one unfortunate soul whose note had been bought by a professional creditor." [22]

> The Charlestown Land Shark my Note he bought,
>   For to make money as he thought;
> The debt must lose, the cost must pay
>   Unless the Shark must run away.
>
> He's Like the Shark, amazing fierce,
>   Such land Sharks may they be more scarce,
> A greater Shark may catch him too,
>   Then he will have what is his due.
>
> Like the great Shark, sees to devour,
>   All that army fall within his power,
> Austere, morose, and Savage too,
>   All you who know, is this not true?
>
> His pay but once that will not do,
>   He wants it twice, they say 'tis true;
> A viler wretch can there be found,
>   If you search the world around?
>
> He likes hush money, as they say,
>   Give him enough and he will stay,
> For a small sum he will not wait,
>   Because his avarice is too great.

He's avaricious as the grave,
    In that a portion he will have,
I think no one will sigh or mourn,
    When to the grave this Shark is borne.

His unjust gain his soul will haunt,
    No pleasure to him will it grant;
His guilty conscience will it sting,
    Down to the grave Death will him bring.

On Negro Hill they say he goes,
    Why is that for you may suppose,
Why does this Shark these Blacks disgrace,
    A Blacker mind a frowning face.

Tis said he once was very sick,
    In consequence of a bad trick,
A certain nurse of him took care,
    And she let out the whole affair.

He boost he's rich-most wretched too,
    What is there bad he will not do?
A vagabond I think he'll be,
    The day will come when we shall see.

In human misery he delights,
    He fiercely barks before he bites,
I sought compassion, one could fine,
    Because there was none in his mind.

In dirty business he is seen,
    His conduct is amazing mean,
His wickedness to be portray'd,
    Volumes before you must be laid.

To gratify his wicked mind,
    Many in jail have been confin'd,
Vile wretched Shark, must pine away,
    His debts must lose, the cost must pay.

Despis'd by all, where he is known,
    Compassion he has never shown.
I hope the shark will leave no seed,
    For of Land Sharks there is no need.

Rejoice, poor man, this Shark must die,
    And be as poor as you and I,
He lives despis'd, his name shall stink,
    And into the lasting contempt sink.

I'm not discouraged nor dismay'd,
    Although a Prisoner I was made,
My mind is tranquil and serene,
    Though in the limits I am seen.

He said in jail I ought to stay,
    Until my flesh did rot away;
The laws tho' mercy are more just,
    The Shark to me has done his worst

No other business does he doe,
    Than to buy notes and people sue;
Both men and women share the same,
    Ah! Wretched Shark! Where is his shame?

If the Coat the Shark doth suit,
    And that it will, none doth dispute,
Then he may wear it if he will,
    At home or upon Negro Hill.

Compos'd on board the "Salem Jug,"
    If once lock'd in twill hold your snug;
'Twill hold you fast till time shall say,
    Now let the Prisoner go his way.

TRADITIONAL – 1815

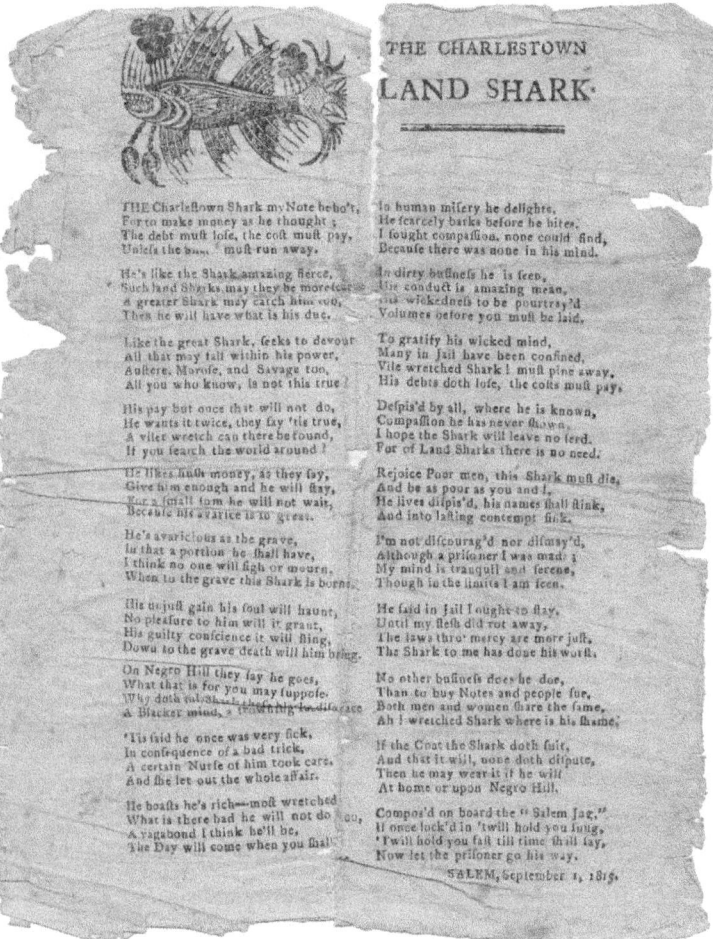

The Charlestown Land Shark, courtesy of Harris Broadside
Collection John Hay Library, Brown University

Susannah Martin

The Witch House, courtesy of Mary Barker

Martin baptized Susannah North, who was one of fourteen women executed during the Salem Witch Trials. Traditional folk singer John Allison sings the song *Susannah Martin* on his *Witches and War-Whoops: Early New England Ballads* LP, and Diane Taraz, a local folk singer, also recorded the song on her CD called *A Silver Dagger ~ Exploring Women's History through* [23] "These ballads recount the sinister tragedy in the year 1692 when the childish fantasies of a handful of adolescent girls touched off a gruesome event, the Salem Witch Persecutions." [24] Allison has been collecting early New England ballads since the 1930s. Of his collections, he states only two ballads have "know authorships," *The Death of Goody Nurse* by Rose Terry Cooke and *Flud Ireson* by John Greenleaf Whittier. Whittier also wrote *The Witch's Daughter* about Susannah Martin.[25]

> Let Goody Martin rest in peace,
> I never knew her harm a fly,
> And witch or not – God knows – not I?
> I know who swore her life away;
> And as God lives, I'd not condemn
> An Indian dog on word of them.

Allsion's LP included the ballads *The Gloucester Witch* or *Old Meg, Giles Corey,* and *Old Mammy Redd*, an accused woman from Marblehead, Massachusetts. Allison also wrote on the back cover of his LP that his daughter, Joan Allison McGee, is a direct descendent of John Willard, who was one of the nineteen executed on *Gallows Hill* in the Village of Salem. [24]

Susannah Martin

Susannah Martin was a witch who dwelt in Amesbury,
    With brilliant eye and saucy tongue she worked her sorcery
And when into the judges court the sheriffs brought her hither,
    The lilacs drooped as she passed by and then were seen to wither.

A witch she was, though trim and neat with comely head held high,
    It did not seem that one as she with Satan so would vie
And when in court when the afflicted ones proclaimed her evil ways,
    She laughed aloud and boldly then met Cotton Mather's gaze.

"Who hath bewitched these maids," he asked, and strong was her reply,
    "If they be dealing in black arts, ye know as well as I"
And then the stricken ones made moan as she approached near,
    They saw her shaped upon the beam so none could doubt 'twas there.

The neighbors 'round swore to the truth of her Satanic powers,
    That she could fly o'er land, stream and come dry shod through showers
At night, twas said, she had appeared a cat of fearsome mien,
    "Avoid she-devil," they had cried to keep their spirits clean.

The spectral evidence was weighed, then stern the parson spoke,
    "Thou shalt not suffer a witch to live, tis written in the Book"
Susannah Martin so accused, spoke with flaming eyes,
    "I scorn these things for they are naught but filthy gossips lies."

Now those bewitched, they cried her out, and loud their voice did ring,
    They saw a bird above her head, an evil yellow thing
And so, beneath a summer sky, Susanna Martin died,
    And still in scorn she faced the rope her comely head held high.

Susannah Martin was a witch who lived in Amesbury,
    With brilliant eye and saucy tongue she worked her sorcery
And when into the judges court the sheriffs brought her hither,
    The lilacs drooped as she passed by and then were seen to wither.

TRADITIONAL – UNKNOWN

A lecture and a song concerning the Robbery at Newbury to some men in jail at Salem

The *Lecture and Song* was printed for and sold by its author, Jonathan Plummer. The song and lecture reveal Plummer was selling his services for healing cancer and for receiving redemption for criminal acts. Levi and Laban Kenniston of Newmarket, New Hampshire, were jailed in Salem on suspicion of having robbed Major Goodrich of Newbury, Massachusetts, on December 19, 1816. Plummer states, "Three pieces of gold were found in the dwelling place of these Kennistons, two of which were under a meat barrel in the cellar." Goodrich could identify one of the pieces of gold "by the paper over it, and the figures marked on the back of it." [26]

The author states that it is not for him to judge these men but up to the Supreme Judicial Court. In the last verse of the song, Plummer writes:

And turn without the least delay, From every base and wicked way, That you salvation may obtain, And with my lovely Jesus reign. At the end of this article, Plummer says, "Any person laboring under that dreadful malady of Cancer by applying in good season to J. Plummer, the author of this lecture, may perhaps obtain a cure: the said Plummer having lately providentially made, a significant discovery, in regard to healing Cancers." [26]

A lecture and a song concerning
the Robbery at Newbury to some men in jail at Salem

Unhappy brothers, friends in grief,
  I come, I haste to your relief!
How can your inward fears be told?
  Who can your dreadful state unfold?

If you have cruel robbers been,
  You'll find some dreadful fruit of sin,
But if you're wrongfully accus'd,
  I hope you'll not be much abus'd.

But whether you have robb'd or not,
    It will be your quite certain lot,
Before my Jesus to appear,
    There for your whole behavior here,

You'll surely have a trial rare,
    A trial holy, just, and fair.
Oh! May you with the Saviour rise,
    To blissful mansions in the skies.

When the last trumpet sounds aloud,
    And wakes in graves the countless crowd,
When the old heav'ns blaze and roll,
    And vanish like a burning scroll!

When all this globe will be on fire,
    And earth and seas, in flames expire!
When he who on Mount Calvary bled,
    From death and hell, will call the dead!

And his holy angels come,
    To endless joy his saints to doom,
And send his foes with grief to hell,
    With Beelzebub the fool to dwell!

What guilt would then your bowels rend,
    If you should find him not your friend!
And find yourself not friends to him,
    But enemies in his esteem!

O for the sake of your poor souls,
    Think while the present moment rolls,
Upon these all important things,
    And honour much the kings of kings:

And turn without the least delay,
    From every base and wicked way,
That your salvation may obtain,
    And with my lovely Jesus reign.

JONATHAN PLUMMER – 1817

~ 4 ~
Social Change

Get Off the Track

tune: *Old Dan Tucker*

Roud # V61860

Get Off the Track was found in the Lester S. Levy Collection of Sheet Music at Johns Hopkins University. [1] The Hutchinson Family Singers had residences in New Hampshire and Lynn, Massachusetts. They used their popularity in the 1840s to support several causes, including women's rights, utopian communities, and temperance. They held a fierce opposition to slavery. [2] Jesse Hutchinson wrote this song to the tune of a lively dance tune that, at the time, was a well-known minstrel melody written by Daniel Emmett called *Old Dan Tucker*.

Get Off the Track was also sung at the New England Anti–Slavery Convention held in Salem on April 11, 1844. [3] Hutchinson used the train to symbolize a "Liberator" coming down the rail as the "pro-slavery multitude were stupidly lingering on the track." [4]

Ho! The car, Emancipation,
Rides majestic thro' our nation;
Bearing on its train, the story,
Liberty! A nation's glory.

Roll it along! Roll it along!
Roll it along! Thro' the nation
Freedom's car, Emancipation

First of all the train, and greater,
Speeds the Dauntless Liberator;
Onward cheered amid hosannas,
And the waving of free banners.

Roll it along! Roll it along!
Roll it along! Spread your banners
While the people shout hosannas.

Men of various predilections,
Frightened, run in all directions;
Merchants, editors, physicians,
Lawyers, priests, and politicians.

Get out of the way! Get out of the way!
Get out of the way! Every station,
Clear the track of 'mancipation.

Let the ministers and churches,
Leave behind sectarian lurches;
Jump on board the car of freedom,
Ere it be too late to need them.

Sound the alarm! Sound the alarm!
Sound the alarm! Pulpit's thunder!
Ere too late, you see your blunder.

Politicians gazed, astounded,
When, at first our bell resounded;
Freight trains are coming, tell these foxes,
With our votes and ballot boxes.

Jump for your lives! Jump for your lives!
Jump for your lives! Politicians,
From your dangerous false positions.

Railroads to emancipation,
Cannot rest on Clay foundation;
And the tracks of 'The Magician',
Are but railroads to perdition.

Pull up the rails! Pull up the rails!
Pull up the rails! Emancipation,
Cannot rest on such foundation.

All true friends of emancipation,
Haste to freedom's railroad station;
Quick into the cars get seated,
All is ready, and completed.

Put on the steam! Put on the steam!
Put on the steam! All are crying,
And the liberty flags are flying.

Now, again the bell is tolling,
    Soon you'll see the car wheels rolling;
Hinder not their destination,
    Chartered for emancipation.

        Wood up the fire! Wood up the fire!
            Wood up the fire! Keep it flashing,
        While the train goes onward dashing.

Hear the mighty car wheels humming!
    Now look out! The engine's coming!
Church and statesmen! Hear the thunder!
    Clear the track! Or you'll fall under.

        Get off the track! Get off the track!
            Get off the track! All are singing,
        While the liberty bell is ringing.

On triumphant, see them bearing,
    Through sectarian rubbish tearing;
Th' bell and whistle and the steaming,
    Startles thousands from their dreaming.

        Look out for the cars! Look out for the cars!
            Look out for the cars! While the bell rings,
        Ere the sound your funeral knell rings.

See the people run to meet us;
    At the depots thousands greet us;
All take seats with exultation,
    In the car, Emancipation.

        Huzza! Huzza! Huzza! Huzza!
            Huzza! Huzza! Emancipation,
        Soon will bless our happy nation.
            Huzza! Huzza! Huzza!

JESSE HUTCHINSON – 1844

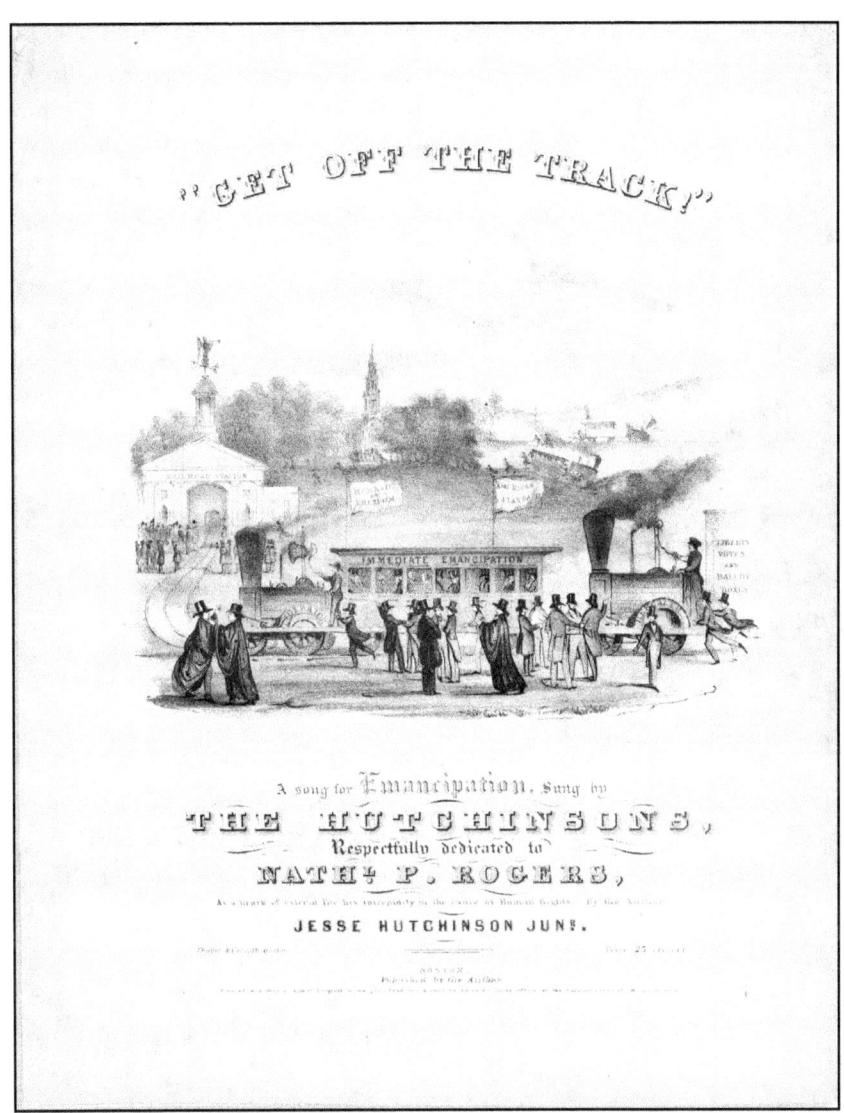

Get Off the Track, courtesy of Lester S. Levy Collection of
Sheet Music, Sheridan Libraries, Johns Hopkins University

Emancipation Hymn

Manuel Fenollosa, a Spanish immigrant, came to Salem from Spain with his brother-in-law Manuel Emilio in 1838. The *Emancipation Hymn* was composed in 1863 by Fenollosa and published by *Oliver Ditson & Co*. The hymn is dedicated to the *Salem Union League*.[5] One year later, Fenollosa held a concert in Salem celebrating Emancipation. Emilio and Fenollosa aided the famous 54th regiment, formed from white Massachusetts officers and black recruits. Their music reflected the abolitionist movement in Salem. [6]

The Civil War Statue in Greenlawn Cemetery, courtesy of Mary Barker

Emancipation Hymn, courtesy of the Library of Congress

Long our land in blood had weltered,
  Blood of dearest sons:
Long had Hero Spirits faltered,
  Not at booming guns:
Long our pray'r to Heav'n ascended,
  Fraught with bondmen's groans;
Long with victory's cheers had blended,
  Fettered manhood's moans!

Chorus: God hath heard us, God hath heard us,
      And in mercy gives us bread for stones.
      God hath heard us, God hath heard us,
      And in mercy gives us bread for stones.

Asking for a Land, for a Land united,
  We forgot the slave.
Pray'd we for our Country, for our Country blighted
  For our falling brave,
Left the bondman, chas'd by blood hounds,
  Scented thro' the cane,
God was with that panting brother;
  Pray'd we thus in vain!

Chorus: Ask, as we would serve another,
      Ask and he will hear again!
      Ask, as we would serve another,
      Ask and he will hear again!

He hath heard; O give Him glory!
  Heard the Bondman's pray'r:
O'er the warpath, red and glory
  Thro' the slave-hound's lair,
Peals the mandate of salvation,
  "Let my people go."
Humbled, bleeding, hear the nation,
  Answer, "Be it so!"

Chorus: Who shall weary! Who shall weary!
      Who shall falter! God is with us now!
      Who shall weary! Who shall weary!
      Who shall falter! God is with us now!

MANUEL FENOLLOSA AND R.T.L. – 1863

Salem Fremont Club

The *Salem Fremont Club* is a political organization consisting of local business leaders and politicians. The group formed to support California Senator and republican John C. Fremont and his run president, not repealing the Missouri Compromise, and to admit Kansas to the Union as a Free State. Despite the lobbying by the *Fremont Club of Salem*, Fremont lost the election to Democrat James Buchanan in 1856 and served as president from 1857 to 1861. In 1854, the Federal government repealed the Missouri Compromise, and three years later, the Supreme Court voted and declared it unconstitutional. The Federal government admitted Kansas to the Union as a free state in 1861, a victory for the anti-slavery movement. [7]

Transcribed from the *Salem Register*, August 4, 1856:

The *Fremont Club of Salem* was organized on Wednesday evening last at the Lyceum Hall, by the choice of officers consisting of representatives of all the political parties. They were reported by a committee, of which A.A. Evans was chairman:

President – Stephen H. Phillips

Vice President – John Bertram, George Choate, Wm. D. Pickman, Aaron Perkins John Chapman, George Wheatland, Eben K. Lakeman, William F. Nichols, John Masury, L.B. Hatch, Stephen C. Phillips, Joseph Andrews, W.P. Goodhue, Stephen B. Ives, Samuel Johnson, James O. Safford, Henry Russell, Walter S. Harris, James H. Battis, Augustus Story, Joseph B.F. Osgood.

Treasurer – Wm. Goodhue, Jr.

Recording Secretaries – Edward, Hodges, Jona Perley, Jr.

Corresponding Secretaries – Nath'l A. Horton, R.S. Rantoul

Executive Committee – Wm. H. Prince, Jas. Kimball, William Hill, Daniel C. Haskell, W.P. Martin

Committee on Finance – David H. Jewett, Thos. H. Frothingham, Wm. Silver, A.A. Smith, L.B. Brooks

The meeting was addressed, in an eloquent manner, by the president, S.H. Phillips, Esq., Hon. C.W. Upham, Wm. S. Bailey, Esq., editor of the anti-Slavery paper in Kentucky, and Robert Rantoul, Esq., and some admirable songs were excellently sung by the *Fremont Glee Club*.

Unanimously adopted: The undersigned, being opposed to the perfidious act of repealing the Missouri Compromise; to the policy of the present administration; to the extension of Slavery into Free Territory; and in favor of the admission of Kansas as a Free State; of the maintenance of the principles promulgated in the Declaration of Independence; and embodied in the Federal Constitution; and restoring the actions of the Federal Government to the principles of Washington and Jefferson; do hereby enroll ourselves as Members of the *Salem Fremont Club*, for the purpose of assisting in the election of John C. Fremont to the Presidency. [7]

Song For the Time

The *Salem Glee Club* sang the *Song For the Time* [8] at the end of the first meeting of the *Salem Fremont Club* in 1856.

O, won't it be a glorious day,
   Hurrah! Hurrah! Hurrah!
When freedom's banner hold the sway,
   Hurrah! Hurrah! Hurrah!
When Freedom's son, and none but he,
Shall take the lead, then you will see
Our glorious Union safe and free,
   Hurrah! Hurrah! Hurrah!

Old James Buchanan's dead and gone!
   Hurrah! Hurrah! Hurrah!
He yielded up the ghost on morn!
   Hurrah! Hurrah! Hurrah!
His spirit since has been transformed
Into a non-descript platform;
There's nothing of him left but form–
   Hurrah! Hurrah! Hurrah!

Then Franklin Pierce, a breathing ghost,
   Hurrah! Hurrah! Hurrah!
Is lingering round his much-loved post,
   Hurrah! Hurrah! Hurrah!
He served his masters faithfully,
And asked once more, most gracefully,
To chew the cud of slavery!
   Hurrah! Hurrah! Hurrah!

But No! th' ungrateful masters say;
   Hurrah! Hurrah! Hurrah!
You've served us well, you've got your pay;
   Hurrah! Hurrah! Hurrah!
To risk you we had rather not;
Another man has tied the knot;
You may retire with what you've got!
   Hurrah! Hurrah! Hurrah!

UNKNOWN – 1856

We're for Freedom Through the Land

tune: *Old Granite State*

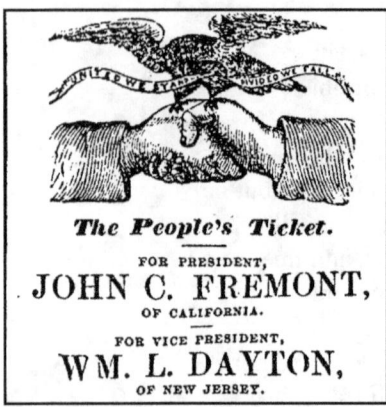

The People's Ticket.

FOR PRESIDENT,

JOHN C. FREMONT,

OF CALIFORNIA.

FOR VICE PRESIDENT,

WM. L. DAYTON,

OF NEW JERSEY.

Salem Register, November 11, 1856

The *Fremont Club of Salem* invited a local group called the *Fremont Glee Club*, an offshoot of the *Salem Glee Club*, to perform and sing several songs supporting the group's mission. The glee club sang the song *We're for Freedom Through the Land* [9] to the tune of the *Old Granite State* by Jesse Hutchinson. The Hutchinson family, a local singing group from Lynn, Massachusetts, performed throughout New England. The group performed temperance songs and songs of social justice and were supporters of the anti-slavery movement.

We are coming, we are coming! Freedom's battle is begun!
No hand shall furl her banner ere the victory be won!
Our shields are locked for liberty, and mercy goes before;
Tyrants tremble in your citadel! Oppression shall be o'er.

Chorus: We are all for Fremont
We are all for Dayton,
We're for Liberty and Justice,
And for Freedom through the land.

We have hatred, dark and deep, for the fetter and the thong;
We bring light for prisoned spirits, for captive's wail a song;
We are coming, we are coming! And "No league with tyrant man."
Is emblazoned on our banner, while our Fremont leads the van!

Chorus: We are all for Fremont
We are all for Dayton,
We're for Liberty and Justice,
And for Freedom through the land.

We are coming, we are coming! But we wield no battle brand;
    We are armed with truth and justice, and our ballot is in our hand,
And our voice which swells for Freedom, Freedom now and evermore!
    Shall be heard as ocean's thunder, when they burst upon the shore!

Chorus: We are all for Fremont
         We are all for Dayton,
      We're for Liberty and Justice,
       And for Freedom through the land.

We are coming, we are coming! Not as comes the tempest's wrath,
    When the frown of desolation sits brooding o'er its path;
But with mercy, such as leaves his holy signet light upon,
    The air in lambent beauty, when the darkening storm is gone.

Chorus: We are all for Fremont
         We are all for Dayton,
      We're for Liberty and Justice,
       And for Freedom through the land.

UNKNOWN – 1856

We're for Freedom through the Land.

Air—"Old Granite State."

We are coming, we are coming! Freedom's battle is begun!
No hand shall furl her banner ere the victory · be won!
Our shields are locked for liberty, and mercy goes before;
Tyrants, tremble in your citadel! oppression shall be o'er.
    We are all for Fremont,
    We are all for Dayton—
    We're for Liberty and Justice,
    And for Freedom through the land.

We have hatred, dark and deep, for the fetter and the thong;
We bring light for prisoned spirits, for the captive's wail a song;
We are coming, we are coming! and "No league with tyrant man,"
Is emblazoned on our banner, while our Fremont leads the van!
    We are all for Fremont, &c.

We are coming, we are coming! but we wield no battle brand:
We are armed with truth and justice, and our ballot's in our hand;
And our voice which swells for Freedom—Freedom now and ever more—
Shall be heard as ocean's thunder, when they burst upon the shore!
    We are all for Fremont, &c.

We are coming, we are coming! not as comes the tempest's wrath,
When the frown of desolation sits brooding o'er its path:
But with mercy, such as leaves his holy signet-light upon
The air in lambent beauty, when the darkening storm is gone.
    We are all for Fremont, &c.

Salem Register,
September 1, 1856

99

Tribute to Reverend Jacob Stroyer

Fred Goldsmith Walker, a local poet, contributed most of his poems and ballads to the local newspapers. In 1892, Walker published a book called *My Leisure Moments*.[10] The book included all his work published in various newspapers. In February of 1908, Walker wrote this tribute to Reverend Jacob Stroyer, published it in the *Salem Evening News*,[11] and read the tribute at his funeral. Nelson Dionne supplied the 1908 article from the *News*.

Transcribed from an article by Polly Wilber written for *Historic Salem*, called *The Frontispiece of My Life in the South*.

"Jacob Stroyer, a former South Carolina slave, lived and ministered to African Americans in Salem for 25 years. Stroyer wrote a memoir of slavery, *My Life in the South*, published in 1879." Wilbert went on to say, "In 1877, at the invitation of the minister of Salem's South Church, Jacob came here, where he preached and ministered off and on for 25 years to Salem's small (about 300) African-American community as founder and pastor of the *Salem Colored Mission*." [12]

'Cause you and I have skins of white
 This doesn't make us great,
I knew a face as black as night.
 A face which showed the Christian light–
In a most happy state.

Men whisper "Jacob Stroyer's dead,"
 Perhaps few eyes are dim,
But o'er that dark and honored head
 Are angles blessing him.

We elevate our heads with pride,
 The dollar is our king,
But Jacob Stroyer worked and died,–
 He hadn't anything.

Only a fortune of Christian love,
 Richer than millionaire,
Oh! He had wealth; in the Things above.–
 Now he is happy there.

FRED G. WALKER – 1908

A Parting Hymn

Charlotte Louise Bridges Forten Grimké was an African American anti-slavery activist, poet, and educator. In 1854, Forten moved to Salem and joined the household of Amy Matilda Cassey and Charles Lenox Remond, where she attended the Higginson Grammar School, a private academy for young women. [13] She was the only non-white student in a class of 200. After graduating, Forten studied literature and teaching at the Salem Normal School (Salem State University). Her first teaching position was in 1856 at the *Eppes Grammar School*, where she became the first African American hired to teach white students in a Salem public school. [14] *The Massachusetts Teacher and Journal of Home and School Education, Volume 9* published Forten's poem *A Parting Hymn*, stating that the poem is a "specimen of the beauty, pure, and philanthropic sentiment, lofty aspiration, and of sublime faith." [15]

When winter's royal robes of white
　From hill and vale are gone,
And the glad voices of the spring
　Upon the air are borne,
Friends, who have met with us before,
　Within these walls shall meet no more.

Forth to a noble work they go:
　O, may their hearts keep pure,
And hopeful zeal and strength be theirs
　To labor and endure,
That they an earnest faith may prove
　By words of truth and deeds of love.

May those, whose holy task it is
　To guide impulsive youth,
Fail not to cherish in their souls
　A reverence for truth;
For teachings which the lips impart
　Must have their source within the heart.

May all who suffer share their love –
　The poor and the oppressed;
So shall the blessing of our God
　Upon their labors rest.
And may we meet again where all
　Are blest and freed from every thrall.

CHARLOTTE L. FORTEN GRIMKE – 1854

O Thou To Whom in Ancient Time

John Pierpont wrote *O Thou To Whom in Ancient Time* [16] for the opening of the Independent Congregational Church at Barton Square in Salem on December 7, 1824. Pierpont was born in 1785 in Litchfield, Connecticut, and was the appointed pastor of the Hollis Street Church in Boston from 1819 to 1845. Pierpont often recited his poetry at antislavery and temperance meetings.

On April 24, 1899, the Independent Congregational Church united with the East Church Society and the Second Church to form one corporation called the Second Church. Pastor Alfred of Manchester held services at the Second Church in Washington Square (now the Salem Witch Museum). [17] The original location of the Independent Congregational church building is now a bank parking lot.

The text discovered in *American Literature with Biographical Sketches and Selections From Their Works* is a compendium of American literature arranged and edited by Salem-born Charles Cleveland. [18]

O Thou to whom in ancient time
    The lyre of Hebrew bards was strung
Whom kings adored in song sublime
    And prophets praised with glowing tongue

Not now on Zion's height alone
    Thy favor'd worshipper may dwell
Nor where at sultry noon thy Son
    Sat weary by the Patriarch's well

From every place below the skies
    The grateful song the fervent prayer
The incense of the heart may rise
    To heaven and find acceptance there

In this thy house whose doors we now
    For social worship first unfold
To thee the suppliant throng shall bow
    While circling years on years are roll 'd

To thee shall Age with snowy hair
    And Strength and Beauty bend the knee
And Childhood lisp with reverent air
    Its praises and its prayers to thee

O thou to whom in ancient time
    The lyre of prophet bards was strung
To thee at last in every clime
    Shall temples rise and praise be sung

DR. JOHN PIEPONT – 1824

The Cornerstone Hymn

Hosea Ballou, an American Universalist clergyman and theological writer, wrote *The Cornerstone Hymn* in 1808, and the song was sung on August 17 of that year, when the First Universalists Society in Salem laid a cornerstone of the building, marking its location on the site. Benjamin Ward donated a plot of land to the Church Trustees on January 22, 1806, so the Universalist Society of Salem could construct a building for their use during service. Ward paid only one-thousand dollars for the building site because of its location on St. Peter Street since the neighborhood considered the area undesirable. St. Peter's Street was also known as "Prison Lane" because of the location of the county jail in the immediate vicinity. [19]

The Universalist Church in Salem was founded in 1805 by seven Salem residents who attended a lecture by Reverend John Murray, a founder of Universalism, on Christmas Eve in a living room on Lynde Street. At that meeting, they decided to form a Universalist Society in Salem. The church building was constructed in 1808, with Reverend Hosea Ballou, a founder of the Universalist Church, laying the cornerstone of the Federal style building. [19]

On the First Universalist Society's 200th birthday, local folk musicians and society members Sarah Smith and her husband Bill organized a concert featuring a small orchestra portraying "the musical history of the church." Sarah, a Salem resident and long-time church member, noted that many of their hymns reflected Universalist themes for social change like abolitionism, anti-war activism, and women's suffrage.[20] For the concert, Bill put the lyrics of the *Cornerstone Hymn* to a new melody.

The Universalist Church closed in 2016 and merged with the First Parish UU church in Beverly, Massachusetts.

The Cornerstone Hymn

On Salem's fair and pleasant shore,
    Thy church, O Lord, in mercy meet;
Display thy grace, display thy pow'r,
    And show the impress of thy feet.

Chorus: On this well tried chief corner stone
        Shall rise to thee a sacred dome.
    It lies here still foundation Strong,
        Our compass for our Blue Boat Home.

Here, on the margin of the tide,
    By thy rich goodness, long shall stand;
Its spacious walls, extended wide,
    And speak the favour of thy hand.

Chorus: On this well tried...

May lib'ral souls, who feel thy grace,
    Build here, in honour of thy name,
And join to consecrate the place,
    Thy cause and honour to maintain.

Chorus: On this well tried...

Yea, from their rich, abundant store,
    May each to thee an off'ring bring,
And from the horn of plenty pour,
    Oblations to their heav'nly King.

Chorus: On this well tried...

In honor of their Saviour's name,
    May Salem's sons and daughters join,
To raise thin Temple to thy fame,
    Their heart in truth and love combine.

Chorus: On this well tried...

As Isra'l, in the days of old,
    To build thine house, rich offerings made,
Of iron, silver, brass, and gold,
    So be our willing gifts display'd.

Chorus: On this well tried...

Succeed our labor and our cost;
    Sustain with strength each workman's arm;
Let the fair prospect not be lost;
    Preserve from accident and harm.

Chorus: On this well tried...

May all who love the Lord rejoice,
    To see these spacious walls ascend;
And join with heart, and soul, and voice,
    To praise their Saviour and their friend.

Chorus: On this well tried chief cornerstone,
    Shall rise to thee a sacred dome.
It lies here still foundation Strong,
    Our compass for our Blue Boat Home.

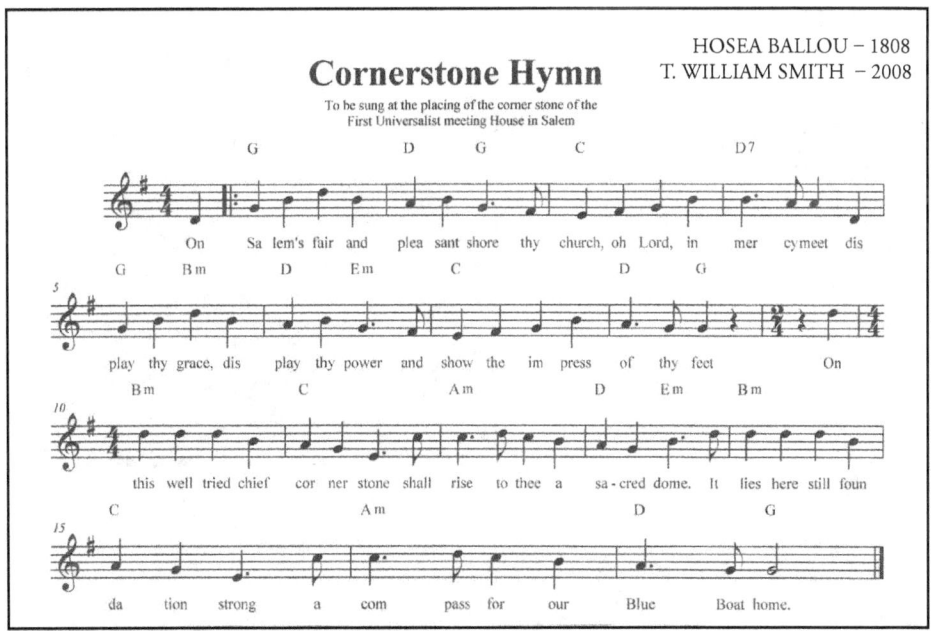

Cornerstone Hymn

HOSEA BALLOU – 1808
T. WILLIAM SMITH – 2008

To be sung at the placing of the corner stone of the
First Universalist meeting House in Salem

Original Hymn
50th Anniversary of the Universalist Church in Salem

Original Hymns.

Sung at the Celebration of the Fiftieth Anniversary of the Dedication of the Universalist Church in Salem, and of the Installation of their first Pastor, on Thursday, August 4, 1859.

WRITTEN BY MR. C. W. SWASEY.

I.

Swift, as the weaver's shuttle plays,
  Have passed th' eventful FIFTY YEARS,
Since first this House of Prayer and Praise
  Was consecrate by Christian seers.

The sainted MURRAY then was here,
  And RICHARDS, with his rapt address;
And SMITH, who asked in fervent prayer
  That God would this new Temple bless.

But where is now that triple band,
  Whose fragrant memory yet remains?
Gone to the blissful "Better Land,"
  Where God is praised in loftier strains!

Our Fathers, too; ah! where are they,
  Who reared in hope this spacious fane,
And bore the burden of that day
  When bigots scorned their cherished name?

For God's great truth they nobly fought,
  As those who battle for the right;
In humble prayer His aid they sought,
  And triumphed in Jehovah's might.

One after one, those warriors brave
  Have laid their Christian armor down,
Till few, yet spared us from the grave,
  Await to share the victors' crown.

May we, on whom their mantles rest,
  Be true and faithful to the last;
So shall our children call us blessed,
  When FIFTY YEARS again have passed.

Original Hymn, 50th Anniversary of the Universalist Church in Salem, Salem Register, August 8, 1859

The *Salem Register* printed the *Original Hymn* on August 8, 1859. The song was written by Mr. C. W. Swasey of Salem and sung at the Celebration of the fiftieth Anniversary of the Dedication of the Universalist Church in Salem on Thursday, August 4, 1859.[21]

Universalist Church, Nelson Dionne Collection, courtesy of the Salem Public Library

Original Hymn
50th Anniversary of the Universalist Church in Salem

Swift, as the weaver's shuttle plays,
    Have passed th' eventful Fifty Years,
Since first this House of Prayer and Praise
    Was consecrate by Christian seers.

The sainted Murray then was here,
    And Richards, with his rapt address,
And Smith, who asked in fervent prayer
    That GOD would the new Temple bless.

But where is now that triple band,
    Whose fragment memory yet remains?
Gone to the blissful, "Better Lands,"
    Where God is praised in loftier strains!

Our Fathers, too; ah! Where are they,
    Who reared in hope this spacious fane,
And bore the burden if that day,
    When bigots scorned their cherished name?

For God's great truth they nobly fought,
    As those who battle for the right;
In humble prayer His aid they sought,
    And triumphed in Jehovah's might.

One after one, those warriors brave
    Have laid their Christian armor down,
Till few, yet spared us from the grave,
    Await to share the victors' crown.

May we, on whom their mantles rest,
    Be true and faithful to the last;
So shall our children call us blessed,
    When Fifty Years again have passed.

MR. C.W. SWASEY – 1859

~ 5 ~

Conflict

Original Ode
The First Shot of Freedom

Original Ode, The First Shot of Freedom, was composed by Miss L.L.A. Very and was sung on the morning of the *Memorial Services at the Centennial Anniversary of Leslie's Expedition to Salem*, on Friday, February 26, 1875.[1] This confrontation known as Leslie's Retreat occurred on February 26, 1775. The British troops, led by Lt. Colonel Alexander Leslie, left Marblehead and arrived in Salem at the North Bridge. The citizens of Salem successfully resisted the advancement of British soldiers without firing a shot:

> This move of the British army was the first open invasion of the rights and freedom of the people and brought out in broad daylight the first actual resistance in arms to the Royal authority of the crown. [1]

The musical program at the service was under the direction of Salem resident Mr. Manuel Fenollosa who wrote the *Emancipation Hymn* in 1863. The singing was by a choir selected from the *Salem Oratorio Society*.

Leslie's Retreat Postcard, courtesy of Sal Pangallo

Original Ode, The First Shot of Freedom

Leslie's Retreat, sounding far through the years!
   Their footsteps are marching, marching today;
Gone are the trials privations and fears
   Our ancestors bore 'neath England's proud sway.
Sown in War's furrows with blood and with tears,
   The harvest of Peace we are reaping today.

Chorus: The first shot of Freedom today we repeat!
         Here's to the memory of Leslie's Retreat!
      A health to the brave ones of old!

Back from our borders by land and by sea,
   Born unto freedom we turn back the feet,
Feet of oppressors who e'er they may be,
   They'll march to the tune of Leslie's Retreat!
Back from our borders by land and by sea,
   We turn back oppressors who e'er they may be.

Chorus: The first shot of Freedom today we repeat!
         Here's to the memory of Leslie's Retreat!
      A health to the brave ones of old!

Between wrong and right let us e'er draw the line,
   Though poverty's here their red coats so fine;
When Georges send down their mandates so wise,
   Our North Bridge shall rival the famed Bridge of Sighs.
Cherish the names of the brave and the true,
   Barnard and Sprague and Pickering too.

Chorus: The first shot of Freedom today we repeat!
         Here's to the memory of Leslie's Retreat!
      A health to the brave ones of old!

MISS L. L. A. VERY – 1875

Col. Leslie's Expedition
tune: *Auld Lang Syne*

The *Salem Register* published the ballad *Col. Leslie's Expedition* in 1848 about Colonel Leslie's retreat from the North Bridge in Salem. Salem resident Mrs. Symonds wrote the song soon after the event in 1775.[2] Mrs. Symonds wrote the song using the tune of *Auld Lang Syne* as a template.

Transcribed from the *Salem Register,* March 23, 1848:

As the attention of your readers has recently been called to Col. Leslie's Expedition to Salem, they will, I think, peruse with interest the following quaint ballad, composed after the events to which it occurred. It was written by Mrs. Symonds, a lady from North Fields. As the lines are from memory, the particular rhythm has occasioned some difficulty in putting them upon paper, especially concerning the last verse, which has proved almost unmanageable. Although the ballad, as will be seen, is incomplete, I have forborne to supply the defect of memory by engraving upon the original any stanza of my own, which laudable example, it is hoped, may be emulated by all succeeding antiquaries. [2]

W.

"On the twenty-sixth of February
The year of seventy-five,
With officers and soldiers
North Bridge was alive.

The Whigs in the North,
Courageously they stood;
They hoisted the channel,
Which was made of wood.

"Why," so says the Colonel,
"My orders run so,
That over this here bridge,
My soldiers must go.

And at my request,
I'll just go thirty rods,
And then I'll return
According to word."

So they, in great haste,
    The channel let fall;
And over went the Colonel,
    The soldiers, and all.

They made a great clamping,
    As they hurried along,
But we didn't mind an atom.
    For we know'd they dare not do wrong.

So, at their request,
    They went thirty rods,
And then they returned,
    According to word.

The Tories in the town,
    Were put to a fright;
Some left their homes,
    And others watched by night.

Prince, he kept close;
    John Sargent, he fled;
And Grant was afraid
    For to sleep in his bed.

The Tory that aided them,
    From Marblehead to Salem,
He came as a Troy,
    And he went as a Whig,
And if you'd know the man
    It was Major Peddrick.

"On the twenty-sixth of February,
    The year seventy-five,
With officers and soldiers
    North Bridge was alive.

The Whigs in the North,
    Courageously they stood;
They hoisted the channel,
    Which was made of wood.

"Why," so says the Colonel,

MRS. SYMONDS – 1848

Col. Leslie's Expedition,
Salem Register,
March 23, 1848

Ode (To Leslie's Retreat)

George Bailey published a book called *Celebration at North Bridge, Salem, July 4th, 1862*. He included Miss Mary E. Todd's song *Ode (To Leslie's Retreat)*. On July 4th, Mayor Webb of Salem met with the residents of North Salem to celebrate the retreat of Lieutenant Colonel Leslie, the first confrontation with the British before the beginning of the Revolutionary War.[3]

> Sons of Freedom, raise the banner!
>   Fling its starry folds abroad;
> Consecrate anew the symbol
>   To our country, and to God!
>
> Traitor hands have marred its lustre!
>   Trailed its honor in the dust!
> Trampled on the hallowed emblem,
>   Our Forefathers' sacred trust.
>
> God, our Heavenly Father! Hear us—
>   Shade of Washington! Draw near!
> As we here renew the compact
>   Sealed by Patriot blood so dear.
>
> We will tarry not, nor falter,
>   Till each darkening strain is borne
> From thy plumage, Bird of Freedom,
>   Now by civil madness torn.
>
> Trusting in the God of Battles,
>   We will hope again to see
> Our proud banner nobly floating
>   O'er a land that's truly free.

MISS MARY E. TODD – 1862

Colonel Pickering's March To Lexington
aka Black Sloven

The Pickering House, courtesy of Mary Barker

The tune *Colonel Pickering's March to Lexington*, aka *The Black Sloven,* is preserved in an old music manuscript book kept at the Phillips Library. Louis Elson, author of *The National Music of America and its Sources*, wrote: "The fife and drum attached to Colonel Pickering's American regiment as it marched from Salem to Lexington on April 19, 1775, played a tune called *The Black Sloven.*" [4]

Colonel Pickering's March to Lexington

TRADITIONAL – PRE 1800

A Funeral Elegy
to the Immortal Memory
of those Worthies who were slain in the Battle of Concord,
April 19, 1775

On April 19, 1875, the *New York Herald* [5] published the contents of an old broadside ballad called *A Funeral Elegy to the Immortal Memory of those Worthies who were slain in the Battle of Concord, April 19, 1775*. The original ballad was published soon after the events in Lexington and Concord. The original broadside, housed at the Phillips Library in Rowley, Massachusetts, can be viewed by appointment.

AID me ye nine! my muse assist,
    A sad tale to relate,
When such a number of brave men
    Met their unhappy fate.
At Lexington they met their foe
    Completely all equip'd,
Their guns and swords made glit'ring show,
    But their base scheme was nipp'd.

Americans, go drop a tear,
    Where your slain brethren lay!
O! mourn and sympathize for them!
    O! Weep this very day!
What shall we say to this loud call
    From the Almighty sent;
It surely bids both great and small
    Seek God's face and repent.

Words can't express the ghastly scene,
    That here presents to view,
When forty-two countrymen
    Sure bid their friends adieu.
To think how awful it must seem,
    To hear widows relent
Their husbands and their children
    Who to the grave was sent.

The tender babes, nay those unborn,
    O! dismal cruel death!
To snatch their fondest parents dear,
    And leave them thus bereft.
O! Lexington, your loss is great!
    Alas! too great to tell,
But justice bids me to relate
    What to you has befell.

Ten of your hardy, bravest sons,
    Some in their prime did fall;
May we no more hear noise of guns
    To terrify us all.
Let's not forget the Danvers race
    So late in battle slain,
Their courage and their valor shown
    Upon the crimson'd plain.

Sev'n of your youthful sprightly sons,
    In the fierce fight were slain,
O! may your loss be all made up,
    And prove a lasting gain.
Cambridge and Medford's loss is great,
    Though not like Acton's town,
Where three fierce military sons
    Met their untimely doom.

Menotomy and Charlestown met,
    A sore and heavy stroke,
In losing five your brave townsmen
    Who fell by tyrant's yoke.
Unhappy Lynn and Beverly,
    Your loss I do bemoan,
Five your brave sons in dust doth lye,
    Who late were in their bloom.

Bedford, Woburn, Sudbury, all,
    Have suffer'd most severe,
You miss five of your choicest chore,
    On them let's drop a tear.
Concord your Captain's fate rehearse,
    His loss is felt severe,
Come, brethren, join with me in verse,
    His mem'ry hence revere.

O 'Squire Gardiner's death we feel,
    And sympathizing mourn,
Let's drop a tear when it we tell,
    And view his hapless urn.
We sore regret poor Pierce's death,
    A stroke to Salem's town,
Where tears did flow from ev'ry brow,
    When the sad tidings come.

The groans of wounded, dying men,
    Would melt the stoutest soul,
O! how it strikes thro' ev'ry vein,
    My flesh and blood runs cold.
May all prepare to meet their fate
    At God's tribunal bar,
And may war's terrible alarm
    For death us now prepare.

Your country calls you far and wide,
    America's sons 'wake,
Your helmet, buckler, and [your?] spear,
    The Lord's own arm now take.
His shield will keep us from all harm,
    Tho' thousands gainst us rise,
His buckler we must sure put on,
    If we would win the prize.

PRINTED AND SOLD BY E. RUSSELL, SALEM – 1775

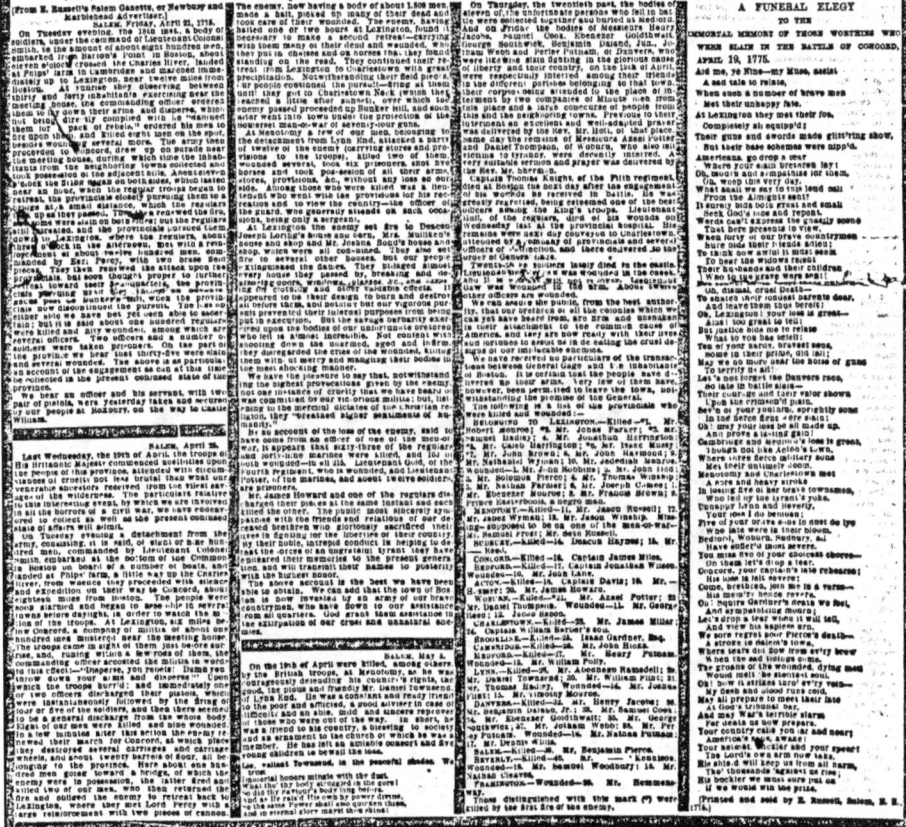

A Funeral Elegy, New York Herald, April 19, 1875 courtesy of the Boston Public Library

Ode of War and Washington
tune: *British Grenadiers*

Salem-born Jonathan M. Sewall wrote the ballad *Ode of War and Washington* during the American Revolution and set the song to the tune called *The British Grenadiers.* Sewall studied at Harvard College, entered the mercantile business, and eventually settled in Portsmouth, New Hampshire, where he "passed the remainder of his life, with a high character for integrity." He died March 29, 1808, at the age of 60. [6]

According to Samuel Kettell, editor of *Specimens of American Poetry*, the *Ode of War and Washington* was a patriotic song that "was sung throughout the country during the Revolutionary War and served to inspire zeal and courage in the cause for independence." [7]

From an article found in the *Salem Mercury* dated October 27, 1789:

The President of the United States is expected to honor this town with a visit on Thursday next, about noon. We are informed that he will come by way of Marblehead, and he will tarry in this town one night and continue his tour eastward the next morning. From the judicious choice made by the inhabitants of this town of the committee for addressing the President and for making arrangements for his reception, we venture to predict that he will be received here in style, becoming the rank of the town and coinciding with the ardent love and affection while every son and daughter of Salem bears this amiable and illustrious perusing. [8]

The Joshua Ward House, courtesy of Mary Barker

The war for independence ended, and George Washington became president. Washington traveled throughout the colonies. On October 29, 1789. he visited Salem to review the troupes and attend a ball at the *Assembly House*. He spent the evening at the private residence of Joshua Ward, a shipping master and rum distiller. [9] The house is located on 148 Washington Street and is now a small boutique hotel called *The Merchant*.

Ode of War and Washington,
Boston Semi-Weekly,
September 7, 1861,
courtesy of the Boston Public Library

Ode of War and Washington

Vain Britons, boast no longer, with fine indignity,
  Your valiant marching legions, your matchless strength at sea.
For we, your loyal sons oppressed, have girded our swords on.
    Huzza! Huzza! Huzza! For War and Washington!

Urged on by North and vengeance, those valiant champions came,
  Loud bellowing Tea and Treason, and George was all on flame,
Yet sacrilegious as it seems, we rebels still live on,
    And laugh at all their empty puffs,—huzza for Washington!

Still deaf to mild entreaties, still blind to England's good,
  You have for thirty pieces, betray'd your country's blood.
Like Aesop's greedy cur, you'll gain a shadow for your bone,
    Yet find us fearful shades indeed, inspired by Washington!

Mysterious! Unexampled! Incomprehensible!
  The blundering schemes of Britain, their folly, pride, and zeal.
Like lions how ye growl and threat! mere asses have you shown,
    And ye shall share an ass's fate, and drudge for Washington!

Your dark, unfathom'd counsels, our weakest heads defeat,
  Our children rout your armies, our boats destroy your fleet,
And to complete the dire disgrace, coop'd up within a town,
    You live, the scorn of all our host, the slaves of Washington!

Great heaven! is this the nation, whose thundering arms were hurl'd,
  Through Europe, Africa, India? whose navy ruled a world?
The lustre of your former deeds, whole ages of renown,
    Lost in a moment, or transferred to us and Washington!

Yet think not thirst of glory, unsheathes our vengeful swords,
  To rend your bands asunder, and cast away your cords.
'T is heaven-born freedom fires us all, and strengthens each brave son,
    From him who humbly guides the plough, to godlike Washington!

For this, Oh could our wishes, your ancient rage inspire,
  Your armies should be doubled, in numbers, force, and fire.
Then might the glorious conflict prove which best deserved the boon,
    America or Albion; a George, or Washington!

Fired with the great idea, our fathers' shades would rise;
    To view the stern contention, the gods desert their skies.
And Wolfe; 'mid hosts of heroes, superior bending down,
      Cry out with eager transport, God save great Washington!

Should George, too choice of Britons, to foreign realms apply?
    And madly arm half Europe, yet still we would defy
Turk, Hessian, Jew, and Infidel, or all those powers in one,
      While Adams guides our senate, our camp great Washington!

Should warlike weapons fail us, disdaining slavish fears,
    To swords we'll beat our ploughshares, our pruning hooks to spears,
And rush, all desperate! On our foe, nor breathe till battle won;
      Then shout, and shout America! And conquering Washington!

Proud France should view with terror, and haughty Spain revere,
    While every warlike nation would court alliance here.
And George, his minions trembling round, dismounting from his throne,
      Pay homage to America, and glorious Washington!

JONATHAN M. SEWALL – 1789

Ode of War and Washington

tune: *British Grenadiers*, transcribed by Dan Mozell

Salem Artillery

The *Salem Artillery* [10] was a popular dance and military tune played in Salem around 1800. The tune was researched and transcribed by T. William Smith, a Salem resident and folk musician, circa 1980. The tune was archived at the *Essex Institute* in Salem (now part of the *Peabody Essex Museum*) and played regularly at contra dances in Salem by the *Salem Country Orchestra* between 1985 – 2010.

TRADITIONAL – 1800

Salem Artillery

Americans to Arms

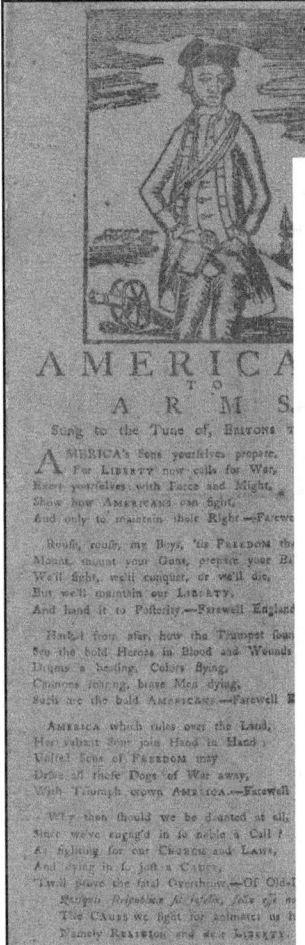

Americans to Arms, courtesy of the Rosenbach Museum and Library

Ezekiel Russel printed the broadside, *Americans to Arms*, in Salem in 1775. The ballad can be sung to the familiar tune *Britons to Arms*, [11]

AMERICA's Sons, yourselves prepare
   For LIBERTY now calls for War.
Exert yourselves with Force and Might,
   Show how AMERICANS can fight,
And only to maintain their Right Farewell England.

Rouse, rouse, my Boys, 'tis FREEDOM that calls;
   Mount, mount your Guns, prepare your Ball;
We'll fight, we'll conquer, or we'll die,
   But we'll maintain our LIBERTY,
And hand it to Posterity Farewell England.

Hark! From afar, how the Trumpet sounds,
   See the bold Heroes in Blood and Wounds;
Drums a-beating, Colors flying,
   Cannons roaring, brave Men dying,
Such are the bold AMERICANS Farewell England.

AMERICA, which rules over the Land,
   Her valiant Sons join Hand in Hand;
United Sons of FREEDOM may
   Drive all those Dogs of War away,
With Triumph crown AMERICA Farewell England.

Why then should we be daunted at all,
   Since we've engag'd in so noble a Call?
As fighting for our CHURCH and LAWS,
   And dying in so just a CAUSE, '
Twill prove the fatal Overthrow Of Old England.

EZEKIEL. RUSSELL – 1775

Song of the Minute Man

The Harris Broadside Collection at the John Hay Library at Brown University and the Frederick E. Berry Library at Salem State University both have a copy of the Broadside ballad.[12] *Song of the Minute Man* was originally written on March 13, 1777, by Mr. Boundbruck. Local businessman George R. Curwen, Esquire, copied and republished the phonetically spelled text from the original manuscript. *The Ladies' Centennial Committee of Salem* reproduced the broadside and was sold by the *Antique Relics & Company* at an exhibition on December 15, 1875, as a fundraiser.[12] Curwen also copied the ballad, *A Funeral Elegy*, and sold the broadside at the same event.

Come rise up Brother minute man and let us have a corous
    The braver and the Bolder the more they will adore us
Oure contry cals for swords and Bals and Drums A loud Doth Rattle
    Oure fifers charmes arise to arms Liberty cals to battle

We have from noble congras men elected for our nurses
    And very joly farmer will assist us with their purses
We let them stay att home we say enjoy their with pleasure
    And we will go and fight oure foes and save there Lives and treasure

So let us not be Dismayed alltho the tories thunder
    Thay only want to Ruin us and live upon oure Plunder
Oure caus is just thirfore we must with heavens kind protection
    With north and Gage in all thair rage will never cum in action

Now tew oure Station Let us march and randevuse with pleasure
    We have ben like Brave minut men to sarve so Great A Treasure
We let them fit amediately that we are men of mettle
    We Jarfey Boys that fere no nois will never flinch for Battle

And when we Do return Again it will be with Glory
    For them that Do remain at home to hear a valiant story
Thay will Draw nere and glad to hear no Douting of the wonder
    That minut men though one to ten should bring tories under

And now poure Gage has tuck his flight and though he has left Commander
    Lord North he has appointed to be his chief Defender
We fere them not though Bullits hot about oure heads Do rattle
    Weal make them fit amediatley in such A Glorious Battle

Long may Georg live and rule the throne and all his loyal Subjects
    That truly stands for liberty and makes these chief objections
For slavith chains we Do Disdain Likewise popesh tiriney
    Such hellish frays we Do Defy and will not to yield to any

Cum fill us up abole Brave Boys it Better Dun than un Dun
    Here is helth to thy Lord mayr and Livery of London
He in pure caus that made no paus Plead Boldly as they intended
    For freedoms right with all oure might my Boys Let us Defend it

Let us be not Dismayd all though the tories should Defious
    There is oure Brave melesi men that shurly will stand By us
That tory Brood that halth with stood that Grait and Glorious joyel
    If theay Advance we will make them Dance the tune Yancadudal *

TRADITIONAL – 1777

[* The text was copied from the original manuscript – RS]

Song of the Minute Man, courtesy
of the Harris Broadside Collection,
John Hay Library, Brown University

Yankee Song

tune: *Yankee Doodle*

Mr. Bigelow of Salem composed the *Yankee Song* [13] and published the song in the *Salem Gazette* in July 1811. This lively song was sung at a military celebration on the 4th of July at the Lynn Hotel in Lynn, Massachusetts, and by the Federalists at *Washington Hall* in Salem.

"Its wit and pleasantry make it a favorite with the Yankees. *Yankee Doodle* will always be a favorite with Americans and "is so much superior to the vulgar ditties generally sung to this tune, that we think proper to preserve it. Some of the provincial phrases of New England are very happily ridiculed." [14]

Yankey Doodle is the tune, Americans delight in;
'Twill do to whistle, sing, or play, And just the thing for fighting.

Chorus: Yankee Doodle, Boys; Huzza!
Down outside-up the middle
Yankee Doodle, fa, sol, la,
Trumpet, Drum, and Fiddle.

Should Great Britain, Spain, or France, Wage war upon our shore, sir,
We'll lead them such a woundy dance, They'll find their toes are sore, sir.

Should a haughty foe we expect? To give our boys a caning,
We guess they'll find our boys have learned, A little bit of training.

Chorus: Yankee Doodle, Boys; Huzza!
Down outside-up the middle
Yankee Doodle, fa, sol, la,
Trumpet, Drum, and Fiddle.

I'll wager now a mug of flip, And bring it on the table,
Put Yankey boys aboard a ship, To beat them they are able.

Then if they go to argufy, I rather guess they'll find, too,
We've got a set of tonguey blades, T'out talk 'em, if they're mind to.

America's a dandy place; The people are all brothers;
    And when one's got a pumpkin pie, He shares it with the others.

        Chorus: Yankee Doodle, Boys; Huzza!
            Down outside-up the middle
        Yankee Doodle, fa, sol, la,
            Trumpet, Drum, and Fiddle.

We work, and sleep, and pray, in peace— By industry we thrive, sir;
    And if a drone won't do his part, We'll scout him from the hive, sir.

And then, on Independent Day, And who's a better right to?
    We eat and drink, and sing and play, And have a dance at night, too.

Our girls are fair, our boys are tough, Our old folks wise and healthy;
    And when we've everything we want, We count that we are wealthy.

        Chorus: Yankee Doodle, Boys; Huzza!
            Down outside-up the middle
        Yankee Doodle, fa, sol, la,
            Trumpet, Drum, and Fiddle.

We're happy, free, and well to do, And cannot want for knowledge;
    For, almost ev'ry mile or two, You find a school or college.

The land we till is all our own; Whate'er the price, we paid it;
    Therefore we'll fight till all is blue, Should any dare invade it.

Since we're so bless'd, let's eat and drink, With thankfulness and gladness:
    Should we kick o'er our cup of joy, It would be satin madness.

        Chorus: Yankee Doodle, Boys; Huzza!
            Down outside-up the middle
        Yankee Doodle, fa, sol, la,
            Trumpet, Drum, and Fiddle.

MR.BIGELOW – 1811

The Patriotic Diggers
tune: *Far off at Sea*

Discovered in the *Salem Observer* dated October 3, 1863, the song, *The Patriotic Diggers* is sung to the melody of *Far off at Sea*.[15] A New York paper first printed the song in 1814 and told how the citizens of New York helped to defend their city during the War of 1812. The writer of the article for the *Observer* recently visited old Fort Lee, on Salem Neck, and Fort Pickering, on Winter Island, and recollected:

> Some scenes of the Wars of 1812, when all classes of citizens on the sea coast volunteered to labor on the fortifications erected to defend those places thought to be in danger of British invasion. Many are now living in Salem who performed wheelbarrow duty at Fort Lee at the time.[15]

To this day, a group of volunteers maintain the Fork Pickering area.

Johnny Bull, beware, keep at proper distance,
    Else we'll make you stare, at our firm resistance.
Let alone the lads who are freedom tasting;
    Recollect our dads gave you once a basting.

Chorus: Pickaxe, shovel, spade, crowbar, hoe, and barrow,
               Better not invade, Yankees have the marrow.

To protect our rights 'gainst your flints and triggers,
    See on Brooklyn Heights our patriotic Diggers.
Men of every age, colour, rank, profession,
    Ardently engage, labour in succession.

Chorus: Pickaxe, shovel, spade, crowbar, hoe, and barrow,
               Better not invade, Yankees have the marrow.

Grandeur leaves her tower, poverty her hovel,
    Here to join their powers, with the hoe and shovel.
Here the merchant toils with the patriotic Sawyer,
    There the labourer smiles, near him sweats the lawyer.

Chorus: Pickaxe, shovel, spade, crowbar, hoe, and barrow,
               Better not invade, Yankees have the marrow.

Here the mason builds Freedom's shrine of glory,
  While the Painter gilds the immortal story;
Blacksmiths catch the flame, grocers feel the spirit;
  Printers share the fame and record their merit.

Chorus: Pickaxe, shovel, spade, crowbar, hoe, and barrow,
      Better not invade, Yankees have the marrow.

Scholars leave their Schools, with their patriotic Teachers;
  Farmers seize their tools, headed by their Preachers:
How they break the soil! Brewers, Butchers, Bakers;
  Here the Doctors toil, there the undertakers.

Chorus: Pickaxe, shovel, spade, crowbar, hoe, and barrow,
      Better not invade, Yankees have the marrow.

Bright Apollo's sons, leave their pipe and tabor,
  Mid the roar of guns, join the martial labour.
Round the embattled plain, in sweet concord rally,
  And in Freedom's strain, sing the foe's finale.

Chorus: Pickaxe, shovel, spade, crowbar, hoe, and barrow,
      Better not invade, Yankees have the marrow.

Plumbers, Founders, Dyers, Tinmen, Turners, Shavers,
  Sweepers, Clerks and Cryers, Jewellers, Engravers,
Clothiers, Drapers, Players, Cartmen, Hatters, Tailors,
  Gaugers, Sealers, Weighers, Carpenters, and Sailors.

Chorus: Pickaxe, shovel, spade, crowbar, hoe, and barrow,
      Better not invade, Yankees have the marrow.

Better not invade; recollect the spirit
  Which our Dads display'd, and their Sons inherit;
If you still advance, friendly caution slighting,
  You may get by chance, a belly-full of fighting.

Chorus: Pickaxe, shovel, spade, crowbar, hoe, and barrow,
      Better not invade, Yankees have the marrow.

TRADITIONAL – 1814 & 1863

The Patriot Song

tune: *Hallelujah Chorus*

The *Salem Observer* [16] published the Civil War song *The Patriot Song* in August 1861. This rousing anthem is sung to the melody of the *Hallelujah Chorus* for the soldiers fighting in the war.

Where, oh where are our city merchants?
Where, oh where are our city merchants?
Where, oh where are our city merchants?
Gone to join the war.

Chorus: Three cheers! Three cheers for our soldiers!
Three cheers! Three cheers for our soldiers!
Three cheers! Three cheers for our soldiers!
And groans of the traitors bold.

Where, oh where are our country farmers?
Where, oh where are our country farmers?
Where, oh where are our country farmers?
Gone to fight for their homes.

Chorus: Three cheers! Three cheers for our soldiers!
Three cheers! Three cheers for our soldiers!
Three cheers! Three cheers for our soldiers!
And groans of the traitors bold.

Where, oh where are our fathers and brothers?
Where, oh where are our fathers and brothers?
Where, oh where are our fathers and brothers?
Gone to defeat old Jeff.

Chorus: Three cheers! Three cheers for our soldiers!
Three cheers! Three cheers for our soldiers!
Three cheers! Three cheers for our soldiers!
And groans of the traitors bold.

They are bound to be good soldiers,
    They are bound to be good soldiers,
They are bound to be good soldiers,
    And bravely they'll beat the South.

Chorus: Three cheers! Three cheers for our soldiers!
        Three cheers! Three cheers for our soldiers!
    Three cheers! Three cheers for our soldiers!
    And groans of the traitors bold.

Hurrah for the constitution!
    Hurrah! Hurrah! For the union!
Hurrah! Hurrah for the soldiers!
    And soon may their labors end.

Chorus: Three cheers! Three cheers for our soldiers!
        Three cheers! Three cheers for our soldiers!
    Three cheers! Three cheers for our soldiers!
    And groans of the traitors bold.

UNKNOWN – 1861

FOR THE OBSERVER.
THE PATRIOT SONG.
(Air—*Hallelujah* Chorus.)

I.

Where, oh where are our city merchants?
Where, oh where are our city merchants?
Where, oh where are our city merchants?
    Gone to join the war.
Chorus.—Three cheers! three cheers for our soldiers!
    Three cheers! three cheers for our soldiers!
    Three cheers! three cheers for our soldiers!
    And groans for all traitors bold.

II.

Where, oh where are our country farmers?
    [Repeat.]
    Gone to fight for their homes.
Chorus.—Three cheers, &c.

III.

Where, oh where are our fathers and brothers?
    [Repeat.]
    Gone to defeat old Jeff.
Chorus.—Three cheers! &c.

IV.

They are bound to be good soldiers,
    [Repeat.]
    And bravely they'll beat the South.
Chorus.—Three cheers! &c.

*The Patriot Song,
Salem Observer,*
August 24, 1861

To Our Salem Boys

To Our Salem Boys [17] was printed in the *Salem Register* on July 28, 1862.

"Come rally round the flag, boys;"
    And craven fear despise;
The blow of murdered martyrs,
    Of brothers, bid ye rise!
Their graves are now appealing,
    Their voices bid ye go.
Can ye hear that silent chiding?
    Forget ye! Who lies low?

Come rally round the flag, boys;
    We bore from British power!
Did we gain it with our freedom,
    To lose it, at this hour?
To give it up to traitors,
    And a heritage of slaves,
And mourn a country fallen?
    No! Sooner gives us graves!

The graves of noble martyrs,
    Where trusting sons lie dead,
Who leave to us the battles
    Since now their souls are fled.
And shall we scorn their warnings?
    No! Let us fear despise!
And should the grave be yawning,
    Those graves should make us rise!

Penny Ballad Seller,
Sunday Boston Herald,
July 24, 1910

Come rally round the flag, boys;
    What though the orphans mourn!
There's virtue in their tears, boys,
    To make our fires burn.
Avenge their cruel wrong, boys,
    And bid the right prevail,
'Tis number in the field, boys
    That makes the coward quail!

Ho! Rally round the flag, boys;
And wrest it from the foe!
The graves of martyred heroes,
Of brothers, bid ye go!
What think we of the parting,
Or what the cost may be;
Let's rally round the flag, boys;
And make the land be free!

UNKNOWN – 1862

FOR THE REGISTER.
To Our Salem Boys.
'Come rally round the flag, boys;'
And craven fear despise;
The blow of murdered martyrs—
Of brothers—bids ye rise!
Their graves are now appealing,
Their voices bid ye go.
Can ye hear that silent chiding ?
Forget ye—who lies low ?

Come rally, round that flag, boys!
We tore from British power!
Did we *gain* it with our freedom,
To *lose* it, at this hour ?
To give it up to traitors,
And a heritage of slaves,—
And mourn a country fallen ?
No!—Sooner give us *graves!*

The graves of noble martyrs,
Where trusting sons lie dead,
Who leave to *us* the battles
Since now *their* souls are fled.
And shall we scorn their warning ?
No!—Let us fear despise!
And should the grave be yawning,
Those graves should *make* us rise!

Come rally round the flag, boys!
What though the orphans mourn!
There's virtue in their tears, boys,
To make our fires burn.
Avenge their cruel wrong, boys,
And bid the right prevail,
'Tis *numbers in the field*, boys,
That makes the coward quail!

Ho! Rally round the flag, boys,
And wrest it from the foe!
The graves of martyred heroes —
Of brothers—bid ye go!
What think we of the parting,
Or what the cost may be;
Let's rally round the flag, boys,
And *make the land be free!*

To Our Salem Boys, Salem Register, July 28, 1862

Departure of the Salem Light Infantry

Departure of the Salem Light Infantry,
courtesy of Harris Broadside Collection
at the John Hay Library, Brown University

The Harris Broadsides Collection at Brown University [18] has a copy of the broadside ballad *Departure of the Salem Light Infantry*. Accepted into state service on April 19, 1861, The *Salem City Guards 7th Massachusetts Volunteer Militia Company H* left Salem and arrived at Faneuil Hall in Boston on April 20, 1861. [19] According to the *Salem Register*, the *Mechanic Light Infantry,* led by Captain Pierson, and the *Salem City Guards,* led by Captain Danforth, under orders of joined Commander Colonel Lawrence's regiment. The *Mechanic Light Infantry* numbered 110 men, and the *Salem City Guards* 64 men. [20]

To arms! To Arms! Our country calls;
    The Salem Infantry reply,
And quickly; leave their armory halls,
    To make the Southern rebels fly.

A company of fearless men,
    In all their youthful strength and force,
'Mid cheers and shouting take the train,
    That bears them on their course.

There's one on whom we can confide,
    On him implicitly rely;
His honor needs not to be tried,
    Temptation he can well defy.

A frame with all the force of youth,
    A mind from folly's shackles clear,
A heart of love, and hope, and truth;
    Our Willie's one whom all revere.

136

His father's pride his mother's joy,
    A brother true, a faithful friend–
May God protect this noble boy,
    In safety to his home to send

And sad was Charlie Dimon's face,
    But duty was his polar guide;
And so with trust, he took his place,
    And ranked himself on Union's side.

May he in Willie's friendship find,
    A balm to soothe the homesick heart;
And may they both forever mind,
    That's good advice, "Act well your part."

Among the troops was one bright face,
    That gleamed with patriotic zeal;
And nobly handsome, full of grace,
    On his pure brow is stamped truth's seal.

The love of country burns within,
    The soul that's large with love for all,
And Johnnie Lakeman deemed in sin
    To answer not his country's call.

Oh! Sad hearts they leave behind–
    And tearful faces, daily met,
Do tell full well that ties that bind,
    We never, never can forget.

"The pride of Salem" – they have gone,
    To battle for their native land;
God grant that they may soon return,
    In safety, and unbroken band.

S.J.C.N. APRIL 19TH – 1861

Lines written for the
Second Reunion of the 23rd Regiment

tune: *Auld Lang Syne*

The Center for Popular Music at Middle Tennessee State University houses a copy of the ballad *Lines written for the Second Reunion of the 23rd Regiment* [21] in their Broadside Collection. Charles Henry Webber wrote the song in 1872. Six companies from Essex County and one from Bristol, Plymouth, Middlesex, and Worcester counties made up the 23rd Regiment. The companies assembled in Lynnfield, Massachusetts, on September 28, 1861. Ten years after their first muster, the surviving soldiers gathered for a reunion in Salem, Massachusetts, formed the 23rd Regiment Association, and read the broadside of the event. [22]

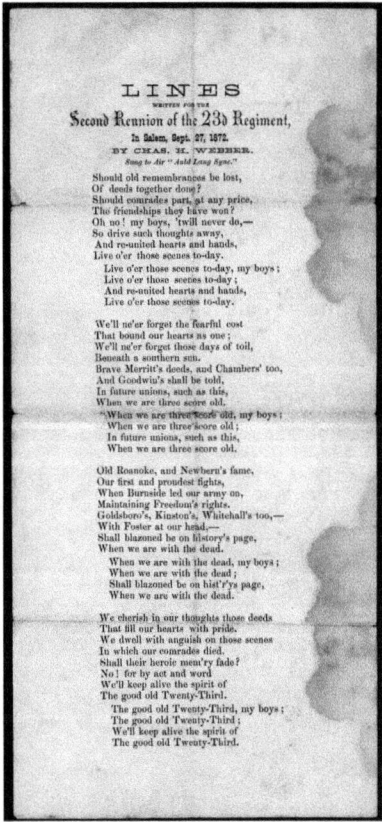

Should old remembrances be lost
    Of deeds together done?
Should comrades part, at any price,
    The friendships they have won?
Oh no! My boys, 'twill never do,
    So drive such thoughts away,
And re-united hearts and hands,
    Live o'er those scenes to-day.

Live o'er those scenes today, my boys;
    Live o'er those scenes today;
And re-united hearts and hands,
    Live o'er those scenes to-day.

We'll ne'er forget the fearful cost
    That bound our hearts as one;
We'll ne'er forget those days of toil,
    Beneath a southern sun.
Brave Merritt's deeds, and Chambers' too,
    And Goodwin's shall be told,
In future unions, such as this,
    When we are three score old,

Second Reunion of the 23rd Regiment, courtesy of the Kenneth S. Goldstein Collection Center for Popular Music, Middle Tennessee State University

When we are three score old, my boys;
    When we are three score old;
In future unions, such as this,
    When we are three score old,

Old Roanoke, and Newbern's fame,
    Our first and proudest fights,
When Burnside led our army on,
    Maintaining Freedom's rights.
Goldboro's, Kinston's Whitehall's too,–
    With Foster at our head,–
Shall blazoned be on history's page,
    When we are with the dead.

When we are with the dead, my boys;
    When we are with the dead;
Shall blazoned be on historys page,
    When we are with the dead.

We cherish in our thoughts and deeds
    That fill our hearts with pride.
We dwell with anguish on those scenes
    In which our comrades died.
Shall their heroic mem'ry fade?
    No! for by act and word
We'll keep alive the spirit of
    The good old Twenty-third.

The good old Twenty-third, my boys;
    The good old Twenty-third;
We'll keep alive the spirit of,
    The good old Twenty-third.

CHARLES HENRY WEBBER – 1872

On September 28, 1905, the Association dedicated a bronze plaque set in a 58-ton boulder, commemorating the 23rd Regiment Massachusetts Volunteer Infantry during the Civil War from 1861 – 1865. The memorial stands on Winter Street, near the Salem Common.

When Johnny Comes Marching Home
Roud# 6673

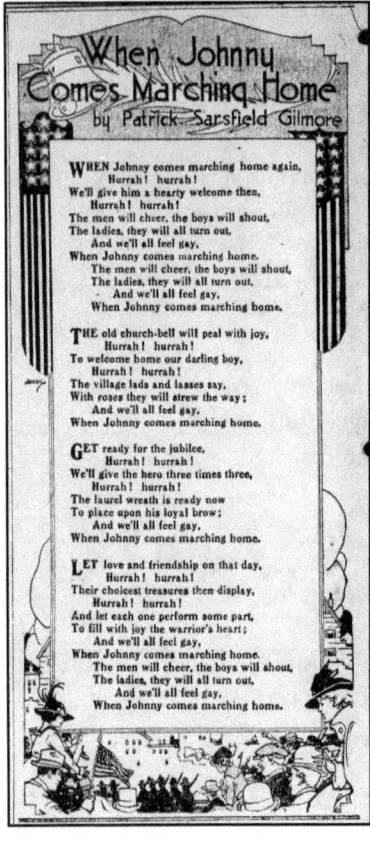

When Johnny Comes Marching Home, Broadside, courtesy of Jarlath MacNamara

Patrick S. Gilmore wrote *When Johnny Comes Marching Home* under the pseudonym of Louis Lambert to celebrate a soldier returning home from the Civil War five years after leaving Salem. Gilmore did not write this song while he was in Salem, but its popularity and importance to the soldiers and their families on both sides of the war warranted inclusion. "It was inspired by the Battle of Gettysburg in July 1863 when the tide of the American Civil War began to turn in favor of the Union." [23]

According to Margaret Bradford Boni, who wrote and compiled the *Fireside Book of Folk Songs*, Gilmore could have heard this tune when it was sung by an "African American," but as Boni pointed out, since Gilmore was an Irishman, it is more likely that the tune had Irish roots.[24] Louis Elson, writer of *The National Music of America and its Sources*, states that *Johnny Comes Marching Home* has a similar melody to the Irish songs *John Anderson, My Jo*, [25] and *Johnny, I Hardly Knew Ye*, an Irish protest song, As stated on the Library of Congress website, "It is possible that this air was written before Gilmore's *When Johnny Comes Marching Home* and that Gilmore unconsciously borrowed from the tune from an African-American spiritual." [26] Discussion continues about the origins of this song.

When Johnny comes marching home again,
　Hurrah! Hurrah!
We'll give him a hearty welcome then,
　Hurrah! Hurrah!
The men will cheer and the boys will shout,
　The ladies they will all turn out,

And we'll all feel gay,
    When Johnny comes marching home.
And we'll all feel gay,
    When Johnny comes marching home.

The old church bell will peal with joy,
    Hurrah! Hurrah!
To welcome home our darling boy,
    Hurrah! Hurrah!
The village lads and lassies say,
    With roses, they will strew the way,
And we'll all feel gay,
    When Johnny comes marching home.
And we'll all feel gay,
    When Johnny comes marching home.

Get ready for the Jubilee,
    Hurrah! Hurrah!
We'll give the hero three times three,
    Hurrah! Hurrah!
The laurel wreath is ready now,
    To place upon his loyal brow,
And we'll all feel gay
    When Johnny comes marching home.
And we'll all feel gay,
    When Johnny comes marching home.

Let love and friendship on that day,
    Hurrah, hurrah!
Their choicest pleasures then display,
    Hurrah, hurrah!
And let each one perform some part,
    To fill with joy the warrior's heart,
And we'll all feel gay,
    When Johnny comes marching home.
And we'll all feel gay,
    When Johnny comes marching home.

LOUIS LAMBERT AKA PATRICK S. GILMORE – 1863

Salem Mechanick Infantry
Quick Step

The *Lester S. Levy Collection of Sheet Music* holds a copy of The *Salem Mechanick Infantry Quick Step.* [27] *Ives & Putman* in Salem published the quick step in 1836. Written and arranged by John Holloway, The *Boston Brass Band* played the tune for the first time on October 13, 1836, on the 29th anniversary of the *Salem Mechanick Light Infantry.*

Salem Mechanick Infantry Quick Step, courtesy of the Lester S. Levy Collection of Sheet Music

Salem Independent Cadet Quick Step, courtesy of the Lester S. Levy Collection of Sheet Music

Salem Independent Cadet
Quick Step

The *Salem Independent Cadet Quick Step* is dedicated to Captain S. B. Foster and the officers and members of the Division Corps of Independent Cadets at their fall parade on October 17, 1848.[28] Found in the *Lester S. Levy Collection of Sheet Music* at John Hopkins University, the piece was composed by Zetzsche, arranged by S. Knaebel, and performed at the parade by the *Flagg's Boston Brass Band.*

Musical Entertainment
at Mechanic Hall, Salem

This concert, sponsored by the New England Women's Auxiliary Sanitary Commission and led by band leader Salem resident Manuel Fenollosa, was held at Mechanic Hall in Salem on January 5 and January 6, 1863, for the benefit of the sick and wounded Massachusetts soldiers who fought in the Civil War. [29] The two-day program raised $423.75 after all expenses. Hattie Safford, E. W. Silsbee, J. F. Tuckerman, E. H. Randall of Salem, E. T. Kemble of Beverly, and M. C. Upton of Danvers performed at the concert. The program consisted of several classical pieces and the singing of two newly composed parlor ballads *Her Bright Smile Haunts Me Still* and *Goodbye, Sweet Heart*.

The song *Her Bright Smile Haunts Me Still* was written by W. T. Wrighton and J. E. Carpenter and was published circa 1858. Recently, the song has had renewed interest through the folk process after being published in *Traditional American Folk Songs* from the Anne and Frank Warner Collection. [30] This program documents one of the first public performances of *Her Bright Smile Haunts Me Still.*

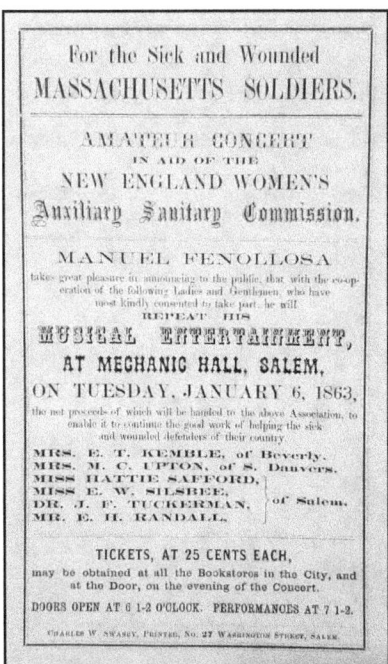

New England Women's Auxiliary
Sanitary Commission Program Booklet,
courtesy of Christine Elizabeth Mistretta

Amateur Concert, *Salem Observer*,
January 3, 1863

Dreaming of Home and Mother

Dreaming of Home and Mother [31] was written in 1868 and composed by John P. Ordway. Ordway was born in Salem on August 1, 1824, and later moved to Boston as a young boy. Ordway wrote popular sentimental songs of the Civil War era. He graduated from Harvard Medical College in 1859 and was one of the first Union surgeons to volunteer at the beginning of the Civil War. He served in the Sixth Massachusetts Militia and tended the wounded after the Battle of Gettysburg. [32] While living in Boston, Ordway was on the school board and in the Massachusetts House of Representatives. James Lord Pierpont, a friend of Ordway, wrote The *One Horse Open Sleigh*, later named *Jingle Bells*, and dedicated the song to John P. Ordway. [33] Peirpont also wrote the songs *No Nothing Polka* and *The Returned Californian*.

Dreaming of Home and Mother,
courtesy of the Prints and Photographs
Division, Library of Congress

Dreaming of home, dear old home.
    Home of childhood and mother–
Oft when I wake 'tis sweet to find
    I've been dreaming of home and mother.
Home, dear home, childhood's happy home!
    When I played with sister and with brother
'Twas the sweetest joy when we did roam
    Over hill and through dale with mother.

Chorus: Dreaming of home, dear old home,
        Home of my childhood and mother–
      Oft When I wake 'tis sweet to find
      I've been dreaming of home and mother.

Sleep, balmy sleep, close mine eyes,
    Keep me still thinking of mother–
Hark! It's her voice I seem to hear–
    Yes, I'm dreaming of home and mother.
Angels come soothing me to rest,
    I can feel their presence as none other,
For they sweetly say I shall be blest
    With bright visions of home and mother.

Chorus: Dreaming of home, dear old home,
        Home of my childhood and mother–
      Oft When I wake 'tis sweet to find
      I've been dreaming of home and mother.

Childhood has come, come again.
    Sleeping I see my dear mother–
See her loved form beside me kneel,
    While I'm dreaming of home and mother.
Mother dear, whisper to me now,
    Tell me of my sister and my brother–
Now I feel thy hand upon my brow–
    Yes, I'm dreaming of home and mother.

Chorus: Dreaming of home, dear old home,
        Home of my childhood and mother–
      Oft When I wake 'tis sweet to find
      I've been dreaming of home and mother.

JOHN P. ORDWAY – 1851

Salem Cadets' March

Elias Howe published the *Salem Cadets' March* [34] in his book called *Howe's School for the Clarinet*. Howe, a lifelong musician, published several music companion books, including *The Musician's Companion* and *The Complete Preceptor for Accordion*. His company, *The Elias Howe Company*, sold sheet music and musical instruments from its Boston location at 88 Court Street.

TRADITIONAL – 1851

Salem Cadets' March, courtesy of the Boston Public Library

Salem Quick Step

Elias Howe included the tune *Salem Quick Step* [35] in his book called *Howe's The Musician's Companion*.

Salem Quick Step, courtesy of the Boston Public Library

TRADITIONAL – 1842

Down on Manila's Bay
tune: *Auld Lang Syne*

Down on Manila's Bay is courtesy of Historic Beverly. The song is sung to the tune of *Auld Lang Syne* and dedicated to the United Spanish War Veterans of America in honor of their 50th Anniversary and to Congressional Medal of Honor recipient Salem's own John P. Riley. [36]

Riley is the only Salem resident to receive the Congressional Medal of Honor. According to the *Salem Evening News*, dated September 2, 1898, he received the honor on May 11, 1898. Riley was one of the crew of the gunboat *Nashville* during the Spanish-American War. He and several volunteers severed a cable linking communication between Cuba and Spain. [37]

A large boulder engraved with his name and surrounded by flagpoles defines the perimeter of Riley's monument near the Salem Post Office. The dedication took place on June 7, 1959. Riley lived at 3 Warner Street in Salem. He worked as a city employee until his retirement in 1944. Riley died on November 16, 1950, and is buried at *Greenlawn Cemetery*. [38]

Down on Manila's Bay

'Twas back in 1898; down on Manila's Bay;
    When Comrades true; in Navy Blue; volunteered that day–
To leave their Battleship of War; to defend a Flag so grand
    To cut the Enemy's Cable; separating Manilas' Mainland.

No questions comrade did you have to ask; no answers to explain;
    For revenge was there in every heart; for the sinking of the *Maine*.
Men stepped forward for the task; in silence; and devotion
    Looking only back; at the Union Jack; the pride of America's Ocean.

You came forward with the others; without hesitation or fear;
    With hooks; knifes; and cutters; brave men abreast; rowed near–
Amid the two sides of the enemy; you found their cabled wire–
    And cut it to hell in pieces; as the enemy opened fire.

UNKNOWN – 1948

147

God Bless America
- A National Anthem -

This version of *God Bless America*[39] was composed and published as a patriotic song from World War I by H. Leander D'Entremont of Salem in 1919.

OUR COUNTRY
God bless America,
The land of liberty
From shore to shore:
May our flag glorious,
Ever victorious,
Be guardian over us
For evermore, For evermore.

OUR PRESIDENT
God bless our President,
The faithful President
Of this country,
That he be wisdom and light
To make the future bright
For Liberty, For Liberty.

THE STARS AND STRIPES
God bless the stars and stripes;
The bright stars and broad stripes
And field of blue:
Each star made history
Each stripe means victory,
That's what makes 'Old Glory'
Faithful and true, Faithful and true.

OUR REPUBLIC
God bless our Republic,
The grandest Republic
In all the world:
It's that posterity,
And all of humanity,
May reap prosperity,
Our flag unfurled, Our flag unfurled.

OUR ARMY AND NAVY

To our noble Army
And our gallant NAVY,
  Thy blessings give:
Behind the guns they stand
To free the sea and land,
  That we may live, That we may live.

AN APPEAL TO GOD

O, Thou, Great God of Love,
Look from Thy Throne above,
  On us mortals:
We are Thy children still,
Grant us peace and goodwill,
And when we're thru life's grill
  Open Thy Portals, Open Thy Portals.

H. LEANDER D'ENTREMONT – 1919

God Bless America, courtesy of the Library of Congress

Ode Deeds of Glory

tune: *America*

The *Salem Register* published the song, *Ode Deeds of Glory*,[40] on July 8, 1850. Songster Edwin Jocelyn, Esq. wrote the *Ode* to be sung at the Celebration of the Fourth of July in Salem.

ODE.

All hail this glorious Festal Day,
   That speaks of FREEDOM's birth!
Let Heaven's broad arches wake the song,
   In echoes round the earth!

CHORUS:
   Deeds of glory,
   That made our peopl
   Let every tongue rehu
   Our Nation's Jubile

Illustrious ADAMS, statesr
   (Be ever green his gra
The primal impulse to the
   Of Revolution gave.
   Deeds of glory, &c.

The hallow'd mound wher
   And gallant WARREN
Now points its granite Sha
   Heroic deeds to tell.
   Deeds of glory, &c.

But on proud SALEM's en
   Where PICKERING da
The crimson drops from p:
   Were earliest made to fl
   Deeds of glory, &c.

Thence rose the vital strea
   Our land from despot po
And bore young Freedom's
   To this triumphant hour
   Deeds of glory, &c.

Then fling your banners to
   And shout the Freeman
In sounding chorus let eacl
   The gladsome notes prol
   Deeds of glory, &c.

Ode Deeds of Glory,
Salem Register,
July 8, 1859

All hail this glorious Festal Day,
   That speaks of FREEDOM's birth!
Let Heaven's broad arches wake the song,
   In echoes round the earth!

Chorus: Deeds of Glory
            That made out people free,
         Let every tongue rehearse on this,
            Our Nation's Jubilee!

Illustrious Adams, statesman bold,
   (Be ever green his grave!)
The prima; impulse to the ball
   Of Revolution gave.

Chorus: Deeds of Glory
            That mdke out people free,
         Let every tongue rehearse on this,
            Our Nation's Jubilee!

The hallow'd mound where Prescott fought,
   And gallant Warren fell,
Now points its granite Shaft to Heaven,
   Heroic deeds to tell.

Chorus: Deeds of Glory
            That makd out people free,
         Let every tongue rehearse on this,
            Our Nation's Jubilee!

150

But on proud Salem's envied soil,
    Where Pickering dared the foe,
The crimson drops from patriot veins,
    Were earliest made to flow.

Chorus: Deeds of Glory
          That made out people free,
          Let every tongue rehearse on this,
          Our Nation's Jubilee!

Thence rose the vital stream that purged
    Our land from despot power,
And bore young FREEDOM's blessing down
    To this triumphant hour.

Chorus: Deeds of Glory
          That made out people free,
          Let every tongue rehearse on this,
          Our Nation's Jubilee!

Then fling your banners to the breeze,
    And shout the Freeman's song!
In sounding chorus let each voice
    The gladsome notes prolong!

Chorus: Deeds of Glory
          That made out people free,
          Let every tongue rehearse on this,
          Our Nation's Jubilee!

EDWIN JOCELYN, ESQ – 1850

~ 6 ~

Commerce

Hardware Advertisement

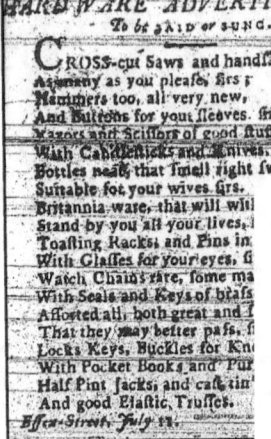

Hardware Advertisement,
Salem Gazette, July 11, 1800

The *Salem Gazette* published this advertisement on July 11, 1800. The unnamed hardware store located in Salem, on Essex Street, used this announcement as an advertisement. [1]

Cross-cut saws and handsaw files,
    As many as you please, Sirs.
Hammers to, all very new,
    And buttons for your sleeves, Sirs.

Razors and scissors of good stuff,
    With Cabinets and knives, Sirs.
Bottles neat, that smell quite sweet,
    Suitable for your wife, Sirs.

Britannia ware, that will with ease,
    Stand by you all your life, Sirs.
Toasting rack, and fins in packs,
    With Glasses for your eyes, Sirs.

Watch chains rare, some made of half,
    With seals and keys of brass, Sirs.
Afforded all, both great and small,
    That they made better pass, Sirs.

Lock keys, buckle for knees,
    With pocketbooks and purses.
Half pint sacks and castin 'd tacks,
    And good elastic Truffles.

TRADITIONAL – 1800

We Are Ped(d)lars

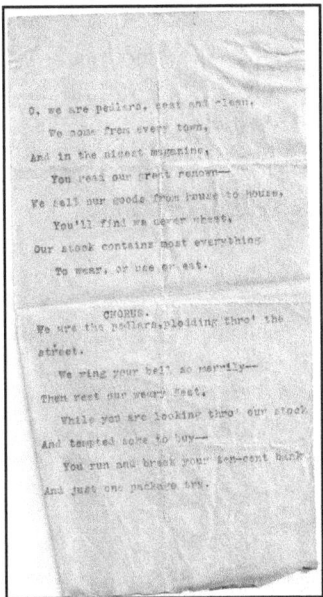

We Are Ped(d)lars, courtesy of the Smith (Burnham) Family Scrapbook

Salem resident Grace Smith recorded the song *We Are Ped(d)lars* [2] in the Smith family scrapbook. Smith is the niece of Salem composer Dexter Smith, who wrote the popular ballad *Ring The Bell Softly, There's Crape on the Door* in 1867. It was common practice to have a diary and record daily events, cut and paste articles from the newspaper, and collect songs, ballads, and poems. There seems to be very little evidence of where the Smith family found this song, *We Are Ped(d)lars*, but worthy of publishing.

Penny Ballad Seller, Sunday Boston Herald, July 24, 1910

O, we are ped(d)lars, neat and clean,
    We come from every town,
And in the nicest magazine,
    You read our great renown–
We sell our goods from house to house,
    You'll find we never cheat,
Our stock contains most everything,
    To wear, or use or eat,

Chorus: We are the peddlers, plodding thro' the street.
        We ring your bell so merrily–
    Then rest our very feet.
        While you are looking throu' our stock
    And tempted more to buy–
        You run and break your ten-cent bank,
    And just one package try.

UNKNOWN – circa 1880

The First Trip

tune: *Oh! Suzanna*

Local writer and contributor to the *Salem Gazette* Edwin Jocelyn wrote *The First Trip* and published the song in the *Gazette* on August 2, 1850. According to Francis C. Bradlee in an article written for the *Essex Institute Collection*, the ballad describes the first trip of the *Salem and Lowell Railroad*. The *Salem Glee Club* sang the song at the opening ceremony of the railroad in 1850. [3]

Twas seven o'clock on Thursday morn,
    And things were ready all,
We step'd on board the Railway cars,
    On neighbors just to call;
The steam was up – the iron horse
    Was proud to bear his load;
Away we shot, on this first trip,
    Upon the Lowell Road!

Chorus: O, the Railroad! You're the way for me!
        No other mode is half so sweet. So jolly, fleet, and free!

We flew across old Danvers town,
    And made the people stare;
And then we pounced on Middleton,
    And found a welcome there;
And, next, we call'd on Reading folks,
    But only left our card;
That we should make so short a stop
    They thought it very-hard.

Chorus: O, the Railroad! You're the way for me!
        No other mode is half so sweet. So jolly, fleet, and free!

At Tewksb'ry, next, we found ourselves,
    And found the people glad,
For who, the jolly, flying cars
    Could view with feelings sad?

Away to Lowell's busy spot
    The speeding train now whirls,
And soon we hail the blessed sight
    Of Fact'ries, Men and Girls!

Chorus: O, the Railroad! You're the way for me!
        No other mode is half so sweet. So jolly, fleet, and free!

Now, here's a note to Phillips' name!
    A noble work he's done,
The int'rests of two cities fair
    Has mingled into one!
He's built a wharf for Lowell's trade,
    Old ocean's wealth to bear,
To ancient Salem's western bound
    Annex'd a city fair!

Chorus: O, the Railroad! You're the way for me!
        No other mode is half so sweet. So jolly, fleet, and free!

Hurrah! the track is ready now!
    And we will have you know
The transport, to and fro, shall be
    A caution to the slow!
Upon our borders, fresh and fair
    The Merrimac shall glide;
And to its favorite city's view
    The ocean open wide.

Chorus: O, the Railroad! You're the way for me!
        No other mode is half so sweet. So jolly, fleet, and free!

EDWIN JOCELYN, ESQ. – 1850

The Salem and Danvers (South) Horse Railroad

Published in the *Salem Observer* on March 14, 1863, the ballad, *The Salem and Danvers (South) Horse Railroad*, [4] celebrates the opening of a horse-drawn railroad from downtown Salem to Danvers Square.

What useful things horse railroads are!
They run so cheap and reach so far;
But half a dime the frugal fare
From Essex Bridge to Danvers Square.
I long to see the S. and D.
With its one horse car.

They take you up where'er you meet,
And leave you handy on the street,
With gentle nod the driver greet,
Arrest the car, and take your seat.
I long to see the S. and D.
With its one horse car.

How many steps they're sure to save
The tired feet on blistering pave!
Whoe'er it was to cites gave
This precious boon, long may he wave!
Soon may we see the S. and D.
With its one horse car.

Lay down the rails! Ne'er mind the frost!
You'll be repaid whate'er the cost!
See to it that no time be lost–
The cry for haste is many-voiced.
All long to see the S. and D.
With its one horse car.

UNKNOWN – 1863

**THE SALEM AND DANVERS (Sou
HORSE RAILROAD.**

What useful things horse railroads are !
They run so cheap and reach so far ;
But half a dime the frugal fare
From Essex Bridge to Danvers Square.

    I long to see the S. and D,
    With its one horse car.

They take you up where'er you meet,
And leave you handy on the street—
With gentle nod the driver greet,
Arrest the car, and take your seat.

    I long to see the S. and D.
    With its one horse car.

How many steps they're sure to save
The tired feet on blistering pave !
Whoe'er it was to cities gave
This precious boon, long may he wave !

    Soon may we see the S. and D.
    With its one horse car.

Lay down the rails ! ne'er mind the frost !
You'll be repaid whate'er the cost ;
See to it that no time be lost—
The cry for haste is many-voiced.

    All long to see the S. and D.
    With its one horse car.

The Salem and Danvers (South) Horse Railroad,
Salem Observer, March 14, 1863

Salem Train Depot postcard, courtesy of Sal Pangallo

Lowell Island

tune: *Dearest Mae*

Lowell, Island, Salem Register, August 25, 1851

The *Salem Register* printed the song *Lowell Island,* [5] on August 14, 1851. A gentleman from Salem wrote the song celebrating the first trip of the steamer *Merrimack* as she took visitors to Lowell Island, located in Salem Harbor. Businessman Stephen C. Phillips formed the *Salem and Lowell Railroad Company* in 1848. The railroad opened in 1850 and connected Salem with Lowell via rail service. The rail line ended at *Phillips Wharf* in Salem. Phillips formed the *Salem Steamboat Company* in 1851 to increase the use of the railroad. Phillips purchased *Children's Island* (formerly *Cat Island*) in Salem Harbor for $1,000.00. The company built a seaside resort on the island and renamed the destination *Lowell Island*. On Tuesday, August 12, the *Merrimack* took the group on a "Moonlight Excursion" in the harbor with Smith's Brass Band on board to promote the new destination. [6]

The North Shore of Massachusetts Bay.
An illustrated Guide and History,
courtesy of the Salem Public Library

Over the years, the island resort house had difficulty attracting customers and changed hands several times. Samuel B. Rindge purchased the resort in January 1878. The Island House continued as a resort under Rindge. Eventually, Samuel's son, Frederick H. Rindge of California, donated the property to *St. Margaret's Home of Boston* for use as *Children's Island Sanitarium.* [7]

Lowell Island

Come, brother, listen to me,
　　We here are jovial met;
The day is fine as day could be,
　　Although it threatn'd wet;
We come to serve the public,
　　We've done the thing "up square,"
And now, of course, our private wants,
　　Come in for lib'ral share.

Chorus: O, Lowell Island! You're the place for me,
　　　　No other Isle is half so fair, in ocean, lake, or sea.

"Cat Island," tho' the name is gone,
　　The substance yet remains,
And tho' old Salem owns a loss,
　　Our neighbor Lowell gains,
But stop, 'tis not secession,"
　　But "annexation," clear,
The "Merrimack" now runs this way,
　　Soon Lowell will be here.

Chorus: O, Lowell Island! You're the place for me,
　　　　No other Isle is half so fair, in ocean, lake, or sea.

And then we'll have the pretty girls,
　　The Factories, and all;
And tho' the spinners plenty be,
　　No spinster, great or small.
The "good time is a coming,"
　　In fact, already here,
For who has seen a better time,
　　Or more abundant cheer.

Chorus: O, Lowell Island! You're the place for me,
　　　　No other Isle is half so fair, in ocean, lake, or sea.

This Island, tho' of rocky make,
    Has ever been "free soil,"
All dwellers here are free to play,
    Or free they are to toil;
Here freely beats the ocean wave,
    And free the breeze blow;
If you can find a freer place,
    Why, I should like to know.

Chorus: O, Lowell Island! You're the place for me,
    No other Isle is half so fair, in ocean, lake, or sea.

'Tis Whig, and Democratic, too,
    Free government is here;
Each one is Ruler for himself,
    No taxes e'er appear;
There are no offices to tempt
    A scramble and a strife;
In Truth this is the very spot,
    To lead a happy life.

Chorus: O, Lowell Island! You're the place for me,
    No other Isle is half so fair, in ocean, lake, or sea.

Here opens wide the Ocean,
    Inviting to "Free Trade,"
Our neighbors all are peaceful,
    No fears that foes invade,
We need no revolution,
    As they of Cuba's Isle,
For here is no oppression,
    But peace and plenty's smile.

Chorus: O, Lowell Island! You're the place for me,
    No other Isle is half so fair, in ocean, lake, or sea.

Around, the fish are plenty,
 And islands, towns, in sight,
And he who "goes on his own hook,"
 May get a fish or bite;
'Tis said, like California, too,
 (But softly be it told,)
It has its quartz, aye, gallons, too,
 Not always though, of gold.

Chorus: O, Lowell Island! You're the place for me,
  No other Isle is half so fair, in ocean, lake, or sea.

Adown the bay, is fair Cape Ann,
 And up the bay, Nahant,
For cooler winds, and better sights
 To rival this they can't.
Then, all in sight, and fair to view,
 Are Marblehead and Lynn,
The first, a famous place of smacks,
 When fishermen are in.

Chorus: O, Lowell Island! You're the place for me,
  No other Isle is half so fair, in ocean, lake, or sea.

But, brothers, time would fail to tell
 The charms that here invest;
We'll now give up the time to cheer,
 Nest year we'll tell the rest.
We find the City lands are safe,
 The islands, anchored fast;
We'll finish here, then, home and tell,
 The jovial times we've passed.

Chorus: O, Lowell Island! You're the place for me,
  No other Isle is half so fair, in ocean, lake, or sea.

UNKNOWN – 1851

Charge of the Ladies' Brigade at Black Alva

Beverly Citizen published the parody *Charge of the Ladies' Brigade at Black Alva* [8] on December 15, 1866. Alfred Lord Tennyson wrote a poem called *The Charge of the Light Brigade* [9] about the battle at Balaklava and the combined forces of England, France, and Turkey against Russia to capture the town of Balaklava on the Crimean Peninsula and part of the city of Sevastopol.[10] Newspapers around the globe printed poems by Tennyson, including *The Charge of the Light Brigade*. The writer of the parody *Charge of the Ladies' Brigade* used Tennyson's model, encouraging residents to shop at the store *Black* in a rushed and confused manner, spending their money for the holidays.

> Halfway down Essex Street,
>   Near to St. Peter's,
> All in the Place of Peace,
>   Strode the six-hundred:
> "Forward the Light Brigade,"
>   "Charge for the goods!" they said;
> Into the store of Black
>   Strode the six-hundred.
>
> "Forward the Light Brigade!"
>   Not a woman dismayed,
> For true all of them knew,
>   No one had blundered;
> There's not to make reply,
>   There's not to reason why,
> There's but to look and buy,
>   Into the store of Black
> Strode the six-hundred.
>
> Cottons to the right of them,
>   Woolens to the left of them,
> Muslins in front of them,
>   Every one wondered!

Penny Ballad Seller, Sunday Boston Herald, July 24, 1910

All low marked down to sell–
  Boldly they bought and well–
Into the store of Black
  In they went pell-mell,
Dashed the six-hundred!

Flashed all their purses there,
  Flashed all their faces fair,
Tossing the goods in air,
  Charging on the clerks, while
All Salem wondered.
  Then amid the noise and smoke
Right through the lines they broke;
  Major Black and his clerks
Stood like brave men the stroke,
  Though so out-numbered,
Then they fell back, the dears,
  All the six-hundred.

Cottons to right of them,
  Woolens to left of them,
Muslins behind them–
  Oh how they wondered!
Clerks to show and tell
  They who had bought so well,
Back from the store of Black
  In good order fell;
With bundles and packages,
  Left the six-hundred.

When can their glory fade?
  Oh! The wild charge they made!
All Salem wondered;
  Honor the charge they made,
Honor the Light Brigade,
  Gallant six-hundred.

UNKNOWN – 1866

Charge of the Light Brigade

First published in a magazine called the *Chelsea Telegraph & Pioneer* and recently found in a January 1875 issue of the *Salem Register*, Mrs. Partington performs this fun ballad called *Charge of the Light Brigade* [11] at a press event and discussions on putting street lights on some of Salem's streets. The *Register* goes on to describe the events.

It will be recollected that a very respectable company of gentlemen connected with the "press gangs" of Boston, Chelsea, and other places and recently inspected, by invitation of Dr. Cutler, the electric method of lighting a portion of the streets of Salem. Among that delegation was the distinguished Mrs. Partington, whose genial presence sheds such radiance that the lesser lights of gas and electricity may be considered almost eclipsed. The venerable woman through her specs made a careful examination of the rival light, and in the effulgence of that illumination, she thus records in merry meter the emotions which then and there animated her intellectualism. We copy the pome(sic) from the *Chelsea Telegraph & Pioneer*: [11]

On a night, on a night,
On a night swarthy,
Down to old Salem town
Rode a choice party,
"Forward the Light Brigade!
Men of the Press" – 'twas said:
Down on the Eastern Road
Rode the choice party.

"Forward the Light Brigade!
Now we will see displayed
What we weren't wise enough
To hold for this city:
How, by a simple art,
Old modes are set apart,
Leaving the foggy chart,
And the street lamps are lit
By electricity.

Gas lights to the right of them,
Gas lights to the left of them,
Gas lights in front of them
Blazed mid the vapors:

Over the slippery street,
    Firmly they moved their feet,
Watching, each way to see
    What the result might be,
      Men of the papers.

Flashed for a moment there
    The blazing lights in air,
Then quickly put out they were,
    Leaving all doubly dark,
While the crowd wondered:
    Plunged in the gloom intense,
All watched in deep suspense –
    Pressman and citizen –
For it to come again:
    Would it? They pondered,
Then it flashed out, amain, –
    Nothing had blundered!

Gas lights to the right of them,
    Gas lights to the left of them,
Gas lights in front of them,
    All brightly gleaming:
Scoffed at by fogies old,
    Condemned by praises cold,
Now it's success was told;
    Over all hostile might,
By press and town confirmed,
    The new electric light
In triumph was streaming.

Who can the value prize
    Of this new process, wise,
Whole towns for lighting?
    Honor to those who made!
Honor the Light Brigade,
    Its praise reciting!

MRS. PARTINGTON – 1875

I Took My Specs

On October 1, 1841, the *Salem Gazette* published *I Took My Specs*.[12]

I took my Specs the other day,
  (For I am getting old,)
I held the paper in my hand
  Its pages to unfold;
The paper filled with wit and news,
  My leisure moments to amuse.

I saw, good readers what think you
  I saw upon that page?
Which came across my scratching view,
  My wand'ring thoughts to engage,
On the firsh page, I saw in full,
  The strangest name: twas; Moses Gull.

'Twas the first Gull I ever heard
  Breathe forth the muse's strain;
Truly he is a daring bird,
  He must possess some brains
Gulls take not oft poetic flight;
  But Moses soars quite out of sight.

The praise of Salem's sunny streets,
  Of Salem girls he sings;
His subject my approval meets;
  For praise of Home still clings
When hope and Joy, and Love beside
  Are gone. Home still remains our pride.

UNKNOWN – 1841

I Took My Specs,
Salem Gazette,
October 1, 1841

Salem Register, January 12, 1852

The Genius of My Glasses

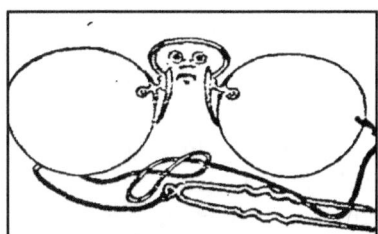

THE GENIUS OF MY GLASSES

You hateful, churlish little sprite
That sits astride my nose,
That never will be left at home,
But watches where one goes.

That like the Salem witches rides
A broomstick, as you please,
That never folds your crystal wings
And never takes your ease.

That like a gilded minion keeps
The door before my eyes.
Perhaps you may a blessing be,
But blessing in disguise!

MARY ANGELL LINCOLN.

The Genius of My Glasses,
Boston Herald,
August 9, 1914

Mary Angell Lincoln, an occasional contributor to the *Boston Herald,* would send in editorials or short ditties. The *Herald* published Lincoln's *The Genius of My Glasses* on August 9, 1914.[13]

You hateful, churlish little, sprite
    That sits astride my nose,
That never will be left at home,
    But watches where one goes.

That like the Salem witches ride,
    A broomstick, as you please,
That never folds your crystal wings,
    And never takes your ease.

That like a guided minion keeps,
    The door before my eyes,
Perhaps you may a blessing be,
    But blessings in disguise!

MARY ANGELL LINCOLN – 1914

"Keeping the North Shore Warm"
Pickering Theme Song

Longtime Salem resident and avid Salem ephemera collector Nelson Dionne discovered this advertising ditty in his travels while collecting. *The Pickering Oil Company* [14] delivered coal and oil to North Shore residents. Located on *Pickering Wharf*, the company had access to coal and oil via the railroad, ocean barges, and trucks. In the 1970s, the company sold the property to a developer to bring locals and tourists back to the negated waterfront and create a mixed-use development that includes restaurants and condominiums. The property is known today as *Pickering Wharf*, a destination for water views, boating, and dining.

We deliver the finest fuels,
  To keep you warm,
They're the best that you can use,
  To keep you warm,
So, let the silver fleet deliver all your heat,
  For Pickering can't be beat,
    To keep you warm,
    To keep you warn.

UNKNOWN – circa 1950s

Pickering Theme Song, courtesy of the Nelson Dionne Collection

On Hearing the Salem Bells Ring for Fire

Salem Register published *On Hearing the Salem Bells Ring for Fire* [15] on November 9, 1843. The newspaper gave credit to Lynn Bard, also known as Alonzo Lewis. Lewis was born in 1794 in Lynn, Massachusetts. He worked as a teacher, poet, reporter, editor, and publisher in Lynn. Lewis was an ardent abolitionist and during his lifetime, edited the *Lynn Weekly Mirror*, the *Lynn Record*, and *Freedom's Amulet*. He surveyed Lynn Beach and Lynn Harbor and created an 1829 map of Lynn for the Federal government. He published three books of poetry, and his complete collection was published posthumously in 1883. [16]

Those Salem Bells! Those Salem Bells!
    I hear their midnight peals!
Their tone a tale of terror tells,
    As on my ear it steals;
And every note the breeze that swells,
    A sigh of wo reveals!

Those Salem Bells! Those Salem Bells!
    How oft in bygone years,
Their tones have ope'd the sacred wells
    Of gladness and of tears;
While sweet and sadden'd memory tells
    A tale of joy and fears!

Those Salem Bells! Those Salem Bells!
    I've roamed the world around,
Yet ne'er amid its hills and dells,
    Such beauty have I found;
With them what love, what friendship dwells,
    With sweetest rapture crowned!

Those Salem Bells! Those Salem Bells!
    O would that One were mine!
I'd pour, what well to her belongs,
    The heart's enrapturing wine;
And round her brow the wreath of song's
    Immortal glory twine.

ALONZO LEWIS – THE LYNN BARD – 1843

Sidewalk Musings

William Jenkins, an occasional contributor to the *Salem Register*, wrote *Sidewalk Musings*, [17] and the *Register* published the ballad on August 2, 1841.

SIDEWALK MUSINGS.

As sung by my particular friend, Mr. Moses Gull.

Oh, Salem streets are bright to view,
And Salem girls are fair,
There's none can match th
That glisten starlike the
Let others roam, and cross
For beauty, gold, or cha
I only ask, in Salem stree
Free scope to loaf and r

They may talk of their pr
Far, far across the sea,
Where they spend the mid
In mirth and revelry.
They may tell of a ruined
Through which the moo
But give to me the shady
Of Salem's sunny stree

Let moonstruck vagrants s
And range beside the st
Or search for flowers in th
By the light of the pale
Let them enjoy their ramb
And sigh in their green
Enough for me, the flower
Old Salem's sunny stree

What though they are not
The bee delights to sip—
The honey of that blushin
Falls sweeter on the lip
That violet blue is fair pe
As any on the plain,
And to the lover's bashful
'Twill answer back agai

They say it is joy to wand
Where the sea breaks w
And the thunder mutters d
And the quick flash ligh
Where the canvass flutters
And strains the quiverin
And with a loud and fearfu
The night winds whistle

But give to me a summer's
And a soft and gentle ai
Around my fevered brow t
And toss my flowing hai
And I will cast my glance
On fair and blooming ch
As I range along the shad
Of Salem's sunny street

Sidewalk Musings,
Salem Register,
August 2, 1841

Oh, Salem streets are bright to view,
  And Salem girls are fair,
There's none can match the eyes of blue
  That glisten starlike there.
Let others roam, and cross the deep,
  For beauty, gold, or change,
I only ask, in Salem streets,
  Free scope to loaf and range.

They may talk of their princely towers
  Far, far across the sea,
Where they spend the midnight hours,
  In mirth and revelry.
They may tell of a ruined castle,
  Through which the moonlight creeps,
But give to me the shady side
  Of Salem's sunny streets!

Let moonstruck vagrants seek the vale,
  And range beside the stream,
Or search for flowers in the dell,
  By the light of the pale moonbeam.
Let them enjoy their rambles long,
  And sigh in the green retreats,
Enough for me, the flowers that throng
  Old Salem's sunny streets.

What though they are not such as those
  The bee delights to sip,
The honey of that blushing rose
  Falls sweeter on the lip!

The violet blue is fair perchance,
    As any on the plain,
And to the lover's bashful glance
    'Twill answer back again!

They say it is joy to wander
    Where the sea breaks wild and high,
And the thunder mutters deep and dread,
    And the quick flash lights the sky,
Where the canvas flutters in the gale,
    And strains the quivering mast,
And with a loud and fearful wail,
    The night winds whistle past.

But give to me a summer's day,
    And a soft and gentle air,
Around my fevered brow to play,
    And toss my flowing hair,
And I will cast my glances wide,
    On fair and blooming cheeks,
As I range along the shady side
    Of Salem's sunny streets.

WILLIAM JENKINS – 1841

Apprenticed In Salem

Apprenticed in Salem [18] recorded on Peter Johnson's CD, *Newport's Fair Town; Traditional Songs and Ballads of North America.* The song *Apprenticed in Salem* is a variation of *Blow the Candle Out* or *The London Apprentice.* Peter states in his liners notes, "This song is not as bawdy as some of its British cousins, but is refreshingly frank in the easy acceptance of the pleasurable aspects of love without doom and gloom of sin and salvation found in many of the southern mountain ballads." [18] The Bodleian Library's digital collections of ballads list early versions of these broadside ballads. [19] The town of "Salem" could be substituted with almost any town's name.

Barn tools, author's personal collection

Apprenticed In Salem

When I was an apprentice in Salem,
    I went to see my dear.
The candles were all burning,
    The moon so bright and clear.
I knocked upon her window,
    To ease her of her pain.
She rose to let me in,
    And she barred the door again.

I like your well'd behavior'
    And thus I often say,
I cannot rest contented,
    With you so far away.
The roads they are so muddy,
    You can gain about,
Come roll me in your arms love,
    And blow the candles out.

Your father and your mother,
    In yonder room do lie,
A-huggin one another,
    So why not you and I?
A-huggin one another,
    Without fear or doubt,
Come roll me in your arms my love,
    And blow the candle out.

If I prove successful love,
    We'll name it after me,
Keep it neat and kiss it,
    And tap it on your knee.
When three years are over,
    My time it will be out,
And I will double my ineptness,
    By blowing the candle out.

TRADITIONAL – 1813

William R. Warner,
The New England Blacking Man

tune: *Yankee Doodle Dandy*

Roud Broadside Index B261623

The Broadside Collection at the Center for Popular Music at Middle Tennessee State University archives this advertising ballad called the *New England Blacking Man*. Warner's Union Oil Polish Company sent salesmen throughout the towns of Lynn and Salem singing the song to the tune of *Yankee Doodle Dandy* while hawking blacking boot polish that "preserves the leather and keeps it from cracking" [20]

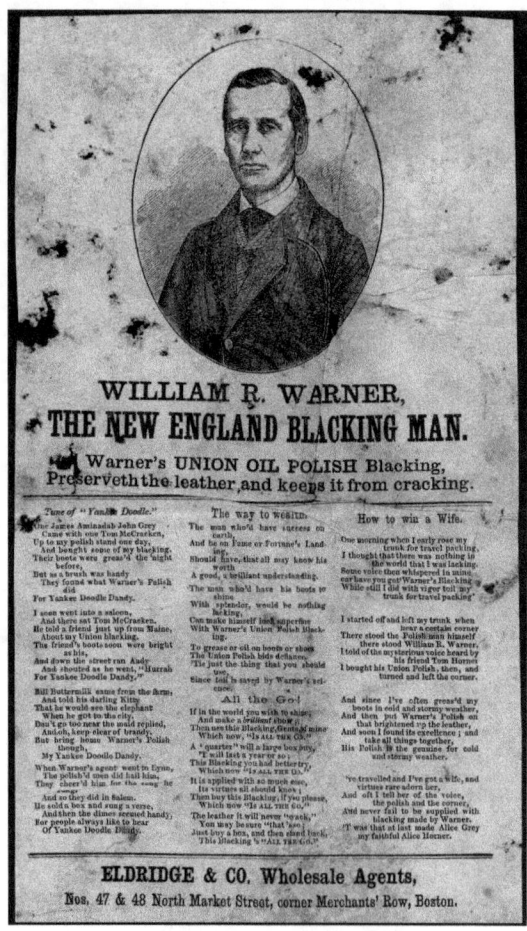

The New England Blacking Man, courtesy of the Kenneth S. Goldstein Collection of American Song Broadsides Center for Popular Music, Middle Tennessee State University

The New England Blacking Man

One James Aminadab John Grey,
    Come with one Tom McCracken.
Up to his polish stand one day,
    And bought some of my blacking.

Their boots were greas'd the night before,
    But as a brush was handy.
They found what Warner's Polish did,
    For Yankee Doodle Dandy.

I went into a saloon,
    And there sat Tom McCracken.
He told his friends just up from Maine,
    About my Union blacking.

The friend's boots soon were bright as his,
    And down the street ran Andy.
And shouted as he went, "Hurrah,
    For Yankee Doodle Dandy."

Bill Buttermilk came from the farm,
    And told his darling Kitty.
That he would see the elephant,
    When he got to the city.

Don't go too near the maid replied,
    And, oh, keep clear of brandy.
But bring home Warner's Polish though,
    My Yankee Doodle Dandy.

When Warner's agent went to Lynn,
    The polish'd men did hail him.
They cheer'd him for the song he sang,
    And so they did in Salem.

He sold a box and sung a verse,
    And then the dimes seemed handy.
For people always like to hear,
    Of Yankee Doodle Dandy.

TRADITIONAL – 1850

Dream
S.F. Rogers

Dream, S.F. Rogers,
Salem Register,
January 6, 1851

The *Salem Register* printed *Dreams* in
their January 6, 1851 issue. The local retail
landmark, S. F. Rogers, is located at 272
Essex Street in Salem. This Christmas and
New Year's advertisement ballad states that
Rogers carries, on hand, a fine assortment
of toys and fancy goods, plus many of
the riches and most beautiful articles for
presents. [21]

One night, not many nights ago,
    I sat me down to music alone,
By grateful fire, that dimm'd and shone,
    With fitful gleam;

The genial warmth around me shed,
    My drowsy eyes to slumber led,
I perched my feet, reclined my head
    And had a dream.

My dream was something on this wise;
    It seemed, and much to my surprise,
The world contracted to a size
    So wonderful small.

That continent, and rolling flood,
    Lake, river, mountain, dale, and wood,
A little Microcosm stood
    I saw it all!

I saw the palace and the cot,
    The Lilliputian men, and what?
Ah! Little woman, that were not,
    Unlike to Dolls.

The steamer, gliding by the store,
    The locomotive, as it tore
Along the track, the ship of war,
    With "wooden walls."

O saw a lion in his liar,
    The tiger, wolf, and grisly bear,
And e'er the little timid hare
    Leap'd over the ground;

The horses, oxen, cows, and hogs,
    And sheep, and goats, and fowls and dogs,
And cats, and rats, and crocking frogs,
    "You'd – better-go-round.

Each Artisan was at his trade,
    And all their tools about them laid,
The husbandmen, with his plow and spade,
    Turned up the ground.

And men, of every occupation,
    Of every clime and every station,
And fabrics, wrought in every nation,
    Were all around.

But all I saw I may not tell,
    On me, as on the world, a spell,
Seemed fixed, and doubting if 'twere well,
    As 'twas before.

I heard a voice say, "What's the price
    Of this?" I started, rubber my eyes,
And found myself, in my surprise.
    In Rogers' Store.

UNKNOWN – 1851

179

A Parody

tune: *In Salem When the Sun Was Low*

The *Salem Observer* [22] published this advertisement ballad for Peabody's Store, a well-known shopping destination on Essex Street in Salem, on November 7, 1863. This advertisement, *A Parody*, uses the melody of the temperance song *In Salem When the Sun Was Low*.

In Salem when the sun was low,
    Before the earliest fall of snow,
Tremendous was the steady flow,
    Of Fashion's tide in Peabody

But Salem saw another sight,
    The Dealers all looked puzzled quite,
And lay awake at the day of night,
    Trying to solve the mystery.

Behind their desks, they look aghast,
    As Fashion's throng went sweeping past,
The tide of trade was setting fast,
    Towards the store of Peabody's.

But soon the cause was plain indeed,
    So even he who ran could read,
The Ladies went with quickening speed,
    To buy their goods at Peabody's.

His styles and fabrics are the best,
    In all the land from East and West,
And ladies who are neatly dressed
    All buy their goods at Peabody's.

The choicest stock you there will meet,
    Comprising all that's new and neat;
The store you'll find on Essex Street,
    The famous store of Peabody's.

On Essex Street, two twenty call,
  Ye young and old both great and small,
We give this kind advice to all,
  Go buy your goods at Peabody's

The largest Stock can there be found,
  Enough for all the country round,
At prices that will suit, We're bound,
  To buy our Goods at Peabody's.

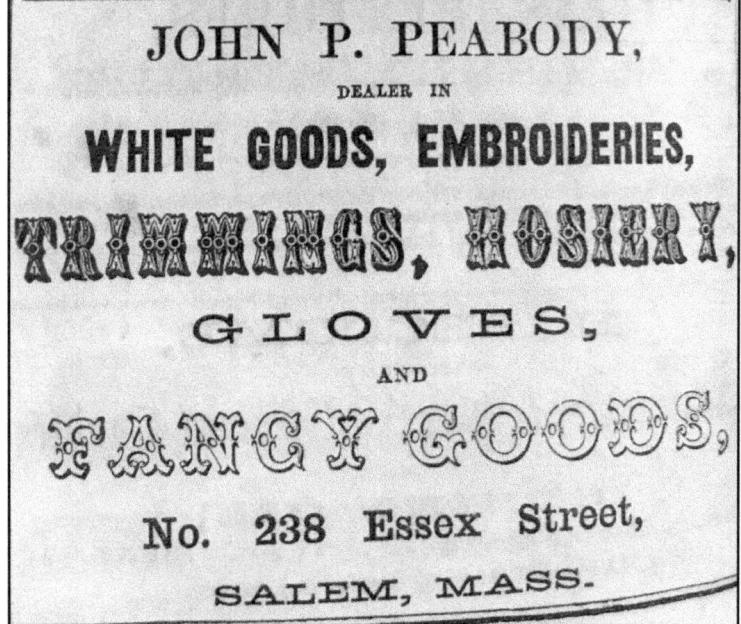

A PARODY.

In Salem ere the sun was low,
Before the earliest fall of snow,
Tremendous was the steady flow,
  Of Fashion's tide to Peabody's.

But Salem saw another sight,
The Dealers all looked puzzled quite,
And lay awake at dead of night,
  Trying to solve the mystery.

Behind their desks they looked aghast,
As Fashion's throng went sweeping past,
The tide of trade was setting fast
  Towards the store of Peabody's.

But soon the cause was plain indeed,
So even he who ran could read,

UNKNOWN – 1863

A Parody, Salem Observer,
July 11, 1863

JOHN P. PEABODY,

DEALER IN

WHITE GOODS, EMBROIDERIES,

TRIMMINGS, HOSIERY,

GLOVES,

AND

FANCY GOODS,

No. 238 Essex Street,

SALEM, MASS.

The Salem Directory, courtesy of the Salem Public Library

Essex Street Rhymes No. 3

Good Photography,
Salem Register,
December 12, 1859

W. Snells' Photographic Gallery, located at 208 Essex Street in downtown Salem, entered a new and innovative industry. The photography company published rhyming ads in the *Salem Observer* [23] in 1863, welcoming everyone to the store to have their picture taken. The gallery offered various types of photography on copper, tin, and glass and the new Hallotype with" soft tones, beautifully colored adapted to many complexions." [24]

To see ourselves as others see us,
    The photograph this gift doth give us,
On copper, leather, tin, or glass,
    Each smirking lad and smiling lass,

Each grandmama and grandpa, too,
    Each pa and ma, and so all through
The lengthy list of their relations,
    All ages, sexes, shades, and stations.

On Essex Street, as oft I wonder
    I stop and on these pictures ponder,
And Snell's and Moulton's view with wonder.

UNKNOWN – 1863

Little Red Riding Hood

The [Boston] *Christian Era* published the ballad *Little Red Riding Hood* [25] on February 18, 1875. Written by Lydia Very, a lifetime Salem resident, poet, and school teacher best known for rewriting and designing the first die-cut book version of the long-lived story of *Red Riding Hood* printed by Boston-based publisher Louis Prang. [26]

Still through the mazes of our early dreams
    We seem to see her tripping through the woods;
The sunshine tints her curls with golden beams,
    And lights with rosy blushed in the seams
        Her crimson hood.

The flowers look upward with tear-spangled cheeks
    And seek to lure her from her coming doom;
But, smiling on them worth her dove-eyes meek,
    She, hastening onward to her granddame sick,
        Reflects their bloom.

The bushes cling around her to impede
    Her fatal progress as she onward walks;
The sunbeams beckon her from hill and mead;
    She pauses not, but to the wolf gives heed,
        And fearless talks.

So children lend a listening ear to sin!
    While Nature's influences around them plead,
Seeking through every sense the soul to win,
    Urging them now, in springtime to begin
        To sow good seed.

And listening oft, their steps will go astray,
    Until the sin that seemed a grand dame old,
From which so easy 'twas to turn away-
    Rises, wolf-like, on its unwilling prey
        With fiercest hold!

LYDIA L.A. VERY – 1875

Red Riding Hood,
courtesy of the
Boston Public Library

~ 7 ~
Courtship, Dancing

The Flirtation

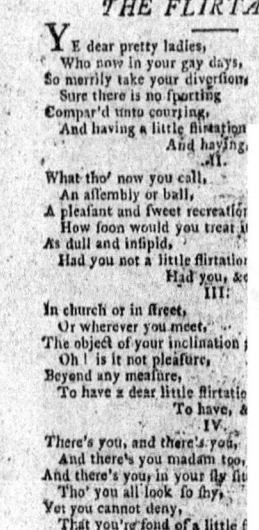

The Flirtation, Salem Gazette,
May 30, 1788

On May 30, 1788, the *Salem Gazette*
published *The Flirtation*.[1]

YE dear pretty ladies,
 Who now in your gay days,
So merrily take your diversion,
 Sure there is no sporting
Compar'd unto courting,
 And having a little flirtation.
  And having a little flirtation.

What tho' now you call,
 An assembly or ball,
A pleasant and sweet recreation;
 How soon would you treat it,
As dull and insipid,
 Had you not a little flirtation?
  Had you not a little flirtation?

In church or in street,
 Or wherever you meet,
The object of your inclination;
 Oh! Is it not pleasure,
Beyond any measure,
 To have a dear little flirtation.
  To have a dear little flirtation.

There's you, and there's you,
 And there's you, madam too,
And there's you, in your sly situation,
 Tho' you all look so shy,
Yet you cannot deny,
 That you're fond of a little flirtation.
  That you're fond of a little flirtation.

TRADITIONAL – 1788

186

Twinkling Stars Are Laughing, Love
Roud # 1549

John C. Schreiner & Son published *Twinkling Stars Are Laughing* [2] in 1855. Salem-born John P. Ordway, leader of the Boston-based *Ordway's Aeolians,* wrote the song and published several additional songs in the 1850s, including *The Death of Taylor, Old Sam Grid Iron, Home Delights*, and the *Know Nothing Polka*. The Lester S. Levy Collection of Sheet Music and the Library of Congress holds copies of the sheet music in their collection.

> Twinkling stars are laughing love,
>   Laughing on you and me;
> While your bright eyes look in mine,
>   Peeping stars they seem to be.
> Troubles come and go, love,
>   Brightest scenes must leave our sight;
> But the star of hope, love,
>   Shines with radiant beams tonight.

> Chorus: Twinkling stars are laughing love,
>   Laughing on you and me;
>   While your bright eyes look in mine,
>   Peeping stars they seem to be.

> Golden beams are shining, love,
>   Shining on you to bless;
> Like the queen of night you fill
>   Darkest space with loveliness.
> Silver stars how bright, love,
>   Mother moon in thronely might,
> Gaze on us to bless, love,
>   Purest vows here made to night.

> Chorus: Twinkling stars are laughing love,
>   Laughing on you and me;
>   While your bright eyes look in mine,
>   Peeping stars they seem to be.

JOHN P. ORDWAY – 1855

Dancing in Salem

Salem has a long history of social dancing and traditional music. The early colonists brought a love for dancing with them, and they continued dancing during hard times.[3] The first evidence of a public dance in Salem comes from the diary of Benjamin Lynde, Jr. On July 14, 1730, Lynde's entry reads: Raining, while at Survey's dance. There are many couples. I did not dance and stayed till 7 o'clock. [4] Since ballrooms were nonexistent, dancing resumed in individuals' homes. Milton Hehr writes in his dissertation, *Musical Activities in Salem, Massachusetts*, "It was recorded in *Mrs. Holyoke's Diary* that she attended at least one dance (in various homes) a year between the years of 1761 and 1781 except the years 1762, 66, 70, 75, 76, and 80." [5] Below are four of Mrs. Holyoke's diary entries:

> January 15, 1761, a dance Jefferies' in the evening.
> January 29, 1761, a dance Jefferies'.
> February 26, 1761, at a dance at Jefferies.
> November 24, 1762, dance, not there, snow. [6]

Assembly House Postcard, courtesy of Sal Pangallo

The *Assembly Hall* at the corner of present-day Chestnut Street and Cambridge Street in Salem opened in 1769. Activities at the hall consisted of lectures, fencing lessons, violin lessons, dance classes, singing concerts, juggling, and feats of strength.[7] Two of the most memorable functions held there during its relatively brief history occurred during the spring of 1774. On April 28, Salem's

Tories gathered at the hall to bid farewell to Governor Thomas Hutchinson as he was preparing to leave for England. Five weeks later, many of the same citizens returned to welcome Hutchinson's replacement, Thomas Gage. [8] On the evening of June 6, a brilliant ball took place at the *Assembly Room* in honor of Thomas Gage. [9]

Cape Ann Advertiser, December 27, 1872

Assembly House, courtesy of Mary Barker

In 1872, a new function hall was built on Federal Street to replace *Assembly Hall* as the gathering spot for the town's wealthier citizens and funded by Salem's merchant class. George Washington was honored with a ball in the hall during his visit to Salem on October 28, 1789. Five years earlier, the *Assembly House* was the scene of a similar party for the Marquis de Lafayette.[10]

Newhall's March

In 1788, Benjamin Gardner of Marblehead and in 1805, Joshua Cushing of Salem notated songbooks documented fife and drum music. Dance tunes like the *Fisher's Hornpipe, Soldier's Joy, Boston March, Yankee Doodle, New Rigged Ship*, and *Jefferson and Liberty* were all performed for dances and played regularly into the next century. Some melodies have a direct Salem connection, including the *Salem Artillery, Lailson's Ride*, and *Newhall's March*.[11] Fred Finkle, a fiddle player from Marblehead, found and shared *Newhall's March* with the *Salem Country Orchestra* circa 2008.

Newhall's March

TRADITIONAL – UNKNOWN

To a LADY Who Admired Dancing

To a LADY Who Admired Dancing[12] was found in the *Salem Mercury*, a local newspaper dated July 29, 1788.

MAY I presume in humble lays,
    My dancing fair, thy steps to praise?
While this grand maxim I advance,
    That all the world is but a dance,

That human-kind, both man and woman,
    Do dance is evident and common.
David himself, that God-like king,
    We know could dance, as well as sing.

Folks who at court would keep their ground,
    Must dance the year attendance round.
All nature is one ball, we find:
    The water dances to the wind;

The sea itself at night and noon
    Rises and capers to the moon;
The moon around the earth does tread
    A Cheshire round in buxom red;

The earth and planets 'round the sun
    Dance, nor will their dance be done
'Till nature in one mass is blended;
    Then we may say the ball is ended.

TRADITIONAL – 1788

To a LADY Who Admired Dancing
Salem Mercury, July 29, 1788

Celebrating "The Night Before"

Grace A. Smith of 10 Foster Street Salem drew the cats *Celebrating "The Night Before"* [13] and included the drawing in her family scrapbook. This humorous sketch depicts several howling cats looking for a mate and singing in harmony, the result of a frustrating evening listening to the mating calls and missing several hours of sleep.

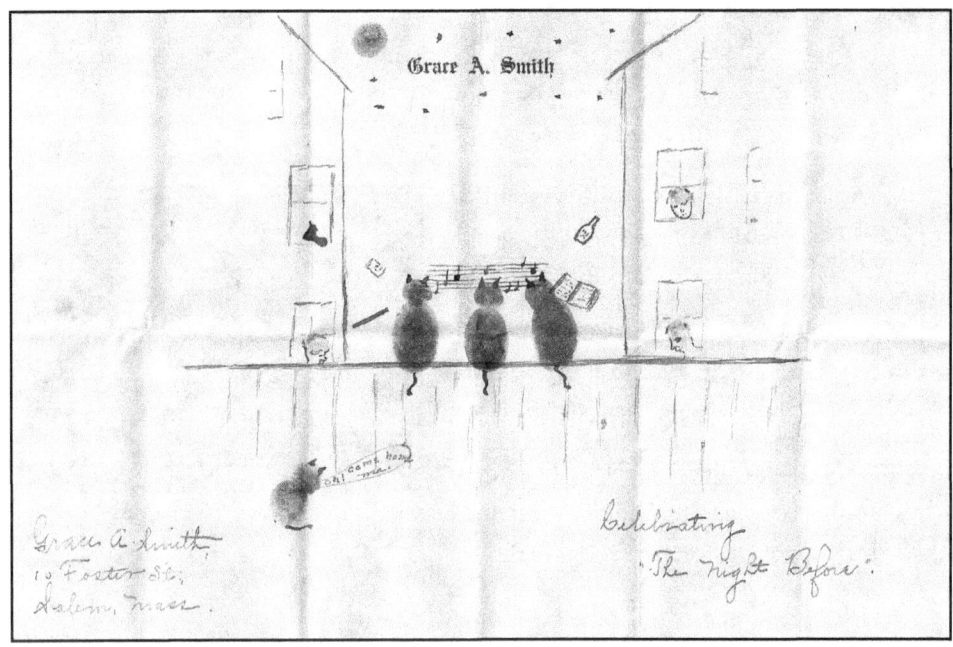

Celebrating "The Night Before," courtesy of the Smith Family's Scrapbook, Salem, Massachusetts

A New Song

Hamilton Hall, courtesy of Sal Pangallo

Marianne C. D. Silsbee of Salem published a book called *A Half Century in Salem* in 1887. Her book consisted of stories Silsbee read at house parties and other events in Salem, stating that she documented the stories "for the amusement of friends who may not be averse to refreshing their memories with harmless gossip." [14]

One of the stories Silsbee wrote was titled *Hamilton Hall*. The author stated the Salem Assemblies (social dances) were revived at Hamilton Hall in 1859 after a two-year hiatus.[15] Mr. Remond, the owner of a catering business at Hamilton Hall since 1805, sent a large bowl to help celebrate the end of the season with a festive dance. [16] Silsbee credits an unnamed "elderly woman" for writing *A New Song* about the famed bowl.

Hamilton Hall, courtesy of Mary Barker

When this old bowl was new
     The magnates of the land.
In numbers not a few,
     Did form a joyous band;
And many a stately dame,
     So beautiful to view,
To our assemblies came,
     When this old bowl was new.

Then ladies bright did shine,
     In loveliness and pride;
While draped in muslin fine
     The maidens fair did glide

Then waved the ostrich plume
    O'er matrons grand and true
In our assembly room,
    When this old bowl was new.

Knee buckles then appeared
    With silken hose they say;
The rules of Fashion feared,
    All bore despotic sway,
Then gentlemen were dressed
    In coat of broadcloth blue,
With white and spotless vest,
    When this old bowl was new.

The courtly minuet
    And long lined country dance
(For beaux and belles as yet
    Had no quadrilles from France)
Were seen upon the floor,
    As the dancers swam or flew,
With graces hovering o'er,
    When this old bowl was new.

When supper time came then,
    The Elder Ladies proud
Were led by gallant men
    Out through the waiting crowd,
The younger came in place,
    Their place full well they knew,
And yielded with a grace,
    When this old bowl was new.

The good old times are fled,
    Have vanished far away;
The stately dames are dead,
    The men oh where are they?
The minuet is a dream,
    Or like a tale that is told;
The light doth faintly beam,
    Now that new bowl is old.

Yet Salem numbers still
　　Her daughter's fresh and fair,
Who dances with right good will,
　　And silks and laces wear,
Their watch spring hoops are wide,
　　Gowns hang in plenteous fold,
And they are Salem's pride,
　　Now that new bowl is old.

Bright eyes are glancing yet,
　　Fair checks are blushing on;
But where Old Ladies sat
　　I gaze they all are gone.
No Elders now are sung,
　　The deed would be too bold;
America is young
　　Now that new bowl is old.

The gallants of today,
　　In solemn suits of black,
Still make the ballroom gay,
　　While outward show they lack.
Yes we can praise them too,
　　Nor leave their worth untold,
Though old times now are new,
　　And that new bowl is old.

BY AN ELDERLY LADY – 1887

After the dance ended, the bowl was returned to Mr. Remond. Remond sent a letter to the *Salem Gazette* describing Hamilton Hall and the bowl's history.[17] Sometime during the two years the Salem Assemblies were not held at Hamilton Hall, the bowl went missing. Mr. Remond found the bowl at "Higginson Square" and returned it to Hamilton Hall. He describes the bowl and concludes, "The writer has no ambition to gratify, and nothing for which to ask but to preserve the *Old Bowl*. Cherish the hall; let it stand and keep it untarnished for its intended purpose."[17]

Social Dancing continued at Hamilton Hall throughout the 1900s and today, and one of Hamilton Hall's oldest traditions is the annual Christmas Dance. The dance is held each December as a fundraiser and dates back to the 1880s.

Dancing Instruction in Salem

M. C. D. Silsbee wrote a book called *A Half Century in Salem*, and she describes various types of social dancing, beginning with the dance called "a voluntary" where the gentlemen were at "liberty to engage their partners," and a draw-dance is a lottery in which the ladies and gentlemen pick numbers and dance with the corresponding number. Silsbee stated the dancers "might or might not be especially pleased with their luck." [18]

Dancing Academy.
MR. PARKS,
INSTRUCTER OF DANCING,

MOST respectfully informs the Ladies and Gentlemen of Salem and its vicinity, that he intends opening a School for the instruction of Masters and Misses in the pleasing and graceful accomplishment of DANCING, at Franklin Hall, on Monday the 10th day of April next.

The most respectable references can be given.

For further particulars please apply at this office, or at the Essex Coffee House.

Salem, March 21, 1820.

Salem Gazette, April 11, 1820

DANCING SCHOOL.
SECOND QUARTER.

MR. P. GUIGON respectfully informs the ladies and gentlemen his patrons and others of Salem, that his Second Quarter in Dancing, for the instruction of young ladies, misses, and young masters, will commence at Concert Hall, on Wednesday afternoon, June 23d

Days of tuition every Wednesday and Saturday afternoon from three till half past five o'clock.

Price $10 per quarter, and $5 extra entrance for novices.

Salem Gazette, June 18, 1830

Dancing and Waltzing School.
MR. J. H. SMITH

RESPECTFULLY informs the Ladies and Gentlemen of Salem, that he will commence a Term of 12 lessons, in the above accomplishment, at Franklin Hall, on MONDAY Evening, Nov. 19th, 1849.

Terms—Gentlemen with Ladies, $4 00.

Hours—Ladies' Class, from 8 to 9; Gents' Class, from 9 to 10 o'clock. The last six nights of the School, Dancing from 8 to 12 o'clock.

Good Quadrille Music will be furnished.

¸ Terms payable at the expiration of the first half term.

Perfect order maintained, and the most fashionable style of Dancing taught.

nov 15

Salem Register, November 19, 1849

In the early 1800s, Salem's prosperity as a shipping center and the wealth that followed gave free time to the well-off. Local instructors and traveling dance teachers placed advertisements in the local newspapers to introduce Salem residents to the latest dancing styles and to educate new dancers on the various dance styles, including the waltz, hornpipes, and quick steps. Mr. Parks, the long-time dance instructor, placed advertisements in the *Salem Gazette* for class meetings at the *Essex Coffee House* in 1820. Mr. P. Guigon placed ads for his *Dancing School* held at Concert Hall in Salem, and long-time Salem instructor Mr. R.J. Davis continually placed ads for his *Dancing Academy* held at Concert Hall.

Dancing Academy.
R. J. DAVIS,

RESPECTFULLY informs the citizens of Salem and vicinity, that as he is about closing one of his Evening Schools, he proposes opening an AFTERNOON SCHOOL, at Concert Hall, on Wednesday and Saturday afternoons, to commence on the 24th of April next, for the purpose of instructing the Youth of both sexes in the polite accomplishment of Dancing.

Mr D. will teach Cotillions, Spanish Dancing, Waltzing, and Fancy Dancing in all its various branches.

The subscriber would inform the citizens that he resides in Salem, and that he will spare no pains on his part to give perfect satisfaction — Having taught in Boston and other places with great success, he confide[nt]

liberal patronage in this

☞ Terms of Tuition half in advance—the re quarter.

☞ N. B. Hours of clock, P M

Those who wish to join the Class, are invited to call at the Hall, on the afternoons of Wednesday and Saturday, the 3d and 6th of April, from two to five o'clock.   March, 19   tf

Salem Gazette, April 19, 1833

Dancing and Waltzing.

R. J. DAVIS respectfully informs the young men of Salem that his last six nights of school will commence on FRIDAY EVENING, Nov. 16.

Tickets for the evening can be obtained at the door. Music—Messrs. Upton and Morse's Band.

nov 12

Salem Register, November 19, 1849

The Bowl

Salem resident Mrs. J.H. Hanaford published the ballad, *The Bowl*, in the *Salem Register* on October 16, 1862. Hannaford wrote and published ballads and songs in the *Salem Register* and the *Beverly Citizen*. Hanaford wrote the ballad after seeing the bowl that George Washington presented to one of his Aids while in Salem. The bowl was decorated and "adorned with representations of national flags. [19]

I saw a bowl 'twas large and fair,
    Its figures traced with talent rare,
And China's curious art;
    But not its pictures, nor the gold,
Which deck'd it near where flags unfold,
    Had power to stir my heart.

Yet, as I touched the ample bowl,
    A chord within my inmost soul,
Thrilled with emotion sweet,
    My spirit wandered far away,
And, where Mount Vernon guards its clay,
    Alone were checked my feet.

I saw the blue Potomac's flow,
    Where hostile armies come and go—
I heard its ripping wave,
    And sadly seemed the stream to glide,
The house of Washington beside,
    And near his honored grave.

The nation which he rescued stand,
    With brother's blood upon her hands—
She'd only in defense
    Of all he prized, of righteous law,
And greater Freedom than he saw,
    Justice without pretense.

Oh, Washington! Baptized in blood,
   Thy country hath looked up to God,
And heard His voice at last;
   And he who fills thine honored place,
Proclaimeth Freedom for a race
   When war is overpast.

Thank God!– this relic, then, of days
   When heroes were their well-earned bays
'Neath Freedom's latest sign,
   Reminds us also that at this age
Is acting deeds for History's page,
   Which will those days outshine.

But over more his name shall stand
   The patrons saint of Freedom's land,
Star of our Nation's dawn!
   And he who guides the Ship of State,
If worthy, e'er shall imitate
   Our matchless Washington!

MRS. J.H. HANAFORD – 1862

The Bowl, Salem Register,
October 16, 1862

The Maid With Elbows Bare

The *Salem Gazette*, #1223, published the song *The Maid With Elbows Bare* [20] in their issue dated May 17, 1803.

> Let Tasteless lover chant their lays,
>   To please the modest, full dress fair;
> The talk remains for me, to praise
>   The charming maid with elbows bare.
>
> Her ruddy cheek, her sparking eyes,
>   Her coral lips, her jetty hair,
> All are the charms I highly prize,
>   But not so much as elbows bare!
>
> The unveiled bosom-neck of snow–
>   May tempt the ill-bred clown of stares,
> But first-rate beaux with deference bow,
>   Before the maid with elbows bare.
>
> Some ladies show the ankle's shape,
>   A fashion too not very rare;
> Others expose a pretty nape,
>   Not mine's the maid with elbows bare.
>
> Let her, in that loose flowing robe
>   Which flaunts and flutters in the air,
> Reflects a heart the ne'er will probe,
>   Unless she leaves her elbows bare.
>
> When winter storms are near and cold,
>   And keenly blows the northern air,
> When muffs and furs the limbs unfold,
>   Still trips my maid with elbows bare.
>
> When summer's scorching heat prevails,
>   And veils shut out the sun's bright glares,
> Still, still my maid will never fail
>   To go with graceful elbows bare.

In winter, summer, fall or spring,
In weather either foul or fair,
In days or night, the charms I sing,
Of my sweat maid with elbows bare.

TRADITIONAL – 1803

Lailson's Ride

T. William Smith, Salem resident, and local contra dance musician, discovered *Lailson's Ride*[21] in the manuscript collection at the Phillips Library. Smith transcribed the tune circa 1980 and played it with the *Salem Country Orchestra* over the next 25 years. The tune's formal connection to Salem is unknown. However, it was first transcribed by a musician in the early 1800s and then stored in the Phillips Library.

Lailson's Ride

TRADITIONAL – UNKNOWN

Pyncheon Lane Capric

Henry O. Upton wrote *Pyncheon Lane Capric* in 1892. The dance tune is one in a series of melodies written for the *House of Seven Gables Series*. The other dance tunes written for the series are *The Caper* (A Dance with Full Explanation) and *Galop "The Crickets."* Upton was born in 1839 in Salem and was a member of the Salem Brass Band and one of the original members of the Salem Cadet Band. He began studying and teaching social dancing in Salem in 1864. [22]

Pyncheon Lane Capric, part of the *House of the Seven Gables Series,* courtesy of the House of the Seven Gables Settlement Association

The Upton family purchased the *House of the Seven Gables* in 1883 and lived there for 25 years. They welcomed visitors to view the house and promoted its connection to Nathaniel Hawthorne. Caroline Emmerton bought the house in 1908, and the Uptons moved to Salem Neck. Henry lived there until he died in 1919. [23]

Pop! Goes the Weasel
Roud # 5249

This version of *Pop! Goes the Weasel* comes from Fred A. Gannon's *Old Salem Scrap Book II.* [24] Gannon noted that young girls in Salem during the 1890s would sing the melody of *Pop! Goes the Weasel* and makeup lines to fit the music. Gannon writes, "When Grandmother was a girl and went to dances at Hamilton Hall or a party, she joined in the singing of songs like this." [24] The Authors James and Dorothy Volo wrote in their book, *Family Life in Seventeenth and Eighteenth Century America*, that the skeining process, the winding of yard to form a skein of uniform thickness, inspired many versions of *Pop! Goes the Weasel.* [25]

Queen Victoria's very sick,
  Napoleon's got the measles
Sebastopol is won at last.
  Pop! Goes the weasel.

All around the cobbler's house
  The monkey chased the people
And after them in double haste
  Pop! Went the Weasel.

When the night walks in as black as sheep
  And the hen and her eggs are fast asleep
When into her nest a serpent creeps,
  Pop! Goes the Weasel.

Of all the dance that ever was plann'd
  To galvanize the heel and hand
There's none (that moved) so gay (and grand)
  Pop! Goes the Weasel.

TRADITIONAL – 1890

Salem Willows for Mine

As social dancing continued in downtown Salem, much larger dance halls were built in an area of Salem called the Willows, overlooking the Atlantic Ocean and Beverly Harbor. The *Salem Evening News* quoted Salem Willows resident John McDonald, saying, "The best bands in the country used to come to the Salem Willows. They played in the ballroom casinos and entertained hundreds of people from Salem and the surrounding area." [26] Lou Collins and trumpeter George Hardy composed *Salem Willows For Mine*. The song was published in 1919 by L. A. Collins and dedicated to Mr. W. E. Brown.[27] Brown was the lessee and manager of the *Casino Ballroom* in the Salem Willows.

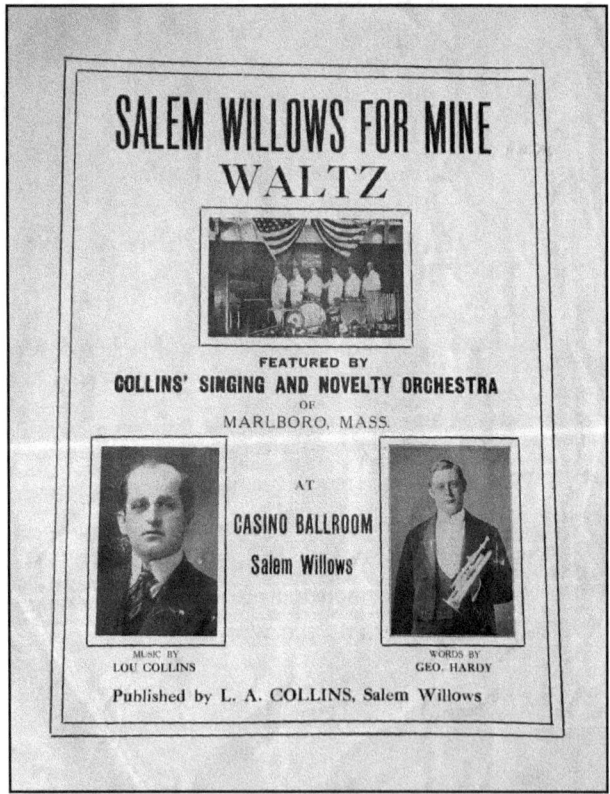

Salem Willows For Mine, Waltz, courtesy of Dee Dee Morneau

Salem Willows For Mine

The place that I long for, the place that I'm strong for,
    Is sure to be in the race,
The boys who will meet you, The girls who will greet you,
    Will all have a smile on their face,

Chorus: It's not very far from Salem, and from Lynn it's a half hour's ride.
        You don't mind the trolley,
    Because you can jolly,
        The nice little girls by your side.

        On moonlights, Gee! it is dandy, and on Sundays its simply divine.
           You can have all your "Coney's"
      To me they're all phoneys
          But Salem Willows for mine.

The dear ballroom floor, is the place I adore,
    The waters with nice shady views,
The music is grand, Makes you dance, understand,
    It's the place where you'll never feel blue.

Chorus: It's not very far from Salem, and from Lynn it's a half hour's ride.
        You don't mind the trolley,
    Because you can jolly,
        The nice little girls by your side.

        On moonlights, Gee! it is dandy, and on Sundays its simply divine.
           You can have all your "Coney's"
      To me they're all phoneys
          But Salem Willows for mine.

LOU COLLINS AND GEORGE HARDY – 1919

Salem Country Dance

Salem residents T. William (Bill) and Sarah Smith offered monthly dances in Salem between 1980 and 2008 at the *Grace Church* and the *Tabernacle Church*. The Smiths' love for traditional dance music and a dance community kept them active and involved in Salem until they moved to Belfast, Maine, in 2009. Chris Greene, a Salem resident and dance enthusiast, designed the *Salem Country Dance* flyer circa 1982. [28]

Salem Country Dance flyer, from Author's Personal Collection

Social dancing continues to this day in Salem. *The Commonwealth Vintage Dancers* celebrated their eleventh annual dance in December 2019. *The Fezziwig's Ball* is held annually at *Old Town Hall* in downtown Salem. The ball highlights the Christmas season during the mid-1800s with vintage dress and dancing. The program consists of Victorian favorites such as *Pop Goes the Weasel*, the *Virginia Reel*, contra dances, simple quadrilles, polkas, and a waltz.[29]

Salem's newest Hamilton Hall dance event, *The Resistance Ball*, celebrates the Colonist's peaceful confrontation with British Colonel Alexander Leslie and his troops in 1775.[30]

High Street

T. William (Bill) Smith wrote *High Street* in 2012. Bill led the *Salem Country Orchestra* for over twenty-five years. High Street is where Bill and his wife Sarah lived while living in Salem. Bill included the tune *High Street* on the CD's *Strawberry Jam* and the Salem compilation CD, *Old Salem in Ballad and Song.*[31]

T. WILLIAM SMITH – 2012

Belle of Tennessee!
A Plantation Love Song
Roud # V49070

Dexter Smith wrote *Belle of Tennessee! A Plantation Love Song*.[32] Smith was born in Salem on November 14, 1837, and as a child, preferred reading to playing with other children. Dexter, not wanting to follow his father's pursuits, was "determined to lead a mercantile life until he should find such a position in the field of literature."[33] It was written in the *Phrenological Journal and Packard's Monthly* that "One reason why his songs are so popular is that the spirit of his mind flows in harmony with that of common humanity like that of (Scottish poet Robert) Burns."[34] Smith continued to write songs that "served to cheer the patriot's heart and to encourage those who took up arms to defend the banner of our country,"[34] including *Follow the Drum, Our Boys in Camp*, and *Hurrah for the Old Flag*. Smith published a book of poetry called *Dexter Smith Poems*[35] in 1868. Dexter died on November 28, 1909.

Does the mockin' bird grow weary
    Of his singin' to his dearie
As they nestle mid the
    White magnolia plumes?
Does the oriole sing clearer
    'cause his mate is hov'rin' nearer
When the night am fragrant
    With summer blooms?

So my heart is singin' sweetly
    As the daylight fades completely
For I know that you'll be
    Waitin' up of me for me
When the moonbeams are a gleamin'
    An the starlight am a streamin'
Then I'll meet you,
    My Belle of Tennessee.

Chorus: Oh my honey! Life is sunny
            For you are more precious more than gold to me;
        Love me sweetie! Love your Petie!
            For I love you, my Belle of Tennessee.

As we sit with arms entwinin',
    While the big moon is a-shinin'
Both our hearts am fondly
    Beatin' to one strain,

As the shafts from Luna's Quiver
    Turn to silver on the river
Somethin' tells me life
    Will never give us pain.

We will share our joys together,
    Thro' life's fair or stormy weather
And the world shall be
    Unending jubilee for me,
If what ever be beside me,
    O! my darlin', my Belle of Tennessee.

Chorus: Oh my honey! Life is sunny
            For you are more precious more than gold to me;
        Love me sweetie! Love your Petie!
            For I love you, my Belle of Tennessee.

DEXTER SMITH & N. HARRIS WARE – 1897

Belle of Tennessee! A Plantation Love Song, from Author's Personal Collection

Salem Tunnel

Salem Press published this humorous ballad, the *Salem Tunnel*,[36] on September 29, 1867.

One summer, while traveling homeward
    To visit my boyhood's haunts,
A trifling incident made it
    One of my happiest jaunts.

A man with a cane gold-headed,
    And hair of silver gray,
Asked me to take charge of his daughter
    As far as Salem, that day.

I bowed most politely and answered,
    As I gave the fair damsel a glance,
And saw her two lips like a rose-bud,
    I'd be "very glad of the chance."

He asked: that when the cars got there,
    If 'twasn't too much of a fuss,
Would I be so very obliging
    As to find his daughter a bus.

I promised, and off we started,
    And quickly were chatting so gay,
I began to wish that Salem,
    Was a thousand miles away.

But soon the city of witches
    Beyond us rose in sight,
And we plunged right into the tunnel
    Where all was dark as night.

'Twas passed, my charge was blushing,
    While her hair was all in a "muss,"
But I'd kept my promise most truly,
    And found the daughter *a buss*!

W.L.W. – 1867

The Dark-Eyed Gypsy, O

Roud #1, Folksong Index (S441235)

Boston Sunday Globe published the old ballad *The Dark Eyed Gypsy, O* [37] on September 26, 1915. Mrs. T. F. F. of Salem sent in the song at the request of J. C. from Boston.

There were three Gypsies in the East,
    They sang so blithe, so Bonnie, O:
They sand so sweet, so very, very, sweet,
    They charmed the heart of the Lady, O.

When Charles came home late at night,
    Inquiring for his lady, O;
"She is gone! She is gone! Said his own servant man,
    She has followed the dark-eyed gypsy, O."

"Go saddle me the milk-white steed,
    The brown was ne'er so speedy, O,
That I may ride through the length of the night,
    Till I find out the dark-eyed gypsy, O."

Then Charles rode thus through the length of the night.
    'Till the next morning early, O.
It's then he met with his own wedded wife,
    And she following the dark-eyed, gypsy, O.

"Will you forsake your houses and land?
    Will you forsake your children, O?
Will you forsake your own wedded lord
    And follow the dark-eyed gypsy, O?"

"What do I care for my houses and lands?
    What do I care for my children, O?
What do I care for my own wedded land?
    While I follow the dark-eyed gypsy, O."

Then she took the garment that she wore
    And wound it as a headdress, O
Saying, "I'll eat the grass and drink the dew,
    And follow the dark-eyed gypsy, O."

TRADITIONAL – UNKNOWN

~ 8 ~
Children Songs

Kid Do Go

William Wells Newell wrote in *The Passover Song of the Kid* and an Equivalent from New England, published in the *Journal of American Folklore*, about *Kid, Do Go*: "I now print," he says, "for the first time a version obtained by myself, many years ago, from the recitation of Miss Lydia R. Nichols of Salem at the time aged 88 years, who retained the words as a reminiscence of her earliest infancy; the date of the rhyme therefore goes back to about 1800." [1]

As I was going over London Bridge,
I found a penny ha'penny, and bought me a kid.
    Kid do go.
Know by the moonlight it's almost midnight,
Time kid and I were home an hour and a half ago.

Went a little further, and found a stick.
    Stick do beat kid, Kid won't go.
Know by the moonlight it's almost midnight,
Time kid and I were home an hour and a half ago.

Went a little further, and found fire.
    Fire do burn stick,
    Stick won't beat kid, Kid won't go.
Know by the moonlight it's almost midnight,
Time kid and I were home an hour and a half ago.

Went a little further, and found water.
    Water do quench fire,
    Fire won't burn stick,
    Stick won't beat kid, Kid won't go.
Know by the moonlight it's almost midnight,
Time kid and I were home an hour and a half ago.

Went a little further, and found ox.
    Ox do drink water,
    Water won't quench fire,
    Fire won't burn stick,
    Stick won't beat kid, Kid won't go.
Know by the moonlight it's almost midnight,
Time kid and I were home an hour and a half ago.

Went a little further, and found butcher.
    Butcher do kill ox,
    Ox won't drink water,
    Water won't quench fire,
    Fire won't burn stick,
    Stick won't beat kid, Kid won't go.
Know by the moonlight it's almost midnight,
Time kid and I were home an hour and a half ago.

Went a little further, and found rope.
    Rope do hang butcher,
    Butcher won't kill ox,
    Ox won't drink water,
    Water won't quench fire,
    Fire won't burn stick,
    Stick won't beat kid, Kid won't go.
Know by the moonlight it's almost midnight,
Time kid and I were home an hour and a half ago.

Rope began to hang butcher, butcher began to kill ox,
    Ox began to drink water,
    Water began to quench fire,
    Fire began to burn stick,
    Stick began to beat kid, Kid began to go.
Know by the moonlight it's almost midnight,
So kid and I got home an hour and a half ago.

TRADITIONAL – 1800

The Cat and the Mouse

The Cat and the Mouse is from the recitation of Miss Lydia R. Nichols of Salem around 1800 and "represents the story as current in New England at the time of the earliest memory of the reciter." [2]

The cat and the mouse went into the oven together.
The cat bit off the mouse's tail,
And the mouse bit off the cat's thread.
The mouse said, " Aye gi' me my own tail again.

I won't without you go the cow and get me some milk.
    Titty mouse hop, and titty mouse run, to the cow I come.
Do cow gi' me milk, I give cat milk,
Cat gi' me my own tail again.

I won't without you go to the barn and get me some hay.
    Do titty mouse hop, and titty mouse run, to the barn I come.
Do barn gi' me hay,
I give cow hay, cow gi' me milk,
I give cat milk, cat gi' me my own tail again.

I won't without you go to the blacksmith and get me a lock and key.
    Titty mouse hop, and titty mouse run, to the blacksmith I come.
Do blacksmith gi' me lock and key,
I give barn lock and key, barn gi' me hay,
I give cow hay, cow gi' me milk,
I give cat milk, cat gi' me my own tail again.

I won't without you go to the sea and get me some coal.
    Titty mouse hop, and titty mouse run, to the sea I come.
Do sea gi' me coal,
I give blacksmith coal, blacksmith gi' me lock and key,

I give barn lock and key, barn gi' me hay,
I give cow hay, cow gi' me milk,
I give cat milk, cat gi' me my own tail again.
I won't without you go to the cock and get me a feather.
    Titty mouse hop, and titty mouse run, to the cock I come.
Do cock gi' me feather,
I give sea feather, sea gi' me coal,
I give blacksmith coal, blacksmith gi' me lock and key,
I give barn lock and key, barn gi' me hay,
I give cow hay, cow gi' me milk,
I give cat milk, cat gi' me my own tail again.

I won't without you go to the miller and get me some corn.
    Titty mouse hop, and titty mouse run, to the miller I come.
Do miller gi' me corn,
I give cock corn, cock gi' me feather,
I give sea feather, sea gi' me coal,
I give blacksmith coal, blacksmith gi' me lock and key,
I give barn lock and key, barn gi' me hay,
I give cow hay, cow gi' me milk,
I give cat milk, cat gi' me my own tail again.

The miller gave him some corn, and he gave it to the cock,
The cock gave him a feather, and he gave it to the sea,
The sea gave him some coal, and he gave it to the blacksmith,
The blacksmith gave him a lock and key, and he gave it to the barn,
The barn gave him some hay, and he gave it to the cow,
The cow gave him some milk, and he gave it to the cat,
And the cat gave him his own tail again.
But after all his trouble,
    the tail was of no use
        to the poor mouse.

TRADITIONAL – 1800

Epitaph on a Favorite Pig

The *Salem Gazette* [3] published the song, The *Epitaph on a Favorite Pig*, on July 4, 1797. The family is reminiscing about the passing of their favorite pig.

Ye dryads weep, ye nymphs bemoan,
　Warble your note in plaintive tone;
　　Let every heart be sad;
Ye chirping birds, your songs refrain,
And join with me in mournful strain,
　　Alas, my Piggy's dead!
　　　Cut off in bloom,
　　　Sent to the tomb,
　　E'er half his days were run;
　　　Relentless death,
　　　Has stop'd his breath,
　　　　My Pig's forever gone!

These sparkling eyes no more shall see
The dawning light, or pleasant day;
His mouth has shut sweet music's door,
And ughs and eeks are heard no more.
His antic tricks no more shall please,
　His social chat is done;
Farewell, dear Pig; I ne'er will cease
　Thy cruel fate to mourn,
While the stars roll round in spheres,
While the queen of night appears,
While the sun his course shall keep,
For little dear Piggy, I will weep.

TRADITIONAL – 1797

Epitaph on a Favorite Pig.
Salem Gazette,
July 4, 1797 #619

Trot, Trot, to Boston

"Trot, trot to Boston

Boston Herald, November 11, 1887

There are several variants to this children's play song. When singing *Trot, Trot to Boston* [4] with a young child on your knee, you bounce the child up and down like trotting on a horse. As the singing progresses, you bounce higher and higher until you collapse your knee, and the child pretends to fall off the horse. The singer can add additional verses to extend the game and excitement.

Trot, trot, to Boston;
   Trot, trot, to Lynn;
Trot, trot, to Salem;
   Home, home again.

TRADITIONAL – UNKNOWN

Additional Lyrics:

Trot trot to Boston.
   Trot trot to Lynn.
Watch out baby you don't fall in!

Trot trot to Boston.
   Trot trot to Dover.
Watch out baby you don't fall over!

Trot trot to Boston.
   Trot trot to Town.
Watch out baby you don't fall down!

TRADITIONAL – UNKNOWN

~ 9 ~

Temperance

The Drunken Soldier

tune: *In a Mouldering Cave Where the Wretched Retreat*

Drunken Soldier[1] was found in the *Salem Mercury* and is sung to the tune of *In a Mouldering Cave Where the Wretched Retreat.*

In a cottage forlorn, with a sigh and a pout,
    Poor Trim sat distracted with care;–
He look'd at his bottle, and saw it was out,
    And gave himself up to despair.

The walls of his cell were he spatted around,
    With the grog he had vomited up!
And even the dirt & the grass on the ground
    Were bestow'd with the dregs of his cup.

The housewife beheld thro, a hole in the wall,
    Him weeping (his whisky half spent).
She cuss'd him, his liquor, his bottle and all,
    And these were the blessings she sent:

"O Trim do forbear, not a grunt nor a swear,
    For your grog, so deservedly lost,
Your bones shall be broke; I will put up my prayer.
    And the answer shall be to your cost.

The boys of the barracks, those soldiers so bold,
    Of gaming have finish'd their talk,
And such in the news, it is currently told–
    They are coming to drink out your stalk.

A council was held ere your eyes were awake,
    And this was the Captain's decree,
That when it is emptied the bottle shall break,
    And the charge they have trusted to me.

To the broomstick straightway, like a fury she flew;
    But he with his bottle began,
And said, shut the door, let me touch it once more,
    And then, they may drink if they can.

With a circle of black the encompass'd his eyes;
    At last into slumbers he sunk,
Then she laid him down snug, left the sight of his jag
    Should tempt him again to get drunk.

TRADITIONAL – 1787

Drunken Soldier,
Salem Mercury,
September 25, 1787

Father Mathew Statue Postcard, courtesy of Sal Pangallo

King Alcohol
a parody, Temperance Glee
tune: *Dame Durden*

The temperance song *King Alcohol,* [2] sung by the Hutchinson Family, supporters of the temperance movement, is a parody of the song *King Andrew* and sung to the tune of *Dame Durden.* The events at the Deacon Giles Distillery in Salem inspired the piece, which claims to be a cautionary tale about negotiating deals with the devil to produce demon rum. The story concerned a Salem deacon who ran a combination Bible manufactory during the day and a rum distillery at night.[3]

King Alcohol has many forms, By which he catches men
He is a beast of many horns, And ever thus has been.

Chorus: For there's rum, and gin, and beer, and wine
And brandy of logwood hue
And hock, and port, and flip combined
To make a man look blue.
He says be merry, for here's good sherry
And Tom and Jerry, champagne and perry,
And spirits of every hue.

O are not these a fiendish crew, As ever a mortal knew.
O are not these a fiendish crew, As ever a mortal knew.

King Alcohol is very sly, A liar from the first
He'll make you drink until you're dry, Then drink because you thirst.

King Alcohol has had his day, His kingdom's crumbling fast
His votaries are heard to say, Our tumbling days are past.

Chorus: For there's rum, and gin, and beer, and wine
And brandy of logwood hue
And hock, and port, and flip combined
To make a man look blue.
He says be merry, for here's good sherry
And Tom and Jerry, champagne and perry,
And spirits of every hue.

222

And now they are a temperate crew, As ever a mortal knew.
    And now they are a temperate crew, And have given the devil his due.

The shout of Washingtonians, Is heard on every gale
    They're chanting now the victory, O'er cider, beer, and ale.

        Chorus: For there's rum, and gin, and beer, and wine
              And brandy of logwood hue
           And hock, and port, and flip combined
              To make a man look blue.
           He says be merry, for here's good sherry
              And Tom and Jerry, champagne and perry,
           And spirits of every hue.

And now they are a temperate crew, As ever a mortal knew.
    And now they are a temperate crew, And have given the devil his due.

JESSE HUTCHINSON – 1850

King Alcohol, Bugle Notes for the Temperance Army, courtesy of hymnary.org

A Parody

tune: *In Salem When the Sun was Low*

Temperance leader and preacher George B. Cheevers wrote the song *A Parody*.[4] The temperance ballad is part of the broadside, called *Deacon Giles' Distillery*, found in the Broadside Collection at the Phillips Library and the Harris Broadside Collection at the John Hay Library, Brown University. The original site of the distillery was on Front Street in Salem, and according to legend and documented in Dale Cockrell's book, *Excelsior: Journals of the Hutchinson Family Singers*, "Deacon Giles inherited both the family distillery and a sense of piety. Unwilling to give up either because of the profit involved with the former and the respectability of the latter, he continued to make rum and enslave his workers with one hand and sell bibles with the other." [5] This broadside from 1835 details the temperance point of view.

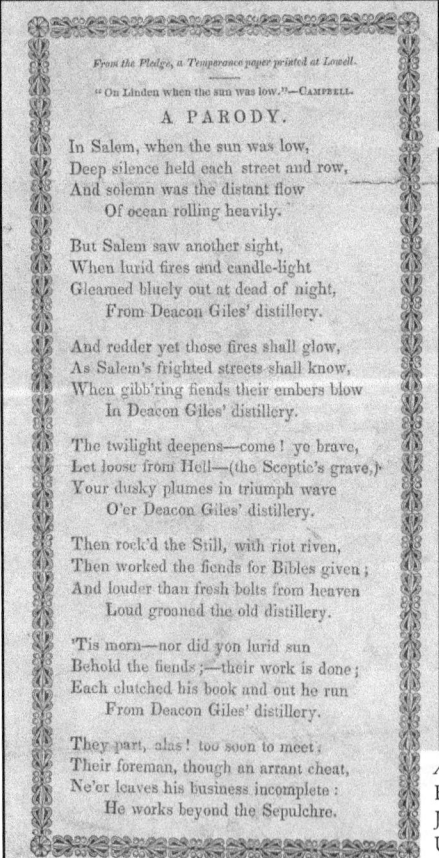

From the Pledge, a Temperance paper printed at Lowell.

"On Linden when the sun was low."—CAMPBELL.

A PARODY.

In Salem, when the sun was low,
Deep silence held each street and row,
And solemn was the distant flow
    Of ocean rolling heavily.

But Salem saw another sight,
When lurid fires and candle-light
Gleamed bluely out at dead of night,
    From Deacon Giles' distillery.

And redder yet those fires shall glow,
As Salem's frighted streets shall know,
When gibb'ring fiends their embers blow
    In Deacon Giles' distillery.

The twilight deepens—come! ye brave,
Let loose from Hell—(the Sceptic's grave,)
Your dusky plumes in triumph wave
    O'er Deacon Giles' distillery.

Then rock'd the Still, with riot riven,
Then worked the fiends for Bibles given;
And louder than fresh bolts from heaven
    Loud groaned the old distillery.

'Tis morn—nor did yon lurid sun
Behold the fiends;—their work is done;
Each clutched his book and out he run
    From Deacon Giles' distillery.

They part, alas! too soon to meet;
Their foreman, though an arrant cheat,
Ne'er leaves his business incomplete:
    He works beyond the Sepulchre.

A Parody, courtesy of Harris Broadside Collection at the John Hay Library, Brown University

A Parody

In Salem, when the sun was low,
　　Deep silence held each street and row,
And solemn was the distant flow,
　　Of ocean rolling rapidly.

But Salem saw another sight,
　　When lurid fires and candlelight,
Gleamed bluely out of the dead of night,
　　From Deacon Giles' Distillery.

And redder yet those fires shall glow,
　　At Salem's frighten street shall know,
When gibb'ring friends their embers blow,
　　In Deacon Giles' Distillery.

The twilight deepens-come! ye brave,
　　Let loose from Hell (the Skeptic's grave,)
Your dusky plumes in triumph wave
　　Over Deacon Giles' Distillery.

Then rock'd the Still, with riot riven,
　　Then worked the fiends from Bible given:
And louder than fresh bolts from heaven,
　　Loud groaned the old distillery.

Tis morn- nor did you lurid sun,
　　Behold the fiends; their work is done;
Each clutched his book and out he run,
　　From Deacon Giles' Distillery.

They part, alas! Too soon to meet,
　　Their foreman, though and arrant cheat,
Ne'er leaves his business incomplete,
　　He works beyond the Sepulcher.

GEORGE B. CHEEVERS – 1835

George B. Cheever

Temperance leader G.W. Bungay wrote this song, *George B. Cheever*,[6] and published the song in the *Liberator* on June 4, 1858. Cheever became the minister of the Howard Street Church in Salem after graduating from Andover Theological Seminary. Controversy followed Cheever, and he left Salem to be the leader of the *American Temperance Society* and published the *Temperance Reformation, Fifth Report of the American Temperance Society*, in the July 1833 issue of the journal *American Quarterly Observer*.[7]

Strike, bold reformer! Strike again!
    For victory echoes in the blow,
And each brave word unlinks a chain,
    And every sentence slays a foe.

Now, while a bleeding nation calls,
    In tones that make the angles weep,
The watchman upon Zion's walls
    Are drugged to dreams and silent sleep.

That Tract Society is dumb,
    No heart to feel, no tongue to speak;
Wake with try fire and thunder drum,
    The dozing Church, and blanch her cheek!

Lift thy broad claymore in the light,
    Of an advancing age, and shame,
The dreaming drones, and put to flight
    Pale tyrants with thy lips of flame!

G.W. BUNGAY – 1858

A Water-Song

George F. Chever of Salem wrote the temperance song, *A Water-Song*, and contributed the ballad to *The Family Fire-side Book or Monuments of Temperance*.[8] Evangelists at the *Old Jerry McAuley Mission* in New York and the *Hadley Mission* in Salem and throughout the United States sang rescue or temperance songs for temperance and enlightenment. The *Hadley Mission* [9] was located on Central Street in Salem and closed on October 31, 1898. [10]

COLD, crystal water to me bring,
    Creation's wide and liquid wealth,
From out whose gushing fountain's spring
    Eternal purity and health.

O! Who can count the precious worth,
    Of such a boon to mortals given,
All other drinks are brewed on earth,
    But water cometh down from Heaven.

Far in the clear, cold upper air,
    The Spirits of God's holy will,
This calm, pure Earth-drink fit prepare,
    And Heaven's unfailing fountains fill.

No soul e'er fell to it a prey,
    No palsied of the mind or limb,
Can trembling point to it, and say,
    "I drank my poison from its brim."

Then crystal water to us bring,
    Creation's wide and liquid wealth,
From out whose gushing fountain's spring,
    Eternal purity and health

GEORGE F. CHEVER – 1851

The Drunkard's Wish

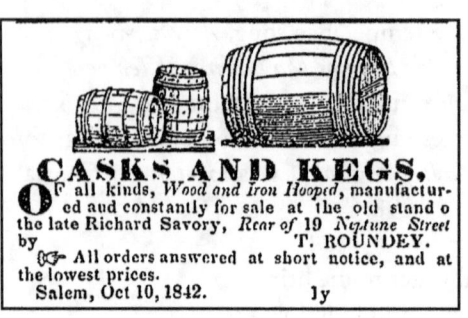

Salem Register, July 20, 1843

The *Salem Gazette* included the temperance song, *The Drunkard's Wish*,[11] in its December 6, 1796 issue. Molasses, processed sugar, was grown in the Caribbean, and Salem merchants imported the molasses and produced rum. Salem Rum had an excellent reputation throughout New England.

Lovely Rum! Enchanting sound!
    So often fought, so often found–
With New England from the still
    Let me know my gullet fill–

This is all I wish to have,
    This is all I ask or grave–
This will raise me from despair,
    And ease my mind of every year.

When my spirits are quite low,
    This will make them briskly flow–
This liquor it does so bewitch,
    When I'm poor it makes, me rich–

When it does its joy impart,
    Light as feathers makes my heart–
Lighter still it makes my head,
    When it's charming fumes are spread.

Bacchanalians hither come,
    And all ye votaries of Rum–
Come and join she jovial throngs,
    Rum inspires the cheerful song–

Liquor that will raise such mirth,
    Sure is of celestial birth,
If a story thrice is told,
    Let it be ne'er so old.

Take another glass or two,
    Suit the story it is new.
Let me with the bottle live,
    Nothing else can pleasure give.

This adds beauty to each grace,
    Lively red it gives the face,
Gives the breath a rich perfume,
    Sweeter than the rose of June.

Fragrant as the balmy fields,
    Or the spice that India yields–
Give me courage when I talk,
    Makes me run, when I can't walk.

Makes me with a proper spirit,
    Resent the ills I do not merit,
Like the infant at the breast,
    So it lulls me quite to rest.

'Till terrific Death shall come,
    I shall ever sing of Rum,
When this groggy life I've past,
    Let me turn to Rum at last.

TRADITIONAL – 1796

The Drunkard's Wish,
Salem Gazette,
December 6, 1796, #557

A Temperance Ode

A Temperance Ode,
Salem Observer,
February 25, 1865

Lydia L.A. Very wrote *A Temperance Ode*,[12] and the *Salem Observer* published the song on February 25, 1865. Very, born in Salem on November 2, 1823, is a well-known writer of poetry and daughter of Reverend Jones Very, Captain during the War of 1812, and brother, Jones Very, a *Transcendentalist* poet and clergyman. She contributed her poetry to local Salem and Boston newspapers.

Away the bowl! though it be wreathed with rose,
    And from its bubbles spicy jets arise,
Though 'neath its wave the siren Mirth reposes,
    To lure you onward with enticing eyes.
        Away the bowl!

Away the bowl! Though social friends may proffer,
    And from your lips so meanly sounds the No!
Regard your health as miser doth his coffer,
    Nor take within your veins a poison slow.
        Away the bowl!

Away the bowl! Thou stern misfortunes press you,
    And friends like leaves, have left you to the blast!
While no kind face beams on your path of bless
    And happiness seems buried with the past.
        Away the bowl!

Away the bowl! Though Death, himself, be near you,
    Pass not in dull unconsciousness away
There is a higher power than wine to cheer you,
    There is a noble guide to endless day!
        Away the bowl!

LYDIA L.A. VERY – 1865

Chug's at Cabot Farm (Broadside)

The temperance movement in Salem was alive and well with local political groups like The *Hadley Rescue Mission*, teetotalist Father Mathew's visit to Salem, the women's movement, and the anti-slavery movement, all gathering for the *Second Annual Picnic at Cabot Farm* in North Salem on September 6, 1897. The broadside promoted the picnic by saying, "Kosy Korners for all" and "Soft Drinks served by bewitching young damsels at the Pavilion," sets the tone for the day. Only non-alcoholic beverages were served at the event. The humorously named *Chug's Orchestra* played at the temperance picnic, entertaining all guests.[13]

GUESTS AT CABOT FARM.
A number of Salem young people were entertained by Helton Jewett at his summer home at Cabot Farm yesterday afternoon. A pleasant time was enjoyed on the lawn watching different games and in social conversation. Refreshments were served during the afternoon.

Guests at Cabot Farm,
Salem Gazette,
September 7, 1897

A notice titled "Guest at Cabot Farm," published in the *Salem Gazette* on September 7, 1897, describes the occasion. "Several Salem young people were entertained by Holton Jewett at his summer home at Cabot Farm yesterday afternoon." [14]

SECOND ANNUAL
PICNIC
OF THE
D. T.'S
CABOT FARM, SEPT. 6, 1897
2-11 P. M.
Balloon Ascension and Boat Races and Kite Flying for the Children.
CHEER UP!
GYMKNA SPORTS FOR ALL.
Expensive Prizes to the Winners.
Band Concert Afternoon and Evening.
ALL IS NOT OVER YET.
An Elaborate* Collation will be Served on the Green.
* (This rests with the ladies.)
Kosy Korners for all. Soft Drinks served by bewitching y[oung] at the Pavilion.

Second Annual Picnic at Cabot Farm, courtesy of Nancy Lutts

Address To A Jug of Rum

The *Salem Gazette* published the temperance ballad *Address to a Jug of Rum* on November 12, 1813. In the early 1800s, a temperance movement began in Salem. Father Mathew was associated with the *Cork Total Abstinence Society*, a movement, started on April 10, 1838, in Ireland visited Salem in September 1849 and laid the groundwork for developing the Salem chapter of *Father Mathew's Catholic Total Abstinence Society*, organized in 1875.[15] The organization purchased the Tucker Estate located on 129 Essex Street in Salem for its headquarters in 1886.[16] To honor Father Mathew, the city erected a statue in 1887. The statue's original location was at the corner of Phenix Hall and Central Street in Salem. In 1916, the statue moved to its current location at the end of Hawthorne Boulevard on Derby Street. There is also a monument of Father Mathew in Philadelphia, a statue on St. Patrick's Street in Cork, Ireland, and one on O'Connell Street in Dublin, Ireland.

ADDRESS TO A JUG OF RUM.

Here, only by a cork controll'd,
And slender walls of earthen mould;
In all the pomp of death repose,
The seeds of many a bloody nose;
The chattering tongue, the horrid oath,
The first for fighting nothing loath;
The passion which no word can tame,
That bursts like sulphur into flame,
The nose carbuncled, glowing red,
The bloated eye, the broken head.
The tree that bears the deadly fruit
Of murder, maiming and dispute,
Assault that innocence assails,
The images of gloomy jails;
The giddy thought on mischief bent;
The midnight hour in riot spent;
All these within this jug appear,
And Jack, the hangman in the rear.

Address to a Jug of Rum,
Salem Gazette,
November 12, 1813

Father Mathew Statue,
courtesy of Mary Barker

Address To A Jug of Rum

Here only by a cork control'd,
    And slender walls of earthen mound;

In all the pomp of death repose
    The seeds of many a bloody nose;

The chattering tongue, the horrid oath,
    The fist for fighting nothing loth,

The passion, which no words can tame.
    That bursts, like sulphur, into flame;

The nose carbuncled, glowing red,
    The bloated eye, the broken head;

The tree that bears the deadly fruit
    Of murder, maiming, and dispute;

As of that Innocence assails,
    The images of gloomy jails,

The giddy thought, on mischief bent,
    The midnight hour in riot spent!

All these within this jug appear,
    And Jack, the hangman, in the rear!

TRADITIONAL – 1813

The Last Glass

The Alcohol, Temperance & Prohibition broadside series at the Brown University Library in Rhode Island houses a copy of this broadside ballad called *The Last Glass*. Franklin's 99 Cent Store on Essex Street in Salem printed the broadside, suggesting you spend your money on clothing instead of liquor.[17]

No, thank you, not any tonight, boys, for me,
  I have drank my last glass, have had my last spree;
You may laugh in my face; you may sneer if you will,
  But I've taken my pledge, and I'll keep it until,
I am laid in the churchyard and sleep 'neath the grass;
  And your sneers cannot move me– I've drank my last glass.

Just look at my face, I am thirsty today,
  It is wrinkled and hollow, my hair is turned gray,
And the light of my eyes that once brilliantly shone,
  And the bloom of my cheek both are vanished and gone.
I am young, but the furrows of sorrow and care,
  Are stamped on a brow once with innocence fair.

Ere manhood its seal on my forehead had set,
  (And I think of the past with undying regret,)
I was honored and loved by the good and the true,
  Nor sorrow, nor shame, nor dishonor I knew.
But the tempter approached me– I yielded and fell,
  And drank of the dark, damming poison of hell.

Since then I trod in the pathway of sin;
  And bartered my soul to the demon of gin;
Have squandered my manhood in riotous glee,
  While my parents, heartbroken, abandoned by me,
Have gone down to the grave, filled with sorrow and shame, *Ballad Seller,*
  With a sigh for the wretch who dishonored their name. *Boston Herald,*
July 24, 1910

God's curse on the glass! Nevermore shall my lip
   Of the fatal and soul burning beverage sip;
Too long has the fiend in my bosom held sway,
   Henceforth and forever I spurn him away;
And never again shall the death-dealing draught
   By me, from this hour, with God's blessing be quaffed.

So good night boys, I thank you, no liquor for me;
   I have drank my last glass, have had my last spree;
You may laugh in my face; you may sneer if you will,
   But I've taken my pledge, and I'll keep it until
I am laid in the churchyard and sleep 'neath the grass;
   And your sneers cannot move me I've drank my last glass.

TRADITIONAL – 1800

The Last Glass,
courtesy of
the Harris Broadside
Collection, John Hay
Library, Brown University

ENDNOTES

I. SALEM

Under the Willows

1. Bob Franke, *Under The Willows, Brief Histories,* Flying Fish, FF–70495, 1992, CD.
2. Eleanor Putnam, *Old Salem* (Boston and New York: Houghton, Mifflin and Company, 1889), 64.

Ode To Salem (City of Peace)

3. "Alumnae and Ivy Day Processions and Other Features of Smith College Commencement Festivities," *Springfield* [Massachusetts] *Republican,* Sunday, June 14, 1925, 6.
4. Alice Osborne Atwood, *Pageant of Salem: Kernwood,* Official Program, Salem, Massachusetts, June 13, 14, 16 and 17, House of the Seven Gables, Settlement Association, 1913, 15.
5. "House of Seven Gables, Caroline Emmerton," retrieved online January 20, 2019, https://7gables.org/history/caroline-emmerton/.

Henry K. Oliver

6. Duane Hamilton Hurd, *History of Essex County, Massachusetts with Biographical Sketches of Many of its Pioneers and Prominent Men, vol. 1, Issue 1* (Philadelphia, PA: J.W. Lewis & Co., 1888), 227.

Federal Street & *Merton C.M.*

7. "Two Famous Hymn Tunes," *Plain Dealer,* August 6, 1885.
8. Charles Charleton Coffin, ed., *Bay State Monthly, A New England Magazine of History, Biography, Literature and State Progress vol. III* (Boston: Boston Bay State Monthly Company), 1885, 304 & T. De Witt Talmage, D.D., ed., *Frank Leslie's Sunday Magazine vol. XVIII July – December 1885* (New York: Frank Leslie's Publishing House, 1885), 658.

To Cold Spring in North Salem

9. G.L. Streeter, "To Cold Spring in North Salem," *Historical Collection of the Essex Institute vol. 2* (Henry Whipple, Institute & Son, 1860), 6.
10. Rachel Valliere Duffalo, *The Lineage of the Goodell Family(s) of Westminster,* retrieved online January 2, 2018, www.usgennet. org /usa/vt/town/ westminster/goodell.html.

A Skating Song
11. "A Skating Song," *Salem Gazette,* Smith Family Scrapbook, Salem, Massachusetts, Date unknown.

Smoking – on 76 Chestnut Street
12. Ship *Ringleader* logbook, Log 1906, Phillips Library, Peabody Essex Museum, Rowley, MA
13. "Registry of Deeds," retrieved online November 13, 2108, www.salemdeeds.com

Chestnut Street
14. H. K. Oliver, S. P. Tuckerman, S. A. Bancroft, *The National Lyre: A New Collection of Sacred Music, consisting of Psalm and Hymn Tunes, with a choice selection of Sentences, Anthems, and Chants* (Boston: Wilkins, Carter and Co. 1848), 54.
15. Hamilton Hall, retrieved online September 15, 2019, https://www. hamiltonhall.org/history.

The Pickering School
16 "The Pickering School," *Salem Gazette,* Smith Family Scrapbook, Salem, Massachusetts, Date unknown.

Only Waiting
17. "Only Waiting," *Salem Register,* December 11, 1854.
18. C.S. Osgood, *Historical Sketch of Salem,* (Salem: Essex institute, 1879), 12 & Jen Ratliff, Blog: *History by the Sea, Almshouse Burial Ground Memorial,* Retrieved online, March 30, 2023. https://www.historybythesea.com/ almshouse-burial-ground-memorial-salem

Gentle Queen, Ascend Thy Throne (May Day)
19. "I Come, I Come! Ye Have Called Me Long (May Day)," *Salem Register,* May 7, 1849.
20. Alfred Tennyson, *The May Queen,* (London: Sampson, Low, Son, & Marston, Crown Buildings, Fleet Street, 1861), 11.
21. Felicia Dorothea Browne, *The Poetical Works of Mrs. Hemans The Landsdowne Poets,* (Boston: Phillips, Sampson, and Company), 1855.

Salem "Great Pasture"
22. J.B.D., "Salem Great Pasture," *Salem Register*, June 8, 1857.

The Latest Song
23. "The Latest Song," *Salem Daily Gazette,* January 26, 1886.

Be Salem Home
24. Alfred, "Be Salem Home," *Essex Register,* March 17, 1826.

Who's to Foot the Bills
25. "Who's to Foot the Bills," *Salem Daily Gazette*, February 1, 1896.

The Origin of the "Salem Shag"
26. Huntress & Dennis Aylward, *The Origin of the "Salem Shag, Essex Institute Collection vol. XXXI* (Salem, Mass.: The Salem Press, 1894 – 95), 216.

Facts About Salem
27. "Facts About Salem," *Salem Gazette*, November 13, 1898.
28. Hiram Ozias Wiley, *Eternity, and Other Poems*, published posthumously, (Salem, Massachusetts: Salem Press, 1874).

Lines on the occasioned by the Author's leaving Salem, Mass.
29. "Lines on the occasioned by the Author's leaving Salem, Mass. To reside in New York," *Portsmouth Oracle*, July 24, 1819.

The Salem Singer
30. Edwin Jocelyn, "The Salem Singer," *Salem Register*, July 8, 1852.

Our Ride to Lynn
31. J. C. Duchow, "Our Ride to Lynn," The Phillip's Library Collection, Salem, 1850.
32. H. S. Thompson, *Willie's on the Dark Blue Sea*, Boston: Oliver Ditson, 1849.

The Legend of the Club House
33. Patricia, "The Legend of the Club House," *Hemet News,* March 18, 1921.

The Moon So Round and Mellow
34. "The Moon So Round and Mellow," Nelson Dionne Collection, unknown year.
35. Matthias Barr, *Children's Poems That Never Grow Old, for Little Folks from Six to Twelve Years Old,* (Chicago, The Reilly & Lee co, 1922), 161.

Observations of Their Travel
36. Thomas Belsham, *The Christian Pioneer Intended To Uphold The Great Doctrines of the Reformation,* vol. IV, September 1829 (Glasgow: James Hedderwick & Son, 1829), 239.

37. Roger Williams, *Observations of Their Travel,* retrieved online September 5, 2018, http://www.hymntime.com/tch/bio/w/i/l/l/williams_roger.htm, & Benedict Gagliardi and Armand Aromin, *The Ocean State Songster,* (Presentation, Pinewoods Camp, Plymouth, Massachusetts, August 2018).

What Cheer or Roger Williams in Banishment
38. Job Durfee & Thomas Durfee, ed., *Whatcheer or Roger Williams in Banishment, Complete Works of the Hon. Job Durfee LL D1 Late Chief Justice of Rhode Island with a Memoir of the Author* (Providence: Gladding and Proud, Boston: Charles C. Little and James Brown, 1849), xiv.
39. Rev. J. Lewis Diman, ed., *Publications of the Narragansett Club: Key into the Language of America,* vol. I (Providence, RI: Providence Press Co., 1866), 2.

Patrick S. Gilmore: Time in Salem 1855 – 1858
40. Marwood Darlington, *Irish Orpheus, The Life of Patrick S. Gilmore Bandmaster Extraordinary* (Philadelphia: Oliver, Maney, Klien Co. 1950), 35.
41. Patrick S. Gilmore, *Sad News From Home*: a ballad/poetry and music. (Boston: Geo. P. Reed & Co.., 1854).
42. *Salem Register*, January 15, 1855.

The Early Days of The Salem Brass Band
43. "The Early Days of The Salem Brass Band," *Salem Register*, March 3, 1859.

Salem Hornpipe (On the Road to Salem)
44. Patrick Sky, ed., *Ryan's Mammoth Collection Fiddle Tunes* (Pacific, MO: MelBay Publication, 1995, originally published in Boston, 1883), 120 & *On The Road To Salem*, Patrick Gilmore (Boston: G.P. Reed & Co., 1853).
45. Jim Dalton, "Gilmore's Road To Salem," *Salem Gazette*, June 3, 2010.

I Never Can Be Thine
46. "I Never Can Be Thine," *Salem Register,* March 3, 1856.

A sampling of Gilmore Concerts with The Salem Brass Band
47. "Grand Concert," *Salem Register*, July 28, 1856.
48. "Program at Gallows, Hill," *Salem Register*, July 28, 1856.
49. Jim McAllister, *Patrick Gilmore and the Salem Brass Band*, Salem Web, Retrieved on line January 1, 2024, https://salemweb.com/about-salem/salem-tales/patrick-gilmore/

50. Grand Concert Broadside, Gilmore's *Salem Brass Band,* 1856.

51. Patrick S. Gilmore, *Sons of Temperance* (Boston: Russell & Fuller, 1858).

World Peace Jubilee

52. *Boston Daily Advertiser,* Thursday, Aug 10, 1871.

53. Patrick Sarsfield Gilmore: *History of the National Peace Jubilee and Great Musical Festival: Held in the City of Boston 1869.* Illustrated with Steel Engravings. Publisher Sale by Lee, Shepard, and Dillingham, New York, 1871.

54. *Boston Daily Journal,* Saturday, June 08, 1872 Boston, MA Vol: XXXIX

Hail, Gentle Peace

55. Henry K. Oliver, "Hail, Gentle Peace," *Salem Register*, July 1, 1872.

The Colored Millionaires, Marching Song

56. C.B. Perkins, Harry J. Ballou, "The Colored Millionaires, Marching Song" (Boston: Oliver Diston Company, 1891).

57. William John Mahar, "Behind the Burnt Cork Mask: Early Blackface Minstrelsy and Antebellum American Popular Culture" (Illinois: University of Illinois Press) 9.

II. ON DYING AND TRAGEDY

Written on Reading an Account of the Execution of Stephen M. Clark

1. *Lines Written on Reading an Account of the Execution of Stephen M. Clark,* Harris Broadsides, Brown Digital Repository, Brown University Library, retrieved online January 10, 2017 https://repository.library.brown.edu/studio/item/bdr:279434/.

2. *Account of the short life and ignominious death of Stephen Merrill Clark,* Salem [Mass.]: T.C. Cushing, 1821, Courtesy of Cornell University Law Library, Trial Pamphlets Collection, retrieved online January 10, 2017 http://reader.library.cornell.edu/docviewer/digital?id=sat:3908#page/1/mode/1up.

3. "Newburyport Fire leads to Execution For Arson," retrieved online July 17, 2107, www.mass moments.org/moment-details/newburyport-fire-leads-to-execution-for-arson.html.

A Funeral Elegy

4. *A Funeral Elegy,* occasioned by the tragedy, at Salem near Boston, Salem, 1875, retrieved online July 18, 2017, Library of Congress, www.loc.gov/item/rbpe.03701700/.

5. Raymond H. Bates Jr., *Shipwrecks North of Boston, vol. I, Salem Bay* (Beverly, Massachusetts: Commonwealth Edition, 2000), 6.

The Salem Tragedy

6. "The Salem Tragedy" Broadside, Boston, 1773. The particulars of the late melancholy and shocking tragedy, which happened at Salem, near Boston, on Thursday, the 17th day of June, Boston, 1773. retrieved online April 2, 2024, Library of Congress, Pdf. https://www.loc.gov/item/2020767530/.

Murder of Joseph White

7. *Murder of Joseph White* (1830), Harris Broadsides. Brown Digital Repository, Brown University Library, retrieved online July 27, 2017, https://repositorylibrary.brown.edu/studio/item/bdr: 281302/ & Robert Booth, *Death of an Empire, The Rise and Murderous Fall of Salem, America's Riches City* (New York: Thomas Dunne Books, St. Martin's Press, 2011).

George A. Brown

8. *Lines composed and sung at the grave of George A. Brown,* Kenneth S. Goldstein Collection of American Song Broadsides Center for Popular Music, Middle Tennessee State University, retrieved online July 18, 2017, http://popmusic. mtsu.edu.

Ballad of Giles Corey

9. John Allison, *Witches and War-Whoops: Early New England Ballads,* Folkways Records, FH5211, 1962, LP.

10. "Giles Corey & Goodwyfe Corey, A Ballad of 1692," *Bulletin of the Essex Institute, vol. I* (Salem, MA: Essex Institute Press, 1870), 15 & Samuel Drake, *The Witchcraft Delusion in New England, vol. V* (Roxbury, Mass.: Munsell Printers, 1865), 113 – 114.

11. Fitch Poole, Esquire, *Salem Observer,* April 13, 1850.

Few Are Our Days

12. Death Notices, *Salem Gazette,* February 8, 1811.

13. Samuel McIntire, *Essex Institute Historical Collection* Vol. 93, (Salem Institute Press, Salem, Mass.), 113 – 222.

Ring The Bell Softly

14. S.R. Wells, ed., *Phrenological Journal and Packard's Monthly* (New York: Samuel R. Wells, Publisher, 389 Broadway, 1870), 313.

III. IMPRISONED

The Escape Of Old John Webb or Billy Broke Locks

1. Barry Phillips, *British Ballads from Maine* As sung by Mrs. S.S. Thornton and Mrs. F.P. Barker of Maine (New Haven: Yale University Press, 1929), 393.
2. Barry Phillips, *British Ballads from Maine* As sung by Mrs. S.S. Thornton and Mrs. F.P. Barker of Maine (New Haven: Yale University Press, 1929), 393.
3. Francis James Child, *The English and Scottish Popular Ballads volume III, Archie O Cawfield*, Variant F (New York: Dover Publications, Inc., 1965), 494.
4. Francis James Child, G. L. Kittredge, *The English and Scottish Popular Ballads* (Boston and New York: Houghton and Mifflin Company, Cambridge: The Riverside Press, 1904), 461.
5. John and Lucy Allison, *Early American Ballads*, Keynote Recordings, K-109, 10", 78 RPM, Album, 1943.
6. Tom Drake, *Kingston Trio, The Escape Of Old John Webb,* Capitol Records, #33625, 45 RPM, 1960.
7. Burl Ives, *The Burl Ives Songbook* (New York: Ballantine Books, 1953), 28.
8. Alan Lomax, *The Folk Songs of North America* (New York: Doubleday & Company, 1960), 14.
9. *The Boston Evening Post*, Monday, October 16, 1738.
10. *The Boston Evening Post*, Monday, October 16, 1738.
11. *The Boston Evening Post*, Monday, October 16, 1738.
12. *The Boston Evening Post*, October 23, 1738.
13. *The Boston Evening Post*, November 20, 1738
14. Kenneth Scott, *Counterfeiting in Colonial Rhode Island.* (Providence, Rhode Island: Rhode Island Historical Society), 1960, 11.
15. Chamberlain Manuscripts Cham F 1.43, *Historical Manuscripts in the Public Library of the City of Boston, Volumes 1–5*, Boston Public Library, (Boston: Published by the Trustees A.D.) 1900, 106.
16. Chamberlain Manuscripts Cham F 1.43, *Historical Manuscripts in the Public Library of the City of Boston, Volumes 1–5*, Boston Public Library, (Boston: Published by the Trustees A.D.) 1900, 107.
17. Chamberlain Manuscripts Cham F 1.43, *Historical Manuscripts in the Public Library of the City of Boston, Volumes 1–5*, Boston Public Library, (Boston: Published by the Trustees A.D.) 1900, 110.
18. Chamberlain Manuscripts Cham F 1.43, *Historical Manuscripts in the Public Library of the City of Boston, Volumes 1–5*, Boston Public Library, (Boston: Published by the Trustees A.D.) 1900, 111.
19. *The Boston Evening Post*, March 31, 1746.
20. *The Boston Evening Post*, September 9, 1754

The Old Salem Gaol

21. *Salem Links and Lore*, Salem Public Library & Jen Ratliff, Blog: *History by the Sea, Old Witch Jail and Dungeon*, January 25, 2022. Retrieved online March 30, 2023. www.libguides.salemstate.edu/home/archives/blog/Old-Witch-Jail-and-Dungeon

The Charlestown Land Shark

22. John Greenway, *American Songs of Protest* (Philadelphia: A.S. Barnes and Company, University of Pennsylvania Press, 1953), 25 & *Charlestown Land Shark* (1815) Harris Broadsides. Brown Digital Repository, Brown University Library, retrieved online July 18, 2017, https://repository.library.brown.edu/studio/item/bdr:267976/.

Susannah Martin

23. Diane Taraz, *A Silver Dagger ~ Exploring Women's History Through Folk Songs*, Raisin Pie Music RP-8, 2008, CD.
24. John Allison, *Witches and War-Whoops: Early New England Ballads*, Folkways Records, FH5211, 1962, LP.
25. John Greenleaf Whittier, *The Complete Poetical Works of John Greenleaf Whittier* (Cambridge: Houghton Mifflin Company, 1894), 64.

A lecture and a song concerning the Robbery at Newbury to some men in jail at Salem

26. Jonathan Plummer, *A lecture and a song, concerning the robbery at Newbury, to some men in jail at Salem*, Printed for the author, and sold by him. 1817, retrieved online July 18, 2017, https://www.loc.gov/resourcrbpe.05101400/.

IV. SOCIAL CHANGE

Get Off the Track!

1. Jesse Hutchinson, *Get Off the Track* (Boston: Published by the Author, 1844), retrieved online, July 16, 2019, https://levysheetmusic.mse.jhu.edu/collection/012/156
2. "Music, Civil War," Americans at War, retrieved online July 20, 2017, https://www.encyclopedia.com/defense/energy-government-and-defense-magazines/music-civil-war.

3. "Popular Songs of the Day," retrieved online July 20, 2017, www.loc.gov/collections/songs-of-america/articles-and-essays/musical-styles/popular-songs-of-the-day/.

4. Philip D. Jordan, *Singin' Yankees* (Minneapolis: The University of Minnesota Press, 1946), 96.

Emancipation Hymn

5. Manuel Fenollosa and R. T L., *Emancipation Hymn* (Boston: Oliver Ditson & Co.), 1863, Notated Music, retrieved online July 20, 2017, http://www.loc.gov/item/ihas.200001094/.

6. Heather Wilkinson Rojo, "Manuel Fenollosa, Spanish Immigrant to Salem, Massachusetts 1838," retrieved online July 20, 2017, www.genealogywise.com/profiles/blogs/manuel-fenollosa-spanish & *Emancipation Hymn, Protest Song Lyrics*, retrieved online July 20, 2017, www.protestsonglyrics.net/Freedom_Songs/Emancipation-Hymn.phtml.

Salem Fremont Club

7. "Salem Fremont Club," *Salem Register*, August 4, 1856.

Song For the Time

8. "Song For the Time," *Salem Register*, November 11, 1856
We're for Freedom Through the Land

9. "We're for Freedom Through the Land," tune: *Old Granite State, Salem Register,* September 1, 1856.

Tribute to Reverend Jacob Stroyer

10. Fred Goldsmith Walker, *My Leisure Moments,* (Salem: Barry and Lufkin, Printers and Publishers), 1892.

11. *Tribute to Reverend Jacob Stroyer For 25 Years Minister to Salem's African-Americans:, Salem Evening News*, February 10, 1908.

12. Wilbert, Polly, Historic Salem, Inc., Excerpts from *My Life in the South, Jacob Stroyer, National Humanities Center* Digital Scanning, Inc., Scituate, MA 02066, originally published, 1879 & McCarthy, B. Eugene, *Bondage to Belonging: The Worcester Slave Narratives* (University of Mass. Press, 2008).

A Parting Hymn (Blessing)

13. Wikipedia contributors, "Charlotte Forten Grimké," Wikipedia, The Free Encyclopedia, retrieved January 16, 2019, https://en.wikipedia.org/w/index.php?title=Charlotte_Forten_Grimk%C3%A9&oldid=851323627.

14. Brenda Stevenson, ed., *The Journals of Charlotte Forten* (New York: Oxford Press, 1988) & "Charlotte Forten," retrieved online January 15, 2019, https://www.salemstate.edu/charlotteforten.
15 . *The Massachusetts Teacher and Journal of Home and School Education, Volume 9,* (Boston: Samuel Coolidge for the Massachusetts Teachers Association, 1856), 140.

0 Thou To Whom in Ancient Time
16. George Barrett, B.A., ed., *Congregational Church Hymnal,* (London: Hodder and Stoughton, 27 Pateroster Row, 1887), 141.
17. Independent Congregational Church Papers, MSS 302, Phillips Library, Peabody Essex Museum, Salem, Mass.
18. Charles Dexter Cleveland & E.C. & J. Biddle, ed., *American Literature with Biographical Sketches and Selections From Their Work. A compendium of American literature,* No. 508 (Philadelphia, PA: Minor Street, 1862), 427 & "Charles Dexter Cleveland," retrieved online November 22, 2017, https://hymnary.org/person/Cleveland_CD3.

The Cornerstone Hymn
19. Lemuel Willis, *A Semi-centennial Address Delivered in the Universalist Church, Salem, Mass., Thursday August 4, 1859, on the Occasion of Celebrating the 50th Anniversary of the dedication of the Church* (Salem: Charles W. Swasey, Register Press, 1859), 66.
20. Amanda McGregor and Tom Dalton, "Universalist Church Celebrates 200th Birthday in Song," *Salem Evening News*, Friday, February 27, 2008.

Original Hymn 50th Anniversary of the Universalist Church in Salem
21. "Original Hymn 50th Anniversary of the Universalist Church in Salem," *Salem Register,* August 8, 1859.

V. CONFLICT

Original Ode: The First Shot of Freedom
1. City Authorities of Salem, *Memorial Services at the Centennial Anniversary of Leslie's Expedition to Salem* (Salem, Mass.: Salem Observer Printing Room 1875), 17.

Col. Leslie's Expedition
2. "Col. Leslie's Expedition," *Salem Register*, March 23, 1848.

Ode (To Leslie's Retreat)
3. George Bailey Loring, *Celebration at North Bridge*, Salem, July 4th, 1862: oration (J.E. Farwell & Company, Boston), 1862.

Colonel Pickering's March To Lexington aka Black Sloven
4. Louis Charles Elson, *The National Music of America and its Sources* (Boston: L.C. Page and Company, 1900), 146.

A Funeral Elegy to the Immortal Memory of those Worthies, who were slain in the Battle of Concord, April 19, 1775
5. "A Funeral Elegy," *New York Herald*, April 19, 1875.

Ode of War and Washington
6. Wikipedia contributors, *War and Washington,* retrieved online September 31, 2017, https://en.wikipedia.org/wiki/War_and_ Washington.
7. Samuel Kettell, *Specimens of American poetry, with Critical and Biographical Notices, vol. 1* (Boston: S. G. Goodrich and Co., 1829), 198 –199.
8. "Ode of War and Washington," *Salem Mercury,* Tuesday October 27, 1789, vol. III, #159.
9. Mary Caroline Crawford, *Little Pilgrimages Among Old New England Inns* (Boston: L.C. Page & Company, 1907, third Impression, 1908), 168.

Salem Artillery
10. "Salem Artillery," Transcriber by T. William Smith, Essex Institute now the Phillips Library, circa 1980.

Americans to Arms
11. "Americans to Arms," The Rosenbach Museum and Library, 2008– 2010 Delancey Place, Philadelphia, PA 19103 & "Poetry & Song on the Outbreak of War," retrieved online September 31, 2017, http:// americainclass.org/sources/makingrevolution/crisis/text8/ outbreakofwar.pdf.

Song of the Minute Man

12. George Rea Curwen and Ladies' Centennial Committee (Salem, Mass.), *Song of the Minute Man* (1875). Harris Broadsides, Brown Digital Repository, Brown University Library, retrieved online September 12, 2018, https://repository.library.brown.edu/studio/item/bdr:290807/.

Yankee Song

13. "Yankee Song," *Salem Gazette*, July 5, 1811.
14. Oliver Oldschool, *Portfolio vol. II*, (Philadelphia: John Watt, 1806), 123.

The Patriotic Diggers

15. "The Patriotic Diggers," *Salem Observer*, October 3, 1863.

The Patriot Song

16. "The Patriot Song," *Salem Observer*, August 8, 1861.

To Our Salem Boys

17. "To Our Salem Boys," *Salem Register*, July 28, 1862.

Departure of the Salem Light Infantry

18. *Departure of the Salem Light Infantry* (1861), Harris Broadsides Brown Digital Repository, Brown University Library, retrieved online August 9, 2017, https://repository.library.brown.edu/studio/item/bdr:270123/.
19. *Fifth Massachusetts Infantry* retrieved online August 9, 2017, www.firstbullrun.co.uk/NEV/Third%2Division/5th-massachusetts-infantry.html.
20. "Departure of Salem Troops," *The Salem Register*, April 23, 1861

Lines written for the Second Reunion of the 23d Regiment

21. *Lines written for the Second Reunion of the 23d Regiment*, Kenneth S. Goldstein Collection of American Song Broadsides Center for Popular Music, Middle Tennessee State University, retrieved online July 18, 2017, http://popmusic.mtsu.edu.
22. Herbert E. Valentine, *Dedication of the boulder commemorating the service of the Twenty-third Regiment, Massachusetts Volunteer Infantry, in the Civil war, 1861–1865, at Salem, Massachusetts, September 28, 1905. United States Army. Massachusetts Infantry Regiment, 23rd (1861 – 1865)* (Salem: Newcomb & Gauss, Mass. 1905), 3.

When Johnny Comes Marching Home

23. Broadside ballad, *When Johnny Comes Marching Home,* retrieved online September 31, 2017, https://digital.nls.uk/broadsidesview/?id=16533.
24. Margaret Bradford Boni, *Fireside Book of Folk Songs* (New York: Simon and Schuster, 1947), 198.
25. Louis Charles Elson, *The National Music of America and its Sources* (Boston: L.C. Page and Company, 1900), 248.
26. Louis Lambert, *When Johnny Comes Marching Home Again.* Library of Congress, Washington, DC, 2002. retrieved online September 31, 2017. Library of Congress, https://www.loc.gov/item/ihas.200000024/.

Salem Mechanick Infantry Quick Step

27. John Holloway, Fitz Hugh Lane (cover art), *Salem Mechanick Infantry Quick Step* (Salem, Mass.: Ives & Putnam, 1836), retrieved online, July 16, 2019, https://levysheetmusic.mse.jhu.edu/collection/055/048.

Salem Independent Cadet Quick Step

28. Zetzsche, and S. Knaebel, *Salem Independent Cadet Quick Step* (Boston: Stephen W. Marsh, Boston, 1848), retrieved online, July 16, 2019, https://levysheetmusic.mse.jhu.edu/collection/084/003.

Musical Entertainment at Mechanic Hall, Salem

29. *Musical Entertainment at Mechanic Hall, Salem,* New England Women's Auxiliary Sanitary Commission Program Booklet (Salem: Charles W. Swasey, Printer, 27 Washington Street, Salem, 1863).
30. W. T. Wrighton and J. E. Carpenter, "Her Bright Smile Haunts Me Still" Anne and Frank Warner, *Traditional American Folk Songs* (Syracuse University Press, 1984), 357.

Dreaming of Home and Mother

31. John P. Ordway, *Dreaming of Home and Mother, ca. 1868.* retrieved online August 6, 2017, Photograph. https://www.loc.gov/item/2001701390/.
32. Oliver Ayer Roberts, *History of the Military Company of the Massachusetts, Now Called the Ancient and Honorable Artillery Company of Massachusetts, 1637 – 1888* (Boston: Alfred Mudge & Sons, Printer, 34 Franklin Street, 1901), 91.
33. J. Pierpont, and J Pierpont, *The One Horse Open Sleigh,* Oliver Ditson, Boston, monographic, 1857, Notated Music, retrieved online January 10, 2019, https://www.loc.gov/item/sm1857.620520/.

Salem Cadet's March

34. Elias Howe, *Howe's School for the Clarinet* (Boston: Oliver Diston & Co. Washington Street Publication, 1851), 21.

Salem Quick Step

35. Elias Howe, *The Musician's Companion* (Boston: Oliver Diston & Co., Washington Street Publication, 1842), 79 & John Jewett's, *National Flutina and Accordion Teacher: Complete Book of Instructions* (Boston: Oliver Diston & Co., Washington Street Publication, 1850), 36.

Down on Manila's Bay

36. *Down on Manila's Bay,* Courtesy of Historic Beverly, www.historicbeverly.net. Catalog Number: 983.36.697
37. *Salem Evening News,* September 2, 1898.
38. "City Pays Final Tribute to Medal of Honor Man Riley," *Salem Evening News,* November 18, 1950.

God Bless America

39. H. Leander D'Entremont, *God Bless America* a national anthem, H. Leander D'Entremont, Salem, Mass., 1919, retrieved online August 6, 2017, http://www.loc.gov/item/2013562539/.

Ode Deeds of Glory

40. "Ode Deeds of Glory," *Salem Register*, July 8, 1859.

VI. COMMERCE

Hardware Advertisement

1. "Hardware Advertisement,*" Salem Gazette*, July 11, 1800 #928.

We Are Ped(d)lars

2. "We Are Ped(d)lars," Smith Family Scrapbook, Date unknown.

The First Trip

3. Francis C. Bradlee, *The Boston and Lowell Railroad* (Salem: Essex, Institute Collection, vol. LIV, Essex Institute, 1918), 222 – 223 & "The First Trip," *Salem Gazette*, August 2, 1850.

The Salem and Danvers (South) Horse Railroad
4. "The Salem and Danvers (South) Horse Railroad," *Salem Observer*, March 14, 1863.

Lowell Island
5. "Lowell Island," *Salem Register*, August 14, 1851.
6. Lowell Island House https://en.wikipedia.org/wiki/Lowell_Island_House
7. Benjamin D. Hill, & Winfield S. Nevins, *The North Shore of Massachusetts Bay*, An illustrated guide and history, 3rd ed., 1880, 107.

Charge of the Ladies' Brigade at Black Alva
8. "Charge of the Ladies' Brigade at Black Alva," *Beverly Citizen*, December 15, 1866.
9. Alfred Lord Tennyson, *The Charge of the Light Brigade at Balaklava* Mary Elizabeth Burt, ed., "Poems That Every Child Should Know," (New York: Grosset & Dunlap, 1904).
10. Terry Brighton, *Hell Riders: The True Story of the Charge of the Light Brigade*, (Henry Holt and Co., 2004).

Charge of the Light Brigade
11. "Charge of the Light Brigade," *Salem Register*, January 1, 1875.

I Took My Specs
12. "I Took My Specs," *Salem Gazette*, October 1, 1841.

The Genius of My Glasses
13. "The Genius of My Glasses," *Boston Herald*, August 9, 1914.

Pickering Theme Song, Keeping the North Shore Warm
14. "Pickering Theme Song, Keeping the North Shore Warm," Nelson Dionne Collection, unknown date.

On Hearing the Salem Bells Ring for Fire
15. Alonzo Lewis, The Lynn Bard, "On Hearing the Salem Bells Ring for Fire," *Salem Register*, November 9, 1843.
16. Alonzo Lewis, aka The Lynn Bard, *The Poems of Alonzo Lewis* (Boston B.B. Mussey & Co. Stereotyped and Printed by S.N. Dickerson & Co., 62 Washington Street, Boston, 1854). 115.

Sidewalk Musings
17. "Sidewalk Musings," *Salem Register*, August 2, 1841.

Apprenticed in Salem
18. Peter Johnson and Friends, *Newport's Fair Town Traditional Songs and Ballads of North America.*, Living Folk Records, LFR 013, Living Folk, 2007, CD.
19. Broadside Collection, Bodleian Libraries and the Bodleian Digital Collections of Ballads, Oxford University, retrieved online October 20, 2018, http://ballads.bodleian.ox.ac.uk/search/printer/Hillatt%2C%20I.

The New England Blacking Man
20. *The New England Blacking Man,* Kenneth S. Goldstein Collection of American Song Broadsides, Center for Popular Music, Middle Tennessee State University, retrieved online July 21, 2017, http://popmusic.mtsu.edu/.

Dreams
21. Dreams, S. F. Rogers," *Salem Register*, January 6, 1851.

A Parody
22. "A Parody," *Salem Observer*, November 7, 1863.

Essex Street Rhymes No. 3
23. "Essex Street Rhymes No. 3," *Salem Observer*, April 11, 1863.
24. "Good Photography," *Salem Register*, December 12, 1859.

Little Red Riding Hood
25. Lydia Very, "Little Red Riding Hood," [Boston] *Christian Era*, February 18, 1875.
26. Lydia Louisa Anna Very, "Red Riding Hood," (Boston, Mass.: L. Prang & Co., no. 159 Washington St., 1863).

VII. DANCING, COURTSHIP

The Flirtation
1. "The Flirtation," *Salem Gazette*, May 30, 1788.

Twinkling Stars Are Laughing Love

2. John P. Ordway, *Twinkling Stars Are Laughing Love* (Boston: J.P. Ordway, Ordway Hall, Washington Street, 1855), retrieved online October 1, 2019, http://levysheetmusic.mse.jhu.edu/collection/023/071.

Dancing in Salem

3. Milton Gerald Hehr, *Musical Activities in Salem, Massachusetts,* 1783 – 1823, Ph.D. dissertation, Boston University, 1963, 87.
4. Milton Gerald Hehr, *Musical Activities in Salem, Massachusetts,* 1783 – 1823, Ph.D. dissertation, Boston University, 1963, 88.
5. F.E. Oliver, ed. *The Diary of Benjamin Lynde and Benjamin Lynde, Jr.* (Boston: 1880), 48.
6. Mrs. Mary (Vail) Holyoke, *The Holyoke Diaries 1709 – 1856* (Salem Mass.: The Essex Institute), 48 – 106.
7. Milton Gerald Hehr, *Musical Activities in Salem, Massachusetts,* 1783 – 1823, Ph.D. dissertation, Boston University, 1963, 90.
8. Robert Rantoul, *A Historic Ball Room* (Salem, Mass.: The Essex institute Historical Collection vol. XXXI #7 & 12, 1894), 69.
9. Milton Gerald Hehr, *Musical Activities in Salem, Massachusetts,* 1783 – 1823, Ph.D. dissertation, Boston University, 1963, 90 & *Essex Gazette*, May 31, 1774.
10. Jim McAllister, *Hamilton Hall, 1805, Salem Tales*, August 11, 2008, retrieved online June 16, 2017, www.salemweb.com.

Newhall's March

11. *Newhall's March,* Transcribed by Fred Finkle, source and date unknown.

To a LADY who admired dancing

12. "To a LADY who admired dancing," *Salem Mercury,* July 29, 1788.

Celebrating "The Night Before"

13. "Celebrating 'The Night Before," Smith Family Scrapbook, date unknown.

A New Song

14. M. C. D. Silsbee, *A Half Century in Salem* (Boston and New York: Houghton Mifflin & Co. The Riverside Press, Cambridge, 1887), i.
15. M. C. D. Silsbee, *A Half Century in Salem* (Boston and New York: Houghton Mifflin & Co. The Riverside Press, Cambridge, 1887), 88.

16. M. C. D. Silsbee, *A Half Century in Salem* (Boston and New York: Houghton Mifflin & Co. The Riverside Press, Cambridge, 1887), 88.

17. M. C. D. Silsbee, *A Half Century in Salem* (Boston and New York: Houghton Mifflin & Co. The Riverside Press, Cambridge, 1887), 91.

Dancing Instruction
18. M. C. D. Silsbee, *A Half Century in Salem* (Boston and New York: Houghton Mifflin & Co. The Riverside Press, Cambridge, 1887), 4.

The Bowl
19. Mrs. J.H. Hanaford, "The Bowl," *Salem Register*, October 16, 1862.

The Maid With Elbows Bare
20. "The Maid With Elbows Bare," *Salem Gazette*, #1223, May 17, 1803.

Lailson's Ride
21. *Lailson's Ride,* Transcribed by T. William Smith circa 1980 from the manuscript collection at the Phillips Library & Elias Howe, *The Musician's Companion* (Boston: Oliver Diston & Co. Washington Street Publication, 1842), 54.

Pyncheon Lane Capric
22. Charles Bancroft, *Illustrated history of Salem and environs: Souvenir edition of the Salem Evening News* (Salem, Mass.: *Salem Evening News*, 1897), 97.

23. Ryan Conary, David Moffat, Everett Philbrook, *House of the Seven Gables,* House of the Seven Gables Settlement Association (Charleston, South Carolina: Arcadia Publishing, 2017), 3 and 18.

Pop Goes The Weasel
24. Fred A. Gannon, *Old Salem Scrap Book ll* (Salem, Mass.: Newcomb & Gauss in City Hall Square, for the Salem Book Co., M.F. McGrath), 21.

25. James M. Volo & Dorothy D. Volo, *Family Life in Seventeenth and Eighteenth Century America* (Westport CT: Greenwood Press, 2006), 264 & Iona Opie & Peter Opie, *The Singing Game* (Oxford: Oxford University Press, 1985), 217.

Salem Willows For Mine

26. Rachel Zoll, "Salem Memorabilia Hunter Uncovers Willows Waltz," *Salem Evening News*, Monday, May 1, 1995, 1.

27. Lou Collin, George Harry, *Salem Willows for Mine Waltz* (Salem, Mass.: L.A. Collins, Publisher, 1919).

Salem Country Dance

28. Salem Country Dance Flyer, Self-published by Chris Green, 1982.

29. Commonwealth Vintage Dancers, *Fezziwig's Ball* at Old Town Hall Salem, retrieved online September 28, 2019   http://vintagedancers.org

30. Hamilton Hall, *The Resistance Ball*, retrieved online September 28, 2019 www.hamiltonhall.org/events

High Street

31. T. William Smith, *High Street, Strawberry Jam,* Salem: Wellspring Studio, 2012, CD & Various Artists, *Old Salem in Ballad and Song*, Self-produced, 2021, CD.

Belle of Tennessee! A Plantation Love Song

32. Dexter Ware Smith, N. Harris, *Belle of Tennessee A Plantation Love Song* Boston: Ent. Sta. Hall, 1897).

33. S.R. Wells, ed., *Phrenological Journal and Packard's Monthly* (New York: Samuel R. Wells, Publisher, 389 Broadway, 1870), 313.

34. S.R. Wells, ed., *Phrenological Journal and Packard's Monthly* (New York: Samuel R. Wells, Publisher, 389 Broadway, 1870), 311.

35. Dexter Smith, *"Dexter Smith Poems,"* (Boston: Russell, 1868).

Salem Tunnel

36. "Salem Tunnel," *Salem Press,* September 29, 1867.

The Dark Eyed Gypsy, O

37. "The Dark Eyed Gypsy, O," *Boston Sunday Globe*, September 26, 1915.

VIII. CHILDREN SONGS

Kid Do Go

1. William Wells Newell, "The Passover Song of the Kid and an Equivalent from New England," *The Journal of American Folklore*, vol. 18, no. 68 (1905): 35 – 36. JSTOR, retrieved online September 17, 2017, www.jstor. orgstable/534260.

The Cat and the Mouse
2. "The Cat and the Mouse," *The Journal of American Folklore*, vol. 13, no. 50 (July – Sept. 1900): 229. JSTOR, retrieved online September 17, 2018, www.jstor.org stable/534260 & William Bernard McCarthy, ed., *Cinderella in America: A Book of Folk and Fairy Tales* (Mississippi: University Press, 2007), 57 – 58.

Epitaph on a Favorite Pig
3. "Epitaph on a Favorite Pig," *Salem Gazette,* July 4, 1797 #619.

Trot, Trot to Boston
4. "Traditional Children's Songs & Nursery Rhymes," *Trot, Trot to Boston*, retrieved online September 17, 2017, www.traditionalmusic.co.uk/ childrens-songs/Trot_trot_to_Boston.htm.

IX. TEMPERANCE

The Drunken Soldier
1. "Drunken Soldier," *Salem Mercury*, Tuesday, September 25, 1787, #50.

King Alcohol, A Parody
2. John Wallace Hutchinson, *Story of the Hutchinson's (tribe of Jesse)* (Boston: Lee and Shepard, No. 10 Milk Street, 1896), 42.
3. Brian Roberts, *Blackface Nation: Race, Reform, and Identity in American Popular Music, 1812 – 1925* (Chicago: University of Chicago Press, 2017), 155.

A Parody
4. George B. Cheever, *A Parody, Alcohol, Temperance & Prohibition* (New York: J.S. Redfield, 1835), Phillips Library Broadside Collection.
5. Dale Cockrell, *Excelsior: Journals of the Hutchinson Family Singers, 1842 – 1846* (New York: Pendragon Press, 1989), 109.

George B. Cheever
6. G.W. Bungay, "George B. Cheever," *Liberator,* June 4, 1858.
7. *Temperance Reformation, Fifth Report of the American Temperance Society, American Quarterly Observer* (Boston: Aaron Russell, 5 Cornhill, New York: John P. Haven, 142 Nassau Street, 1833).

A Water - Song

8. Edward Cornelius Delavan, *The Family Fire-side Book or Monuments of Temperance, Containing: Temperance, Tales, Biography Sketches, Poetry, Essays Pleasing Instructive and Amusing* (Philadelphia: Leary & Getz, Publishers, 1853), 201.
9. City Documents for 1892 (Salem: Salem Observer Book and Job Print, 1893), 72.
10. Henry M. Meek, *The Naumkeag Directory for Salem, Beverly, Danvers, Marblehead, Peabody, Essex, and Manchester* (Salem, Mass.: Henry M. Meek Publishing Company, 1898), 98.

The Drunkard's Wish

11. "The Drunkard's Wish," *Salem Gazette,* December 6, 1796, #557.

A Temperance Ode

12. Lydia L.A. Very, "A Temperance Ode," *Salem Observer*, February 25, 1865.

Chug's at Cabot Farm (Broadside)

13. Second Annual Picnic at Cabot Farm, Nancy Lutts' Collection.
14. "Guests at Cabot Farm," *Salem Gazette*, September 7, 1897.

Address to a Jug of Rum

15. Wikipedia contributors, "Father Mathew," Wikipedia, The Free Encyclopedia, retrieved online July 27, 2018, https://en.wikipedia.org/wiki/TheobaldMathew_%28temperance_reformer%29.
16. Father Mathew, retrieved online July 27, 2018 http://www.noblenet.org/salem/wiki/index.php/Father_Mathew Wiki source, Salem Links and Lore.

The Last Glass

17. "The Last Glass (1860)," *Alcohol, Temperance & Prohibition*, Brown Digital Repository, Brown University Library, retrieved online August 2, 2017, https://repository.library.brown.edu/studio/item/bdr:30273/.

BIBLIOGRAPHY

Account of the short life and ignominious death of Stephen Merrill Clark, Salem, Mass.: T.C. Cushing, 1821.

Adams, George. *The Salem Directory: Contains the City Records, Schools, Churches, Banks, Societies, Etc.* Salem: Henry Whipple & Son, Publishers, 91 Washington Street, 1855.

Allison, John and Lucy. *Early American Ballads*, Keynote Recordings, K-109, 10 inch, 78 RPM, Album, 1943.

Allison, John. *Witches and War-Whoops: Early New England Ballads,* Folkways Records, FH5211, LP, 1962.

Atwood, Alice Osborne. *Pageant of Salem: Kernwood,* Official Program, Kernwood, Salem, Massachusetts, June 13, 14, 16, and 17, House of the Seven Gables, Settlement Association, 1913.

Atlas of the City of Salem, Massachusetts. Philadelphia: G.M. Hopkins & Co., 1874.

Aylward, Huntress & Dennis. *The Origin of the "Salem Shag",* Essex Institute Collection Vol. XXXI. Salem, Mass.: The Salem Press, 1894 – 95.

Bailey, George. *Celebration at North Bridge, Salem, July 4th, 1862.* Boston: J.E. Farewell and Company Printers to the City No. 37 Congress Street, 1862.

Ballou, Harry J., & Perkins, C.B. *The Colored Millionaires, Marching Song.* Boston: Oliver Diston Company, 1891.

Ballou, Hosea. *The Cornerstone Hymn.* Unknown Publisher, 1809.

Ballou, Hosea, & Turner, Edward. *The Universalists' Hymn-Book: A New, Collection of Psalms and Hymns, for the use of the Universalist Societies.* Boston: Munroe & Francis, 1821.

Baltzell, Isaiah. *Excerpt from Gates of Praise: For the Sabbath-School, Praise-Service, Prayer-Meeting, Etc.* Dayton, OH: W. J. Shuey, 1884.

Bancroft, Charles. *Illustrated history of Salem and environs*: Souvenir edition of *The Salem Evening News.* Salem, Mass.: *Salem Evening News,* 1897.

Bancroft, S. A., Oliver, H. K., Tuckerman, S. P. *The National Lyre: A New Collection of Sacred Music, consisting of Psalm and Hymn Tunes, with a choice selection of Sentences, Anthems, and Chants.* Boston: Wilkins, Carter and Co., 1848.

Barber, John Warner. *Historical Collections: Being a General Collection of Interesting Facts, biographical Sketches, Anecdotes & Relating to the History and Antiquities of Every Town in Massachusetts.* Worcester: Warren Lazell, 1844.

Barrett, George, B.A., ed. *Congregational Church Hymnal.* London: Hodder and Stoughton, 27 Paternoster Row, 1887.

Bates Raymond H., Jr., *Shipwrecks North of Boston, Volume I, Salem Bay.* Beverly, Massachusetts: Commonwealth Edition, 2000.

Belsham, Thomas. *The Christian Pioneer Intended To Uphold The Great Doctrines of the Reformation,* Vol. IV. September 1829. Glasgow: James Hedderwick & Son, 1829.

Benoit, Clement F., Compiled by. Barr, Matthias. *Children's Poems That Never Grow Old, for Little Folks from Six to Twelve Years Old.* Chicago: The Reilly & Lee Co., 1922.

Boni, Margaret Bradford. *Fireside Book of Folk Songs.* New York: Simon and Schuster, 1947.

Booth, Robert. *Death of an Empire, The Rise and Murderous Fall of Salem, America's Richest City.* New York: Thomas Dunne Books, St. Martin's Press, 2011.

Boston, Mass. Directory City Records. General Directory of the Citizens. for the year 1864. Boston: Adams, Sampson & Company No. 91 Washington Street, 1864.

Bradlee, Francis C. *The Boston and Lowell Railroad.* Essex Institute Collection, Vol. LIV, Essex Institute, Salem, 1918.

Braithwaite, William Stanley ed., *Anthology of Magazine Verse for 1921.* Boston: Small, Maynard & Company, 1921.

Braithwaite, William Stanley ed., *Yearbook of American Poetry.* Boston: Small, Maynard & Company, 1921.

Brooks, Henry M. *The Olden Time Series, Vol. 6: Literary Curiosities - Gleanings Chiefly from Old Newspapers of Boston and Salem, Massachusetts.* Boston: Ticknor and Company, 1886.

Browne, Felicia Dorothea. *The Poetical Works of Mrs. Hemans.* The Landsdowne Poets. Boston: Phillips, Sampson, and Company, 1855.

Burzynski, Don. *The First Leathernecks: A Combat History of the U.S. Marines from Inception to the Halls of Montezuma.* Open Road Media, 2013.

Chamberlain Manuscripts. Cham F 1.43. *Historical Manuscripts in the Public Library of the City of Boston, Volumes 1–5.* Boston Public Library, Boston: Published by the Trustees A.D., 1900.

Cheever, George B. *A Parody.* New York: J.S. Redfield, 1835.

Cheever, George B. *Liberator,* June 4, 1858.

Childs, Francis James. *English and Scottish Popular Ballads.* Edited from the collection of Francis James Child by Helen Child Sargent and George Lyman Kittredge. Boston and New York: Houghton Mifflin Company, Cambridge: The Riverside Press, 1904.

City Authorities of Salem, *Memorial Services at the Centennial Anniversary of Leslie's Expedition to Salem*. Salem, Mass.: Salem Observer Printing Room, 1875.

City Documents for 1892, Salem: Salem Observer Book and Job Print, 1893.

Cleveland, Charles Dexter & Biddle, E.C. & J. arranged and edited by, *American Literature with Biographical Sketches and Selections From Their Work. A compendium of American literature*. Philadelphia, PA: No. 508 Minor Street, 1862.

Cockrell, Dale. *Excelsior: Journals of the Hutchinson Family Singers, 1842 – 1846*. Stuyvesant, New York: Pendragon Press, 1989.

Coffin, Charles Charleton, ed., *Bay State Monthly, A New England Magazine of History, Biography, Literature and State Progress Volume III*. Boston: Boston Bay State Monthly Company, 43 Milk Street Boston, 1885.

Cole's Thousand Fiddle Tunes. Chicago, IL: M. M. Cole Publishing Co., 1967.

Collins, Lou and Harry, George. *Salem Willows for Mine Waltz*. Salem, Mass.: L.A. Collins, Publisher, 1919.

Conary, Ryan, Moffat, David, Philbrook, Everett. *House of the Seven Gables,* for the House of the Seven Gables Settlement Association. Charleston, South Carolina: Arcadia Publishing, 2017.

Crawford, Mary Caroline. *Little Pilgrimages Among Old New England Inns*. Boston: L.C. Page & Company, 1907, third Impression, November 1908.

Darlington, Marwood. *Irish Orpheus, The Life of Patrick S. Gilmore Band Extraordinary*. Philadelphia: Oliver, Maney, Klien Co., 1950.

Delavan, Edward Cornelius, *The Family Fire-side Book or Monuments of Temperance, Containing: Temperance, Tales, Biography Sketches, Poetry, Essays Pleasing Instructive and Amusing*. Philadelphia: Leary & Getz, Publishers, 1853.

Deese, Helen R., edited. *The Complete Poems By Jones Very*. Athens & London: The University of Georgia Press, 1993.

Diman, Rev. J. Lewis, ed. *Publications of the Narragansett Club: Key into the language of America Volume I*. Providence, RI: Providence Press Co., Printers, 1866.

Drake, Samuel. *The Witchcraft Delusion in New England, Vol. V*. Roxbury, Mass.: Munsell Printers, 1865.

Duchow, J. C. *Our Ride to Lynn*. Broadside Collection at The Phillip's Library Collection. Salem: No publisher given, 1850.

Durfee, Job, Durfee, Thomas, editor. *Whatcheer or Roger Williams in Banishment, Complete Works of the Hon. Job Durfee LL D1 Late Chief Justice of Rhode Island with a Memoir of the Author*. Providence: Gladding and Proud, Boston: Charles C. Little and James Brown, 1849.

Elson, Louis Charles. *The National Music of America and its Sources*. Boston: L.C.
Page and Company, 1900.

Few Are Our Days, Revival Melodies, or Songs of Zion, John Putnam: Boston, No.
81 Cornhill, 1843.

Forbes, Allan. *Taverns and Stagecoaches of New England: Anecdotes and Tales
Recalling the Days of Stagecoach Travel and the Ancient Hostelries where
Strangers Tarried, Volume 1*. Boston: State Street Trust Company, 1953.

Forbes, Allan, & Eastman, Ralph M. *Taverns and Stagecoaches of New England
Volume II*. Boston: State Street Trust Company, 1954.

Forbes, Allan and Eastman, Ralph M., *Town and City Seals of Massachusetts*.
Boston: State Street Trust Company, 1950.

Franke, Bob. *Under The Willows, Brief Histories*. Flying Fish, FF-70495, 1992,
CD.

Gagliardi, Benedict and Aromin, Armand. *The Ocean State Songster*. Providence,
RI: Self-published by Gagliardi & Aromin, 2018.

Gannon, Fred A. *Old Salem Scrap Book*. Salem, Mass.: Newcomb & Gauss in
City Hall Square, Salem Book Co., M.F. McGrath, No copyright date given.

Gannon, Fred A. *Old Salem Scrap Book II*. Salem, Mass.: Newcomb & Gauss in
City Hall Square, Salem Book Co., M.F. McGrath. No copyright date given.

Gilmore, Patrick Sarsfield. *Essex Institute Historical Collection*, XXXVI. Salem
Mass.: Printed for the Essex Institute, 1900.

Gilmore, Patrick Sarsfield. *Sad News From Home: a Ballad*. Boston: Geo. P. Reed
& Co., 1854.

Greenway, John. *American Songs of Protest*. Philadelphia: A.S. Barnes and
Company Inc., University of Pennsylvania Press, 1953.

Hadley, Henry Harrison. *National Christian Men's Temperance Union*. New York:
H.H. Hadley, 1896.

Hehr, Milton Gerald. *Musical Activities in Salem, Massachusetts, 1783 – 1823*.
Ph.D. diss., Boston University, 1963.

Hill, Benjamin D., & Nevins, Winfield S. *The North Shore of Massachusetts Bay.
An Illustrated Guide and History*. 3rd Ed. 1880.

Holyoke, Mrs. Mary (Vail). *The Holyoke Diaries 1709–1856*. The Essex Institute,
Salem Mass. No copyright date given.

Howe, Elias. *The Musician's Companion*. Boston: Oliver Diston & Co.,
Washington Street Publication, 1842.

Howe, Elias. *Howe's School for the Clarinet*. Boston: Oliver Diston & Co.,
Washington Street Publication, 1851.

Hull, Asa, Editor. Oliver, Henry, K. "Hail Gentle Peace." *The Devotional Chimes: a choice collection of new and standard hymns and tunes, adapted to all occasions of social worship, family devotions, and congregational singing.* Publisher: Asa Hull, Philadelphia, 1873.

Hurd, Duane Hamilton. *History of Essex County, Massachusetts with Biographical Sketches of Many of its Pioneers and Prominent Men, Vol. I, Issue 1.* Philadelphia, PA: J.W. Lewis & Co., 1888.

Hutchinson, Jesse. *Get Off the Track.* Boston: Published by the Author, 1844.

Hutchinson, Jesse. *King Alcohol, a Temperance Glee.* Boston: Oliver Diston, 135 Washington Street, 1843.

Hutchinson, John Wallace. *Story of the Hutchinson's (tribe of Jesse).* Boston: Lee and Shepard, Publisher, No. 10 Milk Street, 1896.

Independent Congregational Church Papers, MSS 302, Phillips Library, Peabody Essex Museum, Salem, Mass.

Ives, Burl. *The Burl Ives Songbook.* New York: Ballantine Books, 1953.

Jenkins, Oliver. *Open Shutters, a Volume of Poems.* Chicago: W. Ransom, 1922.

Jewett, John. *Jewett's, National Flutina and Accordion Teacher: Complete Book of Instructions.* Boston: Oliver Diston & Co., Washington Street Publication, 1850.

Johnson, Peter and Friends. *Newport's Fair Town Traditional Songs and Ballads of North America.* Living Folk Records, LFR 013, Living Folk, 2007, CD.

Jordan, Philip D. *Singin' Yankees.* Minneapolis, Minnesota: The University of Minnesota Press, 1946.

Judson, Edward. *The Life of Adoniram Judson.* New York, A. D. F. Randolph & Company, 1883.

Kettell, Samuel. *Specimens of American Poetry, with Critical and Biographical Notices, Vol. I.* Boston: S. G. Goodrich and Co., 1829.

Kuntz, Andrew. "Oh Ned!" *Fiddler Magazine, vol.10, No. 4.* North Sydney, N.S. Canada: Mary E. Larsen, Winter 2003/2004.

Lewis, Alonzo. *The Poems of Alonzo Lewis.* Boston: B.B. Mussey & Co. Stereotyped and Printed by S.N. Dickerson & Co. 62 Washington Street, Boston, 1854.

Lomax, Alan. *The Folk Songs of North America.* Garden City, New York: Doubleday & Company, 1960.

Loring, George Bailey. *Celebration at North Bridge, Salem, July 4th, 1862: Oration.* Boston: J.E. Farwell & Company, 1862.

Lowry, Robert W., & Doane, Howard. *Gospel Hymn and Tune Book: a choice collection of Hymns and Music, old and new, for use in Prayer Meetings, Family Circles, and Church Service*. Philadelphia: American Baptist Publication Society, 1879.

Mahar, William John. *Behind the Burnt Cork Mask: Early Blackface Minstrelsy and Antebellum American Popular Culture*. Illinois: University of Illinois Press, 1999.

Mason, Redfern. *The Song Lore of Ireland*. New York: Wessels & Bissell Co., 1910.

Mason, Lowell. *Carmina Sacra*: or, *Boston Collection of Church Music: comprising the most popular psalm and hymn tunes in eternal use together with a great variety of new tunes, chants, sentences, motetts*. Boston: J. H. Wilkins & R. B. Carter, 1841.

Massachusetts Teacher and Journal of Home and School Education, Vol. 9. Boston: Samuel Coolidge for the Massachusetts Teachers Association, 1856.

McCarthy, B. Eugene. *Bondage to Belonging: The Worcester Slave Narratives*. University of Mass. Press, 2008.

McCarthy, William Bernard, ed. *Cinderella in America: A Book of Folk and Fairy Tales*. Jackson, Mississippi: University Press of Mississippi, 2007.

McCarty, William, ed. *The American National Song-Book, Songs, Odes, and Other Poems on National Subjects*. Compiled from Various Sources by Wm. McCarty. Philadelphia: Wm. McCarty, 1842.

Meek, Henry M., Compiled by, *The Naumkeag Directory for Salem, Beverly, Danvers, Marblehead, Peabody, Essex and Manchester*. Salem, Mass.: The Henry M. Meek Publishing Company, 1898.

Missud, Jean M. *Salem Assemblies Waltzes*. Boston: Ditson & Co., Oliver, monographic, 1878.

Musical Entertainment at Mechanic Hall Salem. Salem: Charles W. Swasey, Printer, 27 Washington Street, Salem, 1863.

Northend, Mary Harrod. *We Visit Old Inns*. Boston: Murray Printing Company, Small Maynard & Co., 1925.

Nutter, Charles S. & Wilbur F. Tillett. *The Hymns and Hymn Writers of the Church*. New York: Methodist Book Concern, 1911.

Oldschool, Oliver. *The Port Folio Vol. II*. Philadelphia: John Watt, Publisher, 1806.

Oliver, F.E., ed. *The Dairy of Benjamin Lynde and Benjamin Lynde, Jr.* Boston: Privately Printed, 1880.

Opie, Iona and Opie, Peter, *The Singing Game*. Oxford: New York: Oxford University Press, 1985.

Ordway, John P. *Dreaming of Home And Mother*. Boston: Oliver Ditson & Co., 1865.

Ordway, John P. *Twinkling Stars Are Laughing Love*. Boston: J.P. Ordway, Ordway Hall, Washington Street. 1855.

Peet, Harriet E. *The School Journal, Volume 75*. New York: A. S. Barnes & Company, 1115 Last Twenty Fourth Street, Vol. LXXV, 1907 and 1908.

Phillips, Barry. *British Ballads from Maine*. As sung by Mrs. S.S. Thornton and Mrs. F.P. Barker of Maine. New Haven: Yale University Press, 1929.

Pierpont, J, and J Pierpont. *The One Horse Open Sleigh*. Boston: Oliver Ditson, monographic, 1857.

Putnam, Eleanor. *Old Salem*. Boston and New York: Houghton, Mifflin and Company, 1889.

Putnam, John. *Revival Melodies, or Songs of Zion*. Boston: 1842.

Rantoul, Robert. "A Historic Ball Room." *The Essex institute Historical Collection Vol. XXXI #7 & 12*, Salem, Mass.: Essex Institute, 1894.

Ratliff, Jen. "Almshouse and Hospital for Contagious Diseases." *History by the Sea*. 2019. https://www.historybythesea.com/almshouse-and-hospital-for-contagious

Ringleader logbook, Log 1906, Phillips Library, Peabody Essex Museum, Rowley, MA.

Roberts, Brian. *Blackface Nation: Race, Reform, and Identity in American Popular Music, 1812 – 1925*. Chicago: The University of Chicago Press, 2017.

Roberts, Oliver Ayer. *History of The Military Company of the Massachusetts, Now Called The Ancient and Honorable Artillery Company of Massachusetts, 1637 – 1888, Vol. IV 1866 – 1888*. Boston: Alfred Mudge & Son, 24 Franklin Street, 1901.

Ropes, Miss Lydia Nichols. *Narrating Facts Given to Her by Her Father, George Nichols*. Salem Mass.: The Salem Press Co., No copyright date.

Ryan, William Bradbury. *Ryan's Mammoth Collection: 1050 Reels and Jigs*. Boston: Elias Howe, 1883.

Salem Mechanick Light Infantry Quick Step. Arranged and Adapted by John Holloway. Salem, Mass.: Ives & Putnam, 1836.

Schmidt, Adolph. *Coliseum Grand March*. G.D. Russell & Co, 1872. doi:https://doi.org/10.5479/sil.980100.mq1683140

Scott, Kenneth. *Counterfeiting in Colonial Rhode Island*. Providence, Rhode Island: Rhode Island Historical Society. 1960.

Seventeenth Annual Report of the Bureau of Statistics of Labor, Massachusetts Bureau of Statistics of Labor. Boston: Wright & Potter Printing Co., 1886.

Sherwin, W. F. & Stearns, J. N., ed. *Bugle Notes for the Temperance Army: a collection of songs, quartettes, and glees, adapted to the use of all temperance gatherings, glee clubs, etc.* Publisher: National Temperance Society and Publishing House, New York, 1871.

Silsbee, M. C. D. *A Half Century in Salem.* Boston and New York: Houghton Mifflin & Co. The Riverside Press, Cambridge, 1887.

Sky, Patrick. ed. *Ryan's Mammoth Collection Fiddle Tunes.* Pacific, MO: MelBay Publication, 1995.

Smith College Commencement Festivities, Springfield [Massachusetts] *Republican.* Sunday, June 14, 1925.

Smith, Dexter. *Dexter Smith Poems.* Boston: G. D. Russell & Company, 1868.

Smith, Dexter. *There's Crape on the Door. Gates of Praise: for the Sabbath-school, praise-service, prayer-meeting, etc.*, Rev. Isaiah Baltzell, Rev. Edmund S. Lorenz. Dayton, OH: W. J. Shuey, 1884.

Smith, T. William. *High Street, Strawberry Jam.* Salem: Wellspring Studio, 2012, CD.

Smith-Dalton, Maggie. *Stories and Shadows from Salem's Past.* Charleston and London: The History Press, 2010.

Streeter, G.L. *Historical Collection of the Essex Institute Vol. II.* Published By Henry Whipple, Institute & Son, 1860.

Stevenson, Brenda, ed. *The Journals of Charlotte Forten.* New York: Oxford Press, 1988.

Stevenson, Burton Egbert, Collected and edited by. *Other Sources: Poems of American History.* Boston: Houghton Mifflin Company, 1908 and reprinted 1922.

Tennyson, Alfred. *The May Queen*, London: Sampson Low, Son & Marston, Crown Buildings, Fleet Street, 1861.

Valentine, Herbert E. *Dedication of the boulder commemorating the service of the Twenty-third Regiment, Massachusetts Volunteer Infantry, in the Civil War, 1861 – 1865, at Salem, Massachusetts, September 28, 1905. United States Army, Massachusetts Infantry Regiment, 23rd (1861 – 1865).* Salem, Mass.: Newcomb & Gauss, 1905.

Volo, D. D. *Family Life in Seventeenth and Eighteenth Century America.* Westport, CT: Greenwood Press, 2006.

Walker, Fred Goldsmith. *My Leisure Moments.* Salem: Barry and Lufkin, Printers and Publishers, 1892.

Warner, Anne and Frank. *Traditional American Folk Songs.* New York: Syracuse University Press, 1984.

Wells, S.R., ed. *Phrenological Journal and Packard's Monthly.* New York: Samuel R. Wells, Publisher, 389 Broadway, 1870.

Whittier, John Greenleaf. *The Complete Poetical Works of John Greenleaf Whittier.* Cambridge: Houghton Mifflin Company, 1894.

Wilbert, Polly. *My Life in the South*, Jacob Stroyer. National Humanities Center, Excerpts from Stroyer, Jacob, *My Life in the South.* Digital Scanning, Inc., Scituate, MA 02066, originally published, 1879.

Wiley, Hiram Ozias. *Eternity, and Other Poems.* published posthumously. Salem, Massachusetts: Salem Press, 1874.

Williams, Alice, Piemonte, Catherine, K., ed., *The Commissioning at Tabernacle Church, Salem's Church with the Lighted Steeple, A History of the Tabernacle Church.* Salem, Massachusetts: Higginson Books Co., 2008.

Williams, Prof. Henry L. *Songs and Ballads of the American Revolution with Preface by Prof. Henry L. Williams, and Notes and Illustrations by Frank Moore.* New York: Hurst & Company, 1905.

Willis, Lemuel. *A Semi-centennial Address Delivered in the Universalist Church, Salem, Mass., Thursday August 4, 1859, on the Occasion of Celebrating the 50th Anniversary of the dedication of the Church.* Salem: Charles W. Swasey, Register Press, 1859.

Zetzsche, and S. Knaebel. *Salem Independent Cadet Quick Step.* Boston: Stephen W. Marsh, monographic, 1848.

WEB RESOURCES

American Antiquarian Society
www.americanantiquarian.org

Ann Lewis Women's Suffrage Collection
www.lewissuffragecollection.omeka.net

Athlone Community Radio Podcast, The Bandmaster
www.athlonecommunityradio.ie

Broadside Ballads Bodleian Libraries Oxford University
www.ballads.bodleian.ox.ac.uk

Cecil Sharp House
www.vwml.org

Center for Popular Music, Middle Tennessee State University
www.popmusic.mtsu.edu

City of Salem
www.salem.com

Commonwealth Vintage Dancers
www. vintagedancers.org

Cyber Hymnal
www.hymntime.com

Dalton, Jim & Smith-Dalton, Maggi
www.singingstring.org

First Bull Run
www.firstbullrun.co.uk

Frederick E. Berry Library at Salem State University
www.salemstate.edu

Genealogy Wise
www.genealogywise.com

Google Books
www.books.google.com

Hadley Genealogy
www.hadleygenealogy.net

Hamilton Hall
www.hamiltonhall.org

Harris Broadside Collection, John Hay Library, Brown University
www.repository.library.brown.edu

Hathi Trust Digital Library
www.hathitrust.org

Historic Beverly
www.historicbeverly.net

History by the Sea
www.historybythesea.com

House of the Seven Gables
www.7gables.org

Hymnary
www.hymnary.org

Internet Archive
www.archive.org

Journal of American Folklore
www.jstor.org

Lester S. Levy Collection of Sheet Music, Johns Hopkins University
www.levysheetmusic.mse.jhu.edu

Library Company of Philadelphia
www.librarycompany.org

Library of Congress
www.loc.gov

Mainly Folk: English Folk and Other Good Music
www.mainlynorfolk.info

Mary Barker, Photographer
www.mabarkerphotography.com
Mass Moments
www.mass moments.org
Mudcat
www.mudcat.org
Music Score Library Project/
Petrucci Music Library
www.imslp.org
Music, Civil War
www.encyclopedia.com
Phillip's Library, Rowley/
Salem, Massachusetts
www.pem.org
Poetry & Song on the Outbreak
of War
www.americainclass.org
Popular Songs of the Day
www.loc.gov
Protest Song Lyrics
www.protestsonglyrics.net
Registry of Deeds
www.salemdeeds.com
Rosie Strom – Graphic Designer
www.rosiestromdesign.com
Roud Folk Song Index at the
Vaughan Williams Memorial
Library
www.vwml.org
Salem Links and Lore, Salem
Public Library
www.noblenet.org
Salem Athenaeum
www.salemathenaeum.net
Salem, Massachusetts
www.salemweb.com
Streets of Salem
www.streetsofsalem.com

Traditional Ballad Index,
Fresno State University
www.fresnostate.edu
Traditional Music Library
www.traditionalmusic.co.uk
Trial Pamphlets Collection,
Cornell University Law
Library
www.awcollections.library.
cornell.edu
USGenNet
www.usgennet.org
Washington University Digital
Gateway Image Collections
& Exhibitions
www.lib-lslv126.wulib
Word on the Street
www.digital.nls.uk

BLOGS

Clark University Professor Janette
Thomas Greenwood, The Camden-
Worcester Connection
https://wordpress.clarku.edu/
jgreenwood/author/jgreenwood/
History by the Sea, Jen Ratliff
https://www.historybythesea.com/
Streets of Salem, Donna Seeger
https://streetsofsalem.com/

PHOTOGRAPHS, POSTCARDS, CLIPPINGS, MAPS

Cover: *Pyncheon Lane Capric*, House of the Seven Gables
George A. Brown, Kenneth S. Goldstein Collection of American Song Broadsides
Winter Island Lighthouse, Mary Barker – Photographer

I. SALEM

Salem Willows Postcard, Sal Pangallo's personal collection
Pageant of Salem Postcard, Sal Pangallo's personal collection
Federal Street, Henry K. Oliver, *Gospel Hymn and Tune Book*,
    Boston Public Library
Pageant of Salem, Boston Herald, May 25, 1913
Henry K. Oliver, Lawrence Public Library, Lawrence, MA
Henry K. Oliver's home, 142 Federal Street, Salem, MA
    Mary Barker – Photographer
Merton C.M., Evangelical Lutheran Hymnal, Boston Public Library
Cold Spring in North Salem, Salem Map 1874, author's personal collection
Chestnut Street Postcard, Sal Pangallo's personal collection
Chestnut Street, Carmina Sacra: or, Boston Collection of Church Music,
    Boston Public Library
Only Waiting, Salem Register, December 11, 1854
The Poor Farm or *Almshouse*, Nelson Dionne Collection & Salem Public Library
May Pole, *Salem Register,* May 1, 1849
The Latest Song, Salem Daily Gazette, January 26, 1896
Be Salem Home, Essex Register, March 17, 1826,
    Christine Elizabeth Mistretta's private collection
Who's to Foot the Bills, Salem Daily Gazette, February 1, 1896
True Facts About Salem, Salem Gazette, November 13, 1898
Lines on the occasioned by the Author's leaving Salem, Mass. To Reside in New York,
    Portsmouth Oracle, July 24, 1819
The Salem Singers, Salem Register, July 8, 1852
Willie's on the Dark Blue Sea, Library of Congress
The Legend of the Club House, Hemet News, March 18, 1921
The Moon So Round and Mellow, Nelson Dionne Collection
    & Salem Public Library
Patrick S. Gilmore, *Essex Institute Historical Collection*, Salem Public Library
Sad News From Home, Lester S. Levy Collection of Sheet Music, Sheridan
    Libraries, Johns Hopkins University

On the Road to Salem, Boston Public Library & Phillips Library, Rowley, MA
Salem Hornpipe, Ryan's Mammoth Collection, Jim and Maggi Dalton's
    personal collection
Grand Concert, *Salem Register,* July 28, 1856
The Salem Brass Band, Concert poster, Smith (Burnham) Family Scrapbook
Program at Gallows Hill, *Salem Register,* July 28, 1856
Grand Concert – Gilmore's *Salem Brass Band*, Jarlath MacNamara
    personal collection
Coliseum Grand March, Patrick S. Gilmore. Boston Public Library
Hail Gentle Peace, The Devotional Chimes: A Collection of New & Standard
    Hymns, Boston Public Library
The Colored Millionaires, author's personal collection

II. ON DEATH AND TRAGEDY

Execution of Stephen M. Clark, Salem Gazette, April 24, 1821
Written on reading an account of the execution of Stephen M. Clark,
    Harris Broadside Collection at the John Hay Library, Brown University
A Funeral Elegy, Harris Broadside Collection at the John Hay Library,
    Brown University
The Salem Tragedy, Library of Congress
Baker's Island Postcard, Sal Pangallo's personal collection
Murder of Joseph White, Harris Broadside Collection at the John Hay Library,
    Brown University
George A. Brown, Kenneth S. Goldstein Collection of American
    Song Broadsides
Few Are Our Days, Revival Melodies, or Songs of Zion, Boston Public Library
Dexter Smith Photograph, Nancy Lutts' personal collection
Ring The Bell Softly, There's Crape on the Door, Gates of Praise: for the
    Sabbath-school, praise-service, prayer-meeting, etc., Boston Public Library

III. IMPRISONED

Boston Evening Post, October 16, 1738, Boston Public Library
Boston Evening Post, October 23, 1738, Boston Public Library
Boston Evening Post, November 20, 1738, Boston Public Library
Boston Evening Post, March 31, 1746, Boston Public Library
Boston Evening Post, September 9, 1754, Boston Public Library

4 Federal Street, the original sight of the Old Salem Jail, Nancy Lutts'
    private collection
Second Salem Jail Postcard, Sal Pangallo's personal collection
The *Charlestown Land Shark*, Harris Broadside Collection at the John Hay
    Library, Brown University
Witch House, Mary Barker – Photographer

IV. SOCIAL CHANGE

Get Off the Track, Lester S. Levy Collection of Sheet Music
Civil War Statue, Greenlawn Cemetery, Salem, Mary Barker – Photographer
Emancipation Hymn, Library of Congress
John C. Fremont, Salem Register, November 11, 1856
We're for Freedom Through the Land, Salem Register, September 1, 1856
Cornerstone Hymn, transcribed by T. William Smith
*Original Hymn, 50th Anniversary of the Universalist Church in Salem,
    Salem Register,* August 8, 1859
Universalist Church Postcard, Nelson Dionne Collection, and the
    Salem Public Library

V. CONFLICT

Leslie's Retreat Postcard, Sal Pangallo's personal collection
Col. Leslie's Expedition, Salem Register, March 23, 1848
The Pickering House, Mary Barker – Photographer
Colonel Pickering's March to Lexington, Phillips Library, Rowley, MA
A Funeral Elegy, New York Herald, April 19, 1875, Boston Public Library
Joshua Ward House, 148 Washington Street, Mary Barker – Photographer
Ode of War and Washington, Boston Semi-Weekly, September 7, 1861,
    Boston Public Library
Ode of War and Washington, tune: *British Grenadier*s, transcribed by Dan Mozell
Salem Artillery, Essex Institute, Salem, MA, now Phillips Library, Rowley, MA
Americans to Arms, The Rosenbach Museum and Library
Song of the Minute Man, Harris Broadside Collection at the John Hay Library,
    Brown University
The Patriot Song, Salem Observer, August 24, 1861
Penny Ballad Seller, Sunday Boston Herald, July 24, 1910
To Our Salem Boys, Salem Register, July 28, 1862

Departure of the Salem Light Infantry, Harris Broadside Collection at the John
  Hay Library, Brown University
Lines written for the Second Reunion of the 23rd Regiment, Kenneth S.
  Goldstein Collection of American Song Broadsides
When Johnny Comes Marching Home, Jarlath MacNamara's personal collection
Salem Mechanick Infantry Quick Step, Lester S. Levy Collection of Sheet Music
Salem Independent Cadet Quick Step, Lester S. Levy Collection of Sheet Music
Musical Entertainment at Mechanic Hall, Salem, Christine Elizabeth Mistretta's
  private collection
Amateur Concert, *Salem Observer*, January 3, 1863
Dreaming of Home And Mother, Library of Congress
Salem Cadets' March, Howe's School for the Clarinet, Boston Public Library
Salem Quick Step, The Musician's Companion, Boston Public Library
God Bless America, Library of Congress
Ode Deeds of Glory, Salem Register, July 8, 1859

VI. COMMERCE

Hardware Advertisement, *Salem Gazette*, July 11, 1800
Penny Ballad Seller, Sunday Boston Herald, July 24, 1910
We Are Ped(d)lers, Smith (Burnham) Family Scrapbook
*The Salem and Danvers (South) Horse Railroad, Salem Observe*r, March 14, 1863
Salem Train Depot Postcard, Sal Pangallo's personal collection
Lowell Island, Salem Register, August 25, 1851
The North Shore of Massachusetts Bay. An illustrated Guide and History,
  Salem Public Library
Penny Ballad Seller, Sunday Boston Herald, July 24, 1910
I Took My Specs, Salem Gazette, October 1, 1841
Salem Register, January 12, 1852
The Genius of My Glasses, Boston Herald, August 9, 1914
Pickering Theme Song, Nelson Dionne Collection
Sidewalk Musings, Salem Register, August 2, 1841
Barn tools, author's personal collection
The New England Blacking Man, Kenneth S. Goldstein Collection of American
  Song Broadsides Center for Popular Music, Middle Tennessee State
  University
Dream, S.F. Rogers, Salem Register, January 6, 1851
A Parody, Salem Observer, July 11, 1863

IX. TEMPERANCE

Drunken Soldier, Salem Mercury, September 25, 1787

Father Mathew Statue Postcard, Sal Pangallo's personal collection

King Alcohol, Bugle Notes for the Temperance Army, hymnary.org

A Parody, Harris Broadside Collection at the John Hay Library, Brown
  University

Casks and Kegs, *Salem Register*, July 20, 1843

The Drunkard's Wish, Salem Gazette, December 6, 1796, #557

A Temperance Ode, Salem Observer, February 25, 1865

Guests at Cabot Farm, *Salem Gazette*, September 7, 1897

Second Annual Picnic at Cabot Farm, Nancy Lutts' personal collection

Address to a Jug of Rum, Salem Gazette, November 12, 1813

Father Mathew Statue, Mary Barker – Photographer

Penny Ballad Seller, Sunday Boston Herald, July 24, 1910

The Last Glass, Harris Broadside Collection, John Hay Library, Brown University

INDEX

- D -

- E -

ACKNOWLEDGMENTS

I want to express my gratitude to my wife, Jennifer, for her support throughout this process, for her work at the Salem Public Library, and for developing the website Salem Links and Lore, a local source for Salem history, found on the Salem Public Library's website. I am particularly thankful to Bill and Sarah Smith, longtime friends, Salem residents, leaders of the *Salem Country Orchestra*, and folk musicians for their continual encouragement and support of this project. Thank you to local historian Jim McAllister for writing the foreword and sharing his vast knowledge of Salem's history with the Salem community. Donna Seeger, Professor of History at Salem State University. Special thanks to Sal Pangallo, Jarlath MacNamara of the Athlone Community Radio, Ireland, Dee Dee Morneau, Professor Jim Dalton of Berkeley College, Joanna Liss, Christine Elizabeth Mistretta, Tyler Twombly, Craig Burnham for the use of the Smith Family Scrapbook, Betsey and Ed Bennett, Nancy Lutts, and Bonnie Hurd Smith, curator of the *Nelson Dionne Collection.* for the use of their private collections. Thanks to folksingers Diane Taraz, John Roberts, Bob Franke, and Peter Johnson for their songs. Special thanks to *Castlebay* folk duo Julia Lane and Fred Gosbee for their support, our late-night discussions, and their newly published book *Songs of Ships and Sailors, Bygone Ballads of Maine, Volume I,* and traditional singer Michael O'Leary, our musical partner and for his research and rediscovery of the Gloucester book, *Fishermen's Ballads and Songs of the Sea.* Thanks to maritime photographer Mary Barker for letting us use her photos of Salem, Gracie Arcand Sabean for editing, and my daughter, Rosie Strom, for sharing her graphic design knowledge, suggestions, and talent.

I would also like to thank all the librarians for their knowledge and support at the following libraries: Boston Public Library, Lawrence Public Library, California State Library, Center for Popular Music, Middle Tennessee State University, David M. Rubenstein Rare Book & Manuscript Library at Duke University, Frederick E. Berry Library at Salem State University, Historic Beverly, House of the Seven Gables, Harris Broadside Collection at the John Hay Library at Brown University, Lester S. Levy Collection of Sheet Music, at Johns Hopkins University, Library Company of Philadelphia, Library of Congress, Philips Library in Rowley Massachusetts, Peabody Essex Museum in Salem, Providence Public Library, Newspapers.com, Genealogy Bank, Washington University Digital Gateway Image Collections & Exhibitions, Salem Public Library, Tabernacle Church's Historical Room in Salem, and William L. Clements Library, University of Michigan. Finally, Steve Roud for cataloging several of the songs in the *Roud Index* and listing them at the Vaughan Williams Memorial Library at the *Cecil Sharp House* in London.

Lastly, I would like to acknowledge all our music friends and local sessions for which we share our love of music and community.

Enjoy Salem and keep singing ~ Bob Strom

PHOTOGRAPHER MARY BARKER

Nautical photographer Mary Barker is the photographer and social media manager for the *Gloucester Marine Railways* and is the official photographer for the *Schooner Adventure.* To add to Mary's resume, she is the official photographer for the *USS Constitution.* Mary has a candid, documentary style of photography focusing on existing light and minimal editing to affect a natural, realistic photographic outcome. Mary strives to capture the essence of historic boat restoration and commercial operations.

Mary continues to publish her photographs in several national magazines, including *Wooden Boat, Marlinspike,* the *National Maritime Historical Society,* local newspapers, brochures, and many travel magazines. Bob Strom features several of her photographs in the two-volume music collection *Old Salem in Ballad* and *Song* and *Old Salem at Sea in Ballad and Song* and the *Unique Book of Songs of the Sea.*

Mary continues to expand her passion for documenting wooden ship restorations on the *Schooners Adventure, Roseway, Ernestina, the Mayflower, Phyllis A,* and *Formidable* to photographing commercial fishing vessels and their operations.

[Every effort was made to use material in the public domain and to contact copyright holders of the extracts in this book. Any unintentional omission of acknowledgment for quoted material will be corrected in future editions. – RS]

www.ingramcontent.com/pod-product-compliance
Lightning Source LLC
Chambersburg PA
CBHW070547130626
46556CB00001B/50